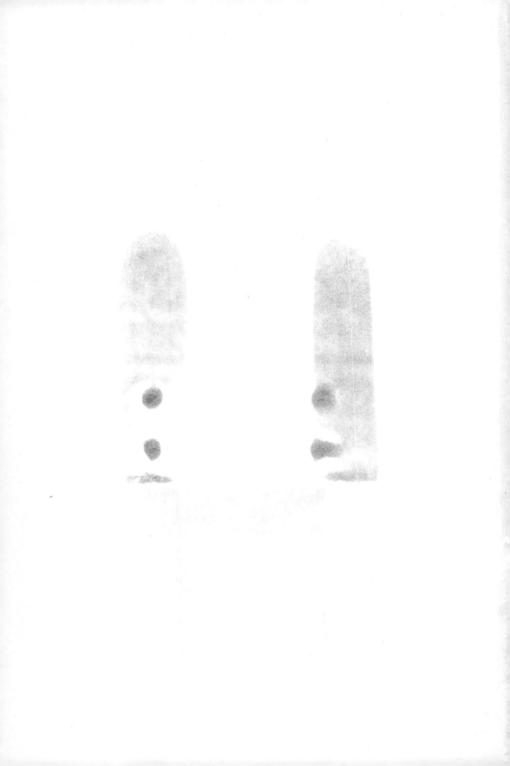

FINDING JIM

FINDING JIM
SUSAN OAKEY-BAKER

RMB

BIOG
OAK

Rocky Mountain Books
www.rmbooks.com

Library and Archives Canada Cataloguing in Publication

Oakey-Baker, Susan, author
Finding Jim / Susan Oakey-Baker.

Issued in print and electronic formats.
ISBN 978-1-927330-70-8 (bound).—ISBN 978-1-927330-71-5 (html).—ISBN 978-1-927330-72-2 (pdf)

1. Oakey-Baker, Susan. 2. Oakey-Baker, Susan—Travel. 3. Haberl, Jim, 1958-1999. 4. Husbands—Death. 5. Adventure and adventurers—British Columbia—Biography. 6. Mountaineers—British Columbia—Biography. 7. British Columbia—Biography. I. Title.

GV191.52.O24A3 2013   796.5092   C2013-902646-0
                             C2013-902647-9

The poem "When we must part" (1977/1986) © Earle Birney, was published in the collection *Last Makings*, with an introduction by Al Purdy (Toronto: McClelland & Stewart, 1991), 116, and is reprinted with permission.

Cover photo: Brooks Range, Alaska by Jim Haberl

Printed in China

Rocky Mountain Books acknowledges the financial support for its publishing program from the Government of Canada through the Canada Book Fund (CBF) and the Canada Council for the Arts, and from the province of British Columbia through the British Columbia Arts Council and the Book Publishing Tax Credit.

 Canadian Heritage / Patrimoine canadien

 Canada Council for the Arts / Conseil des Arts du Canada

 BRITISH COLUMBIA ARTS COUNCIL

This book was produced using FSC®-certified, acid-free paper, processed chlorine free and printed with soya-based inks.

For Joe

"There is no preferred point of view in the universe."
—ALBERT EINSTEIN

CONTENTS

PROLOGUE

There are times in my life when I remember being scared: parachuting from a plane, failing my first exam at university, watching a grizzly sow and her three cubs rip through my campsite.

But nothing prepared me for the news that my 41-year-old husband had been killed in an avalanche.

Why would I be prepared? I believed that with hard work I could achieve my goals. I followed the rules, had everything I was supposed to have: nice friends, good grades, a recession-proof job teaching high school, a loving husband, a beautiful mountain home in Whistler. In return I expected special exemption from the hand of fate. This was the deal I subconsciously concocted: civil obedience, loving kindness for no loss, no pain.

But the impossible happened.

Getting used to my husband's death has taken me 10 years, 30 journals and this book, and it's still a work in progress. At times in my life, fear has kept me alive. At other times, fear has made me feel alive. The intense fear I felt while grieving, however, paralyzed me.

PART 1
BEFORE

Come to the edge.
We might fall.
Come to the edge.
It's too high!
COME TO THE EDGE!
And they came,
and he pushed,
And they flew.
—CHRISTOPHER LOGUE,
"COME TO THE EDGE," *NEW NUMBERS*, 1969

ONE
BEGINNING

(1982–1993)

Jim Haberl first kissed me on a commercial sailing trip in the Queen Charlotte Islands, British Columbia, in 1982. He was 24 and part of the crew; I was 16 and a passenger. After the trip, he wrote postcards to me from all over the world. We drifted apart, and the next time we connected, I was 26. Jim was working to complete his International Mountain Guide certification, and I was teaching languages full time at a high school in Vancouver, while working part time on my master's degree. I had just spent many months breaking up with my boyfriend, who I once thought I would marry. Silently, I vowed I would not get into another relationship for at least a year.

Over the course of the next year, Jim and I went backcountry skiing, backpacking, rock climbing and kayaking. We watched sunsets at the beach together. We teetered on a tightrope. We were friends, but sometimes we were lovers.

One evening we went for Mexican food in Vancouver. My hands dripped with chimichanga sauce when Jim lowered his gaze. "I've been asked to join a Canadian/American expedition led by Stacy Allison to climb K2."

"Where's K2?" I chirped.

"In Pakistan. It's the second-highest mountain in the world. No Canadian has ever reached the summit. I'd be gone three months, next summer. And Dan Culver will be going." He leaned forward on the edge of his seat. "What do you think?"

"It sounds like an amazing opportunity for you, an incredible adventure. I think it sounds great. And it's a good time in your life, no real ties." I nodded my head up and down to convince myself.

Jim and I had slept together. I had dangled from his climbing rope and gone five days without a shower in a tent with him. Still, I would not put my heart on a chopping block and admit that we were tied together.

The K2 team interviewed Jim in Seattle, and Jim accepted their offer.

We continued to see each other. Two months later, at Christmas, Jim invited me on a backcountry ski trip to Rogers Pass with some of his friends. It was –30°C and howling. At a rest stop, Jim brought his face close to mine and yelled over the wind, "How's it goin'?"

I wiggled my fingers and toes and pawed at the icy stream coming from my nose. He ungloved his hand and wiped the half-frozen goo from my upper lip with his warm fingers and gave me a reassuring smile. As cold as I was, my body became still, and I stared at Jim as he strode back to the front to break trail. He's so strong, I thought. So together. So confident. So caring. That night, when he asked to share my bed, my heart pounded. I was falling in love.

The next morning at breakfast, Jim's friends peppered him with questions about the K2 expedition. How long would it take? Three months. Would they use oxygen? No, they had made a decision as a team to go alpine style – without oxygen. When did they plan to summit? The beginning of July. Who would he climb with? He hoped to climb with Dan, but that would be Stacy's decision. How technical was it? It is the second-highest mountain in the world but considered by many to be the most dangerous because it is more technical than Everest.

I didn't say a word. He wouldn't be using oxygen. K2 is more dangerous than Everest.

At the end of our trip, Jim drove to Canadian Mountain Holidays' Bobbie Burns Lodge near Golden to guide heli-skiing, and I returned by bus to Vancouver to my teaching. My older sister, Sharron, picked me up from the bus station, and I sat in the car only half listening to her news as my body inhaled and forgot to exhale.

I burst and gushed out how I had fallen in love with Jim Haberl, how he was kind and generous and honest and brave and strong, yet gentle and inspiring.

For the next five months, before Jim left for k2 at the end of May, we spent as much time together as possible between my teaching and his guiding jobs. Our letters and phone calls intensified with that free-fall abandon of young, threatened love.

The day Jim left for Pakistan, he reassured my parents, "Don't you worry, I'm coming back." Dad hugged him and wished him luck.

Jim turned to me, raised his eyebrows and exclaimed, "Wow, a hug from your dad!"

TWO
K2

(MAY–JULY 1993)

At the Seattle Airport, Jim stood amongst his six teammates – Stacy Allison, John Petroske, Steve Steckmeyer, John Haigh, Phil Powers and Dan Culver – and 45 pieces of luggage, labelled with purple and white K2 stickers. I grew anxious. A current travelled up my body and left me frazzled. I pulled my face tight to stop tears from leaking out, moved into Jim's open arms, kissed his face and pushed a letter into his hand. My voice warbled, "Be careful. I love you. Come home. Have a wonderful time."

Back in Vancouver, I prepared my students for their exams, moved into my first big purchase – a condominium in Kitsilano – biked and rock climbed with friends, worked on my master's, went on a horseback riding trip in the Rocky Mountains and planned a ski trip to Chile and Argentina.

I wrote to Jim every week and envisioned my letters' journey, first by plane to Skardu, then by truck to Askoli and finally by foot up the Baltoro Glacier into Jim's hands at Base Camp, elevation 5000 metres. I sent them special delivery but was not sure it made a difference.

Jim sent letters every four or five days, and I received all but one. Only half of mine made it to him, and the first one took six weeks. None of our letters arrived in the proper order. What follows are excerpts from Jim's letters to me.

May 25, 1993

Dear Sue,

Greetings from Pakistan. I'm sitting on my bed in the hotel room in my underwear, sweating. It's over 40°C outside, and the air conditioning unit is old and can't cope. It's hot, but otherwise things are going very well. The logistics are rolling along smoothly. Tomorrow we leave for the north: Skardu by 24-hour bus along the famous Karakoram Highway, an old silk-traders' route. We had planned to fly, but our reservations didn't make the computer translation from Seattle to Karachi. And flights to Skardu are booked for another 17 days. But though the bus ride will be brutal, it should offer a spectacular view of the countryside and a taste of the local culture.

We spent today changing our 32 kg planeloads into 25 kg porter loads. It looks like we will have 100 porters into Base Camp. It sounds huge to me but Gulam (our cook) said the last Japanese team to K2 had 1300 porters for 25 climbers, and there are only seven of us.

The whole scene here is amazing. Everything is pretty well figured out: porter requirements, helicopter rescue, insurance for porters, cook's equipment, everything regulated and followed to the letter. It is kind of like organizing by numbers – just look at the list and do the next job.

So we're on the move again tomorrow and hope to be on the trail, *Inshallah* (God willing), on May 30th. Our team has been lucky since I joined it last August, and I have a really good feeling. Keep your fingers crossed.

Much Love, Jim XOX

May 28, 1993

Dear Sue,

We're in Skardu now, our final jumpoff point for K2. In fact, if the weather cooperates, we'll leave tomorrow by jeep for Askoli and begin the approach on Sunday. Very exciting. The pace of the journey so far has been far more hectic than I imagined. It will be fantastic to get on the trail and have long sleeps and steady physical activity.

The bus ride from Islamabad to Skardu was the wildest part of our trip so far. The bus itself, painted and covered in more dingle balls and chimes than all the cars in Surrey, was solid mechanically and came with the world's most durable driver, which was a good thing. For the most part, the road we travelled, the Karakoram Highway, follows the route the Indus River has carved through the Himalayas since the beginning of time. The valley is thousands of metres deep and the road is literally etched into the side of the canyon. I have been on some wild roads – South America, Africa and even at home in British Columbia – where there were blind corners and long stretches of exposed driving, but nothing like this. The Karakoram Highway is on the verge of dropping into the Indus River. It's hard to describe, but if anything had gone wrong with the bus – flat tire, brakes, kingpin on the steering column – we would have been toast. I bet we turned more than 5,000 blind corners, horn blasting to warn would-be oncoming traffic. The entire road is single lane.

Yesterday, Dan, Phil and I tried to figure out how many porters we would need, and thus how much food to buy. We have seventy-seven porter loads, about 1900 kg, but then we need porters to carry the food for the seventy-seven porters, and more porters to carry food for the porters who are carrying food. Then, as we eat the food – 104 porters plus our team members will eat almost 91 kg of food per day – the number of porters we need decreases. So ... how many kilos of wheat flour do we buy? Try 460 kg! Our next job is to load our 2500 kg of food and gear into jeeps and drive to Askoli. The numbers are quite staggering to me. All to climb a mountain!

Hugs and kisses though the mail can't match the real

thing, but that will come soon.
Love Always, Jim.

May 31, 1993
Dear Sue,
The road from Skardu to Askoli was another scary, eight-hour affair. For the final few hours, from Dasso to Askoli, the road was etched into the sides of a canyon formed by the violent Braldu River. The drivers negotiated switchbacks requiring two or three-point turns in 4WD low overlooking 150 metres of nothing to the water of the Braldu Gorge, and bridges suspended by cables and free to sway under the weight of our loaded jeeps.

Finally we are walking and tonight is the second on our approach march. The area is spectacular. Big peaks and stark beauty and we are still days from the "real" name mountains of the Karakoram. From today's camp, we can just glimpse the top of Paiyu Peak, the first of the big boys. It is an area of history, fables of mountain travel, summits where heroes are born; and now I'm walking into the heart of it all. Romantic, exciting and just a bit intimidating. I know that once we get going on the mountain, familiar actions and the process of decision-making in a mountain environment will chase any goblins from my head.

🦎

It's now June 1 and we are camped at Paiyu, the final camp before heading onto the Baltoro Glacier, our highway to K2. I just had a wash in the freezing Braldu River, one of those situations that is totally uncomfortable but you know the rewards will be worth it. Rain is pouring on the tent fly and I am thinking of you as I snuggle deeper into my sleeping bag.

🦎

It is now June 2. This morning it was hot and sunny and we caught our first glimpse of the Baltoro Glacier. Behind one spectacular summit, the west ridge of K2 was barely discernible, 50 kilometres away. The objective draws nearer. With good weather, Inshallah, we'll arrive at Base Camp in four days. Then our work will begin in earnest.

Today was Eid al-Adha, the Islamic celebration of Abraham's faith in God through his willingness to sacrifice his son Isaac. I guess God came to Abraham in a dream. In Christianity, God stops Abraham as his sword is poised for the kill. In Islam, Isaac is turned into a goat. Hence the ceremonial slaughter of goats, or whatever animal the family can afford, on Eid. Our porters sacrificed a Zoa (ox) through a ritual slaughter using slow cuts across the neck artery, so that the meat would bleed without stopping the heart – scenes of *Apocalypse Now*. It was disgusting but an event that is part of the trip and the porters' lives.

Photography has been going well, ten rolls so far and we're just getting into the mountains. I'll be shooting most of my 50 rolls. The people shots, particularly the porters, have been exciting. Lots of expressions and the long line of porters weaving their way along the trail etched into the steep canyon carved by the Braldu River. Both Dan and I are working at the "job" of photography, and we seem to feed off of each other's enthusiasm. I think the final product will be a pretty high standard. Ideas grow daily for writing projects.

June 4. At 4300 metres the altitude is starting to take my breath away. We're just past halfway to the top, and I figure it's only going to get tougher. I found out today that a German couple is heading down the Baltoro Glacier and they're willing to carry out our mail. A chance to send my love to you – don't want to miss that! You are always on my mind. Some of the thoughts look to the future; some stay tuned to the moment.

Two weeks into the trip now and everything has gone according to plan. I wonder if that pattern will continue on the mountain. I am not going to push things, but with some weather breaks and if everyone continues to share such a great attitude and stays healthy – who knows? Dan and I are getting along famously, and the whole team is doing well. Stacy continues to keep a solid grip on most aspects of the trip. How that control will manifest itself on the mountain remains to be seen. I don't anticipate any problems. Phil has been a fountain of knowledge of Pakistan and the Karakoram; our smooth transition from North America to here is a huge credit to his experience and connections. Doctor John from Calgary is very good; his preparation has been excellent. Steve and John, the Seattle connection, are both team players and round out the K2 unit well. Everyone is healthy and keen – so far!

The Baltoro is spectacular, in a teasing kind of way. We catch glimpses of the great peaks around it, and then clouds veil the summits. It is surely one of the most amazing places on the globe, and the scale is beyond my descriptive abilities and must really be seen to be understood.

Love, Jim XOXO.

June 11, 1993
Dear Sue,

Things are going exceptionally well. Keep your fingers crossed. Today I made my first carry to Camp One, at 6100 metres. K2 Base Camp is at 5000 metres, so the journey to Camp One was a substantial effort. I felt strong and moved surprisingly well for my first crack on the mountain. Dan and Phil went up a few days ago. Dan and I have been split temporarily, but that is not a problem. When the time came for a first carry to Camp One, I decided to give my chest an extra day to clear. The doc, John Haigh, listened to my breathing and sensed tightness in my lungs. I am still convinced it is an allergy, and coming into a clean environment has helped, but the complications of altitude have left me feeling a bit congested. The doc has me using an inhaler, Beclovent, to help with the inflammation. Anyways, to make a long story even longer, my sense is that the chest is clearing up and today's effort to 6100 metres didn't make it feel any worse and made the goblins in my head disappear. I feel competent and strong and very much at home, rejuvenated by the technical terrain. The more time I spend with my "hands on" the mountain, the more comfortable it will become. The summit is still very far away, but I feel strongly that I can look after myself. Stronger every day. Stress is one thing I don't need if I'm going to make a dent on this hill. I feel good!

Tomorrow I rest while Dan and Phil return to Camp One, spend the night and then on the 13th carry on to Camp Two, at 6900 metres! While they're going to Two, Steve and I will return to Camp One with our sleeping bags, spend the night, and the next day carry on to Two and then return all the way to base. Meanwhile, Stacy, John and John will carry for the first time to One tomorrow, rest on the 13th, and then return to One to sleep on the 14th. That's the plan, anyway! Got all that?

The route is great. There are plenty of positive aspects, probably the most encouraging being that the terrain from Advanced Base Camp to Camp Three will be mostly fixed with a series of ropes. This means that it will be relatively easy to back off the mountain quickly in the event of bad weather or altitude complications. It took me less than one hour to descend from Camp One to Advanced Base Camp this afternoon – a vertical distance of 760 metres.

❧

June 12. Another glorious day, our fourth in a row. And to top it all off, it's Dan's 41st birthday. I got up at 5 a.m. to see Dan, Phil, Stacy, John and John off to Camp Two. Hopefully the weather will hold and Steve and I will get back to Camp One and carry to Two.
Love Always, Jim XOXO

June 16, 1993
Dear Sue,
Just listened to Blue Rodeo's "Lost Together" and my mind really focused on you. Your memory brings such a warm feeling into my heart. I wonder how you're doing. I am anxiously awaiting news from you. I know you're thinking of me. I can sense that, so I don't need your letters, but I want them. I know you and I talked of my being a different person when I get back. It seemed inevitable, after time spent in such a place, on such a mountain. It still does, though how I'll be affected is not clear. Whether I'll want to return to such high and desperate mountains is certainly not a given. I have been exploring the value of this trip in my mind, the nature of the climbing, the people I'm here with and the quality of the experience. The ledger is still being examined. Probably the real outcome won't be fully analyzed until some time after, maybe years.

On Friday I will have been gone four weeks. I wonder if we dictate our own lives by the way we reach for goals or new directions. I think that in many ways we do, but that reshaping requires courage. I'm searching for some of that courage. It's not always easy or comfortable, and in many ways ease and comfort are precisely what we are seeking in life.

Dan is doing great. He focuses incredibly well and has his sights set on the top. I think these forced rest days affect him more than me. We've talked about patience, and maybe K2 is one of his learning experiences. K2 will require patience:

patience to slowly achieve altitude given the nature of the weather and the route conditions. Eventually, however, there will come a time for a bold step toward the summit. Too soon and the margin of safety dwindles; too late and the opportunity is gone for the season. We talk about it a lot.

It's now a cool June 18th at 7 in the morning. I'm under a mountain of down trying to keep my fingers warm enough to write this. Yesterday Dan and I did a carry to Camp One from Base Camp. It was a physically tough day in marginal weather and the rest of the team decided not to go. With all of the new snow we were trail-breaking, which added 3 hours to our previous times. I feel good this morning, though, so I guess we are getting acclimatized. Dan and I are now at least one carry ahead of the rest of the team. It's the Dan Culver School of Impatience and Motivation. I've been around it before and will be careful, as the stakes get higher, not to be drawn into the whirlwind. We talk about it and recognize our different personality traits. In many ways we complement each other; it's simply a matter of the correct personality dominating at the right time. Our cook, Gullam, has the best advice: "Going slowly. K2 is not going anywhere, not to China, not to India, you going slowly." Sound advice.

It's starting to warm up now and my fingers are able to hold the pen continuously.

K2 Base Camp is becoming a real international show. There is a Dutch team, a Slovenian team, a Swedish team and our team: all this activity, drama, intrigue. The Dutch team brought a satellite communications system. It's an amazing deal. A small dish, about 120 cm in diameter, automatically tracks a satellite when the system is engaged. We can call home anytime we want to, but it is not private and costs $25 a minute. Dr. John phoned his wife Carol in Calgary today, who wasn't expecting the call. He said it was tough because he has semi-successfully taken that component of his life (wife

and one-year-old son) and placed it in the back of his mind. His call, one minute and 58 seconds, only served to open the emotions. I don't intend to use the phone unless I summit or if something goes badly wrong with our team.
Love Always, Jim.

June 22, 1993
Dear Sue,
Dan, Phil and I got off the mountain last night after pushing our high point to Camp Three, at 7500 metres. It was a long, hard day and I struggled more than Dan and Phil, but it's just a matter of acclimatization. It is the most technically serious part of the climb, but with the strong work of the Slovenians and the gaps filled in by our team and now the Dutch down below, there are fixed ropes everywhere and so escape is fast. Yesterday we descended in two hours and 45 minutes. Granted we had good weather, but even in worse weather I know we could descend quickly. From Camp Three to the top of K2 is a walk, except for a few hundred metres on summit day. Our biggest concern, other than lack of oxygen, is finding the route in poor weather. We've brought 250 wands to mark the way.
   I thought for sure we'd receive mail today as the other Canadian team arrived, but no luck. Tough mail service around here. Though I'd love to hear from you, I know in my heart you're with me up here. Your warmth gets me through the long nights and your love keeps me focused when the going gets toughest.
Love Always, Jim.
P.S. The porters say the weather on June 21 dictates the type of weather for the summer. This year ... hot and sunny, YES!

June 24, 1993
Dearest Sue,

It looks like a mid-winter storm in Whistler out there, the winds howling and the snow continuing to fall. Weather changes are wild and dramatic here. All is well, our team is comfortably secure in Base Camp – warm, well read and certainly well fed!

No big news since my last letter, but this one won't get away for a few days, so I doubt you'll see it before the 20th of July. The only real news today was that Stacy picked the first summit team: Phil, Dan and me. This is great news in many ways. First, it's a strong team – safety in strength and experience. Second, it would be great to summit with these guys; they're going very well and I have the strongest bonds with them.

There's plenty of work ahead, lots of unknowns, and these are obstacles we'll have to deal with once the storm breaks. We have to sleep at Camp Three and then move to establish Camp Four at 7900 metres, sleep there and then hope we're feeling up to going another 600 metres to the top. We're a ways from the summit, but there's a good feeling among us.

Today we established that we'll carry a Gamow bag to Camp Three, the bag we're sharing with the Swedish team. It's a pressure contraption designed to effectively lower the altitude within the bag. It's an emergency deal. If a climber is feeling the effects of altitude, he or she can crawl inside and the pressure is changed with the use of a pump. This bag can change the altitude at Camp Three from that of 7500 metres to something more like 4000 metres. Apparently the history of these bags is startling, many reversals of cerebral edema and other high altitude illnesses. One more safety feature in our favour.

Now it's the 25th of June and nothing has changed from yesterday. The snow continues to fall steadily and we have been reduced to reading and eating machines. I suppose there have been a few hours of sleep thrown in as well.

I just finished reading *Leaven of Malice* by Robertson Davies, the second of his *Salterton Trilogy*. The books are going fast; my selection will be done soon. Fortunately, there are lots of books about camp that I am anxious to read if the mountain doesn't want us on its slopes.

It's a funny thing, but until these past couple of days there has been no opportunity to really relax and let my mind drift. These trips are often ripe with such chances, but this one has been paced very quickly and with so many new experiences invading my brain, and the many chores that consume our days, there has been little chance of a clean slate in my head to allow new or developing thoughts to grow. So, despite my desire to get on with the task at hand, learning to enjoy and grow with this idle time is my new, tough assignment. The *Tao of Pooh* talks about it, they sang about it in *The Life of Brian*, and it's up to me to let life's flow of energy work for me instead of trying to force it in some direction it doesn't want to go. Easy to say, tough to live.

June 26th. The weather has shifted and the skies have cleared. Lots of snow from the past few days is sloughing off the steep mountain slopes surrounding us. As the day's heat builds, we'll certainly see an increase in avalanche activity from the steep, rocky slopes. Our latest plan is for Phil, Dan and I to leave soon, probably at 2 a.m. tomorrow, and make an attempt on the summit. That would take four days up and two days down, so our weather window needs to be pretty long. We'll see how it goes. We'll also have to feel comfortable sleeping at Camp Three and then at Camp Four at 7900 metres. Lots of questions to be answered and the only way is to make the move.

I'm a bit nervous, only about the altitude, and I will be doing a good job of listening to my body up there. The altitude will affect our decision-making abilities, and decision making is crucial at this stage of the climb. It will take an incredible mental and physical push to reach the summit, but we don't want to step over the line just to summit K2. I feel fit and rested, however, so we'll go and check it out. There is still lots of time, though it would be fantastic to have it all behind us quickly. We're all packing and deciding what we can do without, how to lighten our loads without endangering our lives. There is a hesitant buzz of excitement, our first summit bid and everyone is feeling the drama. The four who aren't on the first summit team – Stacy, John, John and Steve – will be following behind Dan, Phil and I, supporting us from one or two camps below. Here we go.

Well, Sue, my stomach is full of butterflies but they'll calm down once I'm on the hill. I'll use you to help me make my decisions; you're a big part of my future. If we get a big weather window, who knows how it will all work out. I am anxious to hold you and to know your sweet smile again in my life. Take care of yourself, Sue, and I'll be seeing y'all soon.
Love Always,
Jim XOXOXOXOXO

June 28, 1993
Dearest Sue,
I'm sitting in my tent in Base Camp listening to "Unplugged" by Eric Clapton. Bonnie Raitt will come on soon with "Let's Give Them Something To Talk About." It reminds me of Rogers Pass and the way you and I fell in love. My memories of time spent with you carry me these days on K2.

The weather is still not cooperating. We had such an excellent start, but the momentum has died and the energy will have to be rekindled when the time is right. K2 is a waiting game.

🦎

It's now after dinner, the light is fading and I'm huddled under my mound of down, writing. The weather is showing some signs of improvement. In the past couple of hours, the wind screaming across K2's summit has stalled and the skies are trying to change from obscured to clear. We'll be up at 1 a.m. to take a look and make a decision about whether this is an appropriate window for a summit attempt. Dan is anxious to the point of being fidgety, but patience is the name of the game. We'll see how we handle the thin air when the time is right. Not before.

K2 has provided some great personal insights for me. I don't think it is because I'm simply away and have time for thought, though significant time away from the pleasantries of Western Canada is something that allows thought processes to jell. I really feel that K2 itself, the nature of the climbing and the seriousness of the mountain, play a huge part in how my thoughts are going. For the past 17 years, mountains have played an increasing role in my identity and my persona. I think you've clearly seen that in the past year. K2 and this trip and my time with you in the past are changing my perspectives. It's a difficult thing to describe, particularly since it's not clear in my own head, but I sense it is in the process of focusing in my thoughts. I'll keep you posted.

So, my love, it's time I turned in so the 1 a.m. alarm doesn't find me too groggy. If tomorrow is yet another rest day, I'll add to this; if not I'll be off to Camp Two.
Love Always,
Jim

July 2, 1993
Dearest Sue,
Happy Canada Day. I came off the mountain yesterday after a three-day stint into unsettled weather. I wish I could tell

you our schedule here for K2, but it all depends on the weather. We've been waiting now since June 21st for our "break" for the summit. Patience is a learned virtue and we are all learning; K2 insists on it. There is some hope for tomorrow. The Swedish team down the glacier gets weather reports from the Swedish Meteorological Service via some elaborate set-up, and they are calling for a shift tonight and a four-day window of weather. We'll see.

My last trip up the mountain revealed some new insights into both myself and the challenges of K2. Dan, Phil and I left at 2 a.m. on the 29th and pushed right through to Camp Two at 6700 metres. We arrived at 3 p.m. after a long and tiring day. The next day we were to go to Camp Three to sleep, but after about 150 metres, I knew I couldn't do it. I turned around, knowing that Dan and Phil could be going to the top. Lots of thoughts ran through my head, but the bottom line was that I wasn't acclimatized and going on would have been dangerous. It was one of those threshold things and now that I've passed it and dealt with it, the decisions in the future should be easier and clearer.

Anyway, I returned to Camp Two by myself and worked there on the camp and spent another, much better night, which will help with acclimatization. Dan and Phil ended up turning around too, because of poor weather. Back in Base Camp, Doctor John has me on a prophylactic course of Diamox now to help with the acclimatization process. Stacy, John, John and Steve have been using it with success. Dan, Phil and I had a different philosophy. But now, for me, philosophy is out the window and "better living through chemistry" is in! I'm the control in the Diamox experiment, so I'll keep you posted after my next shot at Camp Three, and beyond.

We're doing well and have established many safeguards: Gamow bag, fixed lines from BC to Camp Three, the latest high altitude drugs, well stocked camps in terms of food and fuel, three-person teams, etc. All of us are keen on returning home, me most of all. I sometimes wonder if I've got the guts to climb K2. I still don't know how close to the line one has to wander, but I feel I may not have the ability to wander too close. You know me. I'm your basic wimp-chicken. Things will have to be going very well for me to reach the top.

I wonder if you'll recognize me when I get home. I'm certainly not losing any weight, probably gaining with all of these days in Base Camp, and my body is changing from biceps to belly. My climbing goals are shifting a bit, too. 5.12 on rock is the next plan.

It's dinnertime. Who knows, maybe we'll wake up at 1 a.m. and the Swedish report will have been right and the push will be on. The sooner we climb this great mountain and I can fly home to your arms the better. I've been gone six weeks now and we're halfway at worst. I am hopeful for August 1st, but I'll let you know somehow once the dates become more fixed and the summit is a done deal.

Love Always,

Jim XOXO

Back in Vancouver, I checked the mail every day and read Jim's letters over and over, especially before I went to bed. Some nights I went to sleep dreaming of marrying my brave, confident love, and other nights, especially as he neared the summit, I could only think of running away from him as fast as possible.

By July 12, 1993, Jim had been gone for almost two months. Rays of mid-morning summer sun plunged through the windows of my apartment. Humming to myself, I let a cool ocean breeze in through the balcony door. What to do today? A jog along the seawall? A bike ride? I was making the bed when the phone rang. "Hello?"

"Hi, Sue. It's me, Patti." Her voice trailed off. It was Dan's wife.

"Oh hi, Patti, how are you?" I pinned the phone to my shoulder with my cheek and flicked the sheet.

"Sue, I have bad news. Dan is dead."

"No!" I shouted and dropped the sheet. What about Jim? Where's Jim? But I was too scared of the answer to ask.

Patti sighed. "Yes, he is."

"No!" I yelled again and gripped the phone with both hands.

"Jim called last night. The Dutch team let him use their satellite phone. Jim is fine. Dan fell on the way down. They couldn't find his body." Patti spoke methodically.

I slumped to the bed in relief. Jim was not dead. "Oh, Patti. Is there anything I can do?" The phone shifted in my sweaty palm.

"No, thank you, honey."

"Is anyone with you?"

"Ryan is here. My brother is coming." Ryan is her 13-year-old son from her first marriage.

"Oh, Patti, I am so sorry."

"Yes."

We said goodbye, and I sat there paralyzed and vibrating internally all at once, still clinging to the phone. The news of Dan's death ricocheted through my body. My arm felt like cement when I lifted the receiver to call my father.

"Hullo?"

"Hi, Dad. It's me, Sue," I wavered.

"Hi, Sue. What's wrong?"

"Dan is dead. He fell." I fingered my bottom lip.

"Oh dear, oh, Sue. Is Jim okay?"

"Yes, he's fine." I got up and paced.

I knew Jim was not fine. He was alive but he had watched his friend fall. I wondered if he would ever be the same again.

"Oh, Sue, you know, I'm not all that surprised." Dad pressed on in a soft voice. "That's why I hugged Jim when he left. I knew there was a good chance we would not see him again." His words hit me like a wall of ice-cold water.

"It could have been Jim" is what Dad was saying. It could have been Jim. Later, I read that 33 per cent of the climbers who attempt the summit of K2 are killed. So of course it could have been Jim, but I was not even aware of that statistic at the time. I shook my head to push the painful truth aside. It could have been Jim.

I walked for hours along Jericho Beach until there was no more sand, and I climbed the steep embankment up to the university library. Inside, I ran my fingers along the book spines and pulled out a volume of poems by Earle Birney. I scanned them, looking for key words: grief, husband, wife, mountains, fall. Back and forth until I decided on a poem from *Last Makings*.

When we must part

sweetheart, think that my death
swings wide your harbour's mouth
to welcome in the young & joyful
the quick eyes ready for the searoads
time is yours for choosing
the love to sail the world with

(and the father to make with you
the unborn waiting to be loved)

if clouds hang heavy now
remember how your gentle sun
wheeled my rough planet round you
believe in my belief
that you were made to shine
with love
and being loved

swim proud dear princess
let no one dim
the brilliance of your mind
let no one bind
the courage of your heart

my small one so tall in patience
i think you will grow wise as Orcas
yet never lose your dolphin curves.

I copied the words on the inside of a card I bought for Patti. On the way home, I picked up a few bags of groceries for her. I couldn't decide if I should get comfort food or healthful food. The bags bulged with potato chips and mixed greens.

When I arrived at Dan and Patti's log home on the banks of Indian Arm, the front door was open a crack. I tapped on the swollen wood and felt the salty residue stick to my knuckles. No answer. I eased the door open and peered inside as if I expected a burglar to appear. Swoosh, swoosh, a tall man strode toward me, hand outstretched. "I'm Patti's brother."

"Hi, I'm Sue." I shook his hand.

"Patti and Ryan are in there." He relieved me of my shopping bags and pointed with his chin.

I tiptoed to the door of Patti's bedroom and heard sniffles. "Come in, Sue." Patti's voice was high and strained. I stood in the doorway. Ryan, Patti's son, sat on the bed facing her and held her hand. Patti dabbed at her red nose with tissue. "We're coming out now anyway, right, Ryan?" Patti tried to smile and raised herself jerkily from the bed.

"Are you okay, Mom?" Ryan reached forward, ready to steady her.

"I'm fine, honey." She laid her hand gently on his arm.

I moved forward to hug Patti. "I'm so sorry, Patti."

In the living room, Patti patted the couch beside her and I sat down.

"This card is for you." I placed the white envelope in her palm.

"Thank you." Patti opened the card, and I watched her eyes roam over the words. About halfway down the page, she crumpled at the waist. "Oh, God." She closed the card, crying, and looked at me, "Thank you. I'll have to finish reading it later."

She must have come to the part in the poem about having a baby. It was too late to take the poem back. I wanted to take away some of her pain. I didn't want to cause her more. At the same time, I knew that nothing I said or did would bring Dan back. And this poem honoured their dreams together.

"Jim sounded strong when he called. He was crying but his voice was strong," Patti reassured me.

"If there's anything I can do…" I held her hand.

"My family is here." The room was so quiet I could hear the ocean lapping outside.

Four days later, Jim's parents picked me up to go to Dan's memorial service. Entering the church was like walking into a forest. Evergreen trees towered and waved through the floor to ceiling windows and skylights. People flowed in like water, some eddying around a collage of photos of Dan. He looked so happy.

Patti took big gulps of air before she stepped up onto the stage-like platform.

"Thank you for coming, everyone. I've brought some vegetables and flowers from our garden because Dan and I really enjoyed the garden. It represents so much life. I am so proud…" Patti lowered her head for a second and then continued, "I am so proud of Dan for being the first Canadian to summit both Everest and K2. And I think it is very important for us to acknowledge Jim's achievement of summiting K2. He will need our love and support when he gets home." A lump formed in my throat, and I sat on my hands in the wooden pew.

After the service, I waited in my seat for the crowd to disperse.

A friend leaned over to me and whispered, "I wish Jim were here." I covered my mouth with my hand and sobbed as silently as I could.

On the way home in the car, Jim's mother, Mom Haberl, turned around in her seat to ask me, "What do you think Jim would like best for an airport reception? A lot of people are talking about going down to meet him – Matt, Alastair, Kevin. What do you think?"

"It would be great for Jim to see his closest buddies there. That would be a huge show of support."

"We'll see." She faced forward again. I pondered her question, and by the time they dropped me off I wasn't so sure of my answer. I wanted to do what would be best for Jim.

That night, I dreamed that I met Jim at the airport and gave him a hug but he didn't return it. I squeezed harder, but he just gazed off into the distance.

Shortly after I woke up, Jim's younger brother called to say that the family thought it best if I went alone to meet Jim at the airport in Seattle. I was the one he would want to see. Jim would be home in two weeks.

The Sunday morning of Jim's arrival dawned beautiful and sunny and I walked to the beach for a swim. It will relax me, I thought. After a shower, I scrutinized my closet and soon covered the bed in discarded outfits. The clock ticked. My nervousness turned into procrastination, and I left 15 minutes later than planned. "Why do you do that?" I berated myself. I was often late. I drove down to the Canada–US border and clenched my jaw when I saw the lineup of cars and the estimated one-hour wait. I had only allowed 45 minutes for the border. I planned to be holding the eight-foot-long poster I had made that read "Welcome Home! Congratulations!" as Jim arrived. Now, Jim would arrive and I wouldn't be there. The car heated up as I waited, and the skin on my thighs stuck to the seat when I raised my legs to get some relief from the burning, sweaty feeling.

I pulled up to the arrivals area of the airport just in time to see some K2 shirts and team members loading a car. I ran over. Steve said that Jim went back into the airport one last time to find me because he knew I was coming. I turned to see him striding toward me.

"Hey, there you are!" He beamed.

I ran to him, squeezed him and kissed his smooth cheeks, his lips, and we laughed. I felt his flesh and knew without a doubt that he was alive.

"God, it's good to see you," I gasped while I buried my nose and mouth in the warm earthy smell of his neck.

"You too. You look great." Jim grinned as he scanned my tanned shoulders.

My cheeks ached from smiling.

"Where's all your stuff?" I asked without letting go of his hand.

Together we hefted two square burlap packages containing handmade carpets into the trunk. Beside them we crammed his climbing pack and duffle bags. At every opportunity, I ran my hand down his arm, rested my fingers on his shoulder or grazed the back of his neck. Each touch set off another adrenaline high. He was alive.

As we drove to one of the climbers' houses in Seattle to go over the details of Dan's accident, I focused on directions. I chatted with the energy of a small bird and laughed at nothing. As we pulled into the driveway, Jim's facial muscles tightened to pull in a breath. I followed his gaze to the front door where Dan's father slumped, eyebrows raised in Jim's direction. I squeezed Jim's leg, leaned over and kissed his cheek.

"Dan's family is keen to talk to the team alone so we thought it would be best if all of the other partners and spouses went for a walk together. Okay?" Jim glanced at me and looked back at Dan's father.

"That's fine. I love you," I said quietly.

"I love you, too." Jim ambled away from me. He was swallowed by the arms, voices and gut-wrenching sobs of those who desperately needed to hear his story. The juxtaposition of the two groups struck me. We were ecstatic to have our loved ones home, while Dan's family and friends were torn apart.

An hour later our group returned from our stroll, laughing and enjoying each other's company. I squinted into the sun to see Jim smiling down at me from the balcony. I covered my mouth and stopped laughing, but when we got close enough he said, "It's nice ... to hear the laughter." I breathed a sigh of relief.

Driving home to Vancouver, Jim rested his hand in mine as he always did in the car, but it felt lighter, as if the slightest movement would jar its hold. Our words skipped around as if they were not certain whether or not they wanted to be heard. I alternated my gaze between the road and Jim and was grateful not to have to keep eye contact.

"Jim ... I," and my gaze flipped back to the road, "want to be there for you, but I'm not really sure what to do." This was unfamiliar territory for me. Generally Jim took care of me and requested very little attention in return. In fact, he was uncomfortable as the one in need. He didn't like to feel indebted.

"This is great, Sue, you don't have to do anything," he reassured me.

"But I mean if you want to talk about it, I'm happy to..." I trailed off.

"It's just great to be home," he said and kissed my neck. It was going to be okay. We were going to be okay. For the rest of the trip we exchanged stories, news and plans for the future. Where did he want to stay in Vancouver? He had no fixed address. He could stay with his parents. I offered for him to come and stay with me. He agreed immediately, but there were butterflies in my stomach telling me that he was uncertain. Usually he was so thoughtful, deliberate and confident about his decisions. Now I second-guessed him silently.

At my condominium, Jim fielded phone calls from newspaper

and television reporters. Everyone wanted to hear the story of how Dan died. Soon the living room was full of portable studio lighting, huge camera lenses and microphones. Jim was emotional as he described how he and Dan walked arm in arm to the summit of K2. In short childlike sentences, he described how Dan fell. The headlines didn't hold much back:

K2 Scaled, Draws Blood

K2 Climbed, Claims Yet Another Life

Climber Recalls Deadly K2 Day: Jim Haberl Watched Dan Culver "Roll By"

Climber Who Died After Besting K2 Eulogized As "Bright Shining Blade"

A Life Lived To the Outer Limit

K2 Assault: His Ambition Was To Preserve the Wilderness

Dan Culver Had Died Doing What He Wanted To Do

When all of the cameras were gone, Jim sat motionless on the couch. He would tell his story many more times.

THREE
AFTER K2

(SEPTEMBER–NOVEMBER 1993)

Mountain Equipment Co-op sponsored Jim to give a κ2 slide-show at John Oliver Secondary School in Vancouver. One thousand people stamped their feet and shook their umbrellas as they squished into the auditorium. More than a hundred people clamoured at the door where tickets were being scalped. Jim surveyed the throng of people, some standing at the back and down the sides of the auditorium, and clasped his hands in front of him. "Wow!" he exclaimed. Eleven members of my family occupied the row right in front of Jim's podium. I grabbed both of his hands, kissed his cheek and wished him luck. He wore a κ2 T-shirt and jeans and stood alone onstage.

The show began with photos of Jim's close friends: his younger brothers Pat and Kevin, buddy Matt from Camp Potlatch, high-school friends Eric and Geoff, climbing partners Michael and Mike. His voice choked up and his hands trembled as he thanked these people for being in his life. "Here we go," he half joked to the crowd. "Shake it out, Jim." And the climbers in the audience chuckled at this climbing expression used to calm the jitters.

The natural storyteller in him took hold, and he relaxed as he detailed the long trek into base camp, the countless storm days, the slow ascent to the summit. The audience watched silently as Jim simulated just one step of his 13-hour summit day. He breathed slowly and heavily into the microphone 15 times, then stopped and said, "And then I took another step." For 13 hours he used this as his mantra to keep forward momentum, 15 breaths and then a step. And if he couldn't take a step after 15 breaths, he made up for it with the next step. Thirteen hours to gain an elevation of 600 metres, and there he was, just below the summit. Jim dug out a little platform in the ice and sat down to wait for Dan. It was their dream to reach the summit together. When Dan arrived, 45 minutes later, they linked arms and walked the final steps to the summit and hugged.

There was a holding in the crowd then, as if people had taken a deep breath.

Jim explained, "You know, we could see clear down to China from there. It was a pretty neat feeling." With those unassuming words so typical of Jim, the crowd let out its breath and laughed, and applause erupted. Jim and Dan were the first two Canadians to reach the summit of the world's second-highest peak and the crowd celebrated what it must have felt like to be at the top of the world.

When the noise died down, the screen went black and the light from the podium carved shadows in Jim's face. "This is going to get harder," he said and took a deep breath, "But anyways…"

I leaned forward in my seat.

Jim gripped the sides of the podium, closed his eyes and cocked his head. He ground out each word through his stiff jaw. He rocked his head from side to side as if trying to dodge the pain.

"We were focused now on getting down safely to camp," Jim explained. Jim led the way and had descended the technical bottleneck section when he heard a loud crack behind. He turned and saw a shock of blond hair and Dan cartwheeling down the steep slope. Dan stabbed repeatedly at the snow with his ice axe, trying to get a purchase. Seconds passed and then he was gone. Jim opened his mouth and then closed it. He opened it again and a cry for help came out, and then he followed the body imprints. They became progressively farther apart and deeper and more jagged. Jim retrieved Dan's hat. He carefully picked his way down the slope until it dropped off the impossibly steep south face of K2. He sat down in the snow and felt the salt of his tears stinging his cracked lips. Dan was dead. He knew it. But a voice inside of him nagged. What if he got caught up somewhere and is waiting for me to come and rescue him? What if? But logic told him Dan was dead, and now Jim needed to get it together to survive. So, he put his heart into a bottle and set about climbing back up to Camp Four. Partway there, he met up with his team members Stacy, John and Steve, who were dressed for rescue. They had heard Jim's call. Jim managed to breathe out, "Dan is dead," and he crumpled backward into the snow.

As I listened to Jim's story, my body tensed. "No," I wanted to scream. I wanted to wrap myself around him. I wanted to rewind the story and rewrite it so that Dan and Jim descended safely and returned home to a hero's welcome.

The last slide of the show was of Dan – a tribute. Jim finished by saying, "Reaching the summit of K2 was an incredible experience, but I would trade it in a heartbeat to have Dan back."

It was a choice he did not have. He made a different choice by climbing K2.

As the applause built to a roar, I beamed at Jim. The lights came on and excited murmurs filled the space. Jim hung around the podium, and people moved forward to congratulate him. I waited until he was alone. He squeezed most of the air out of my lungs with his hug.

Despite Jim's letter detailing how much weight he'd put on at Base Camp, he had actually lost 10 kilograms on the mountain, and weighed about 55 kilograms. One morning, he clutched at his stomach and grimaced but insisted he was fine. I convinced him to see a doctor, who prescribed Flagyl to treat giardia. The next night, my stomach turned; it was clear that I had caught whatever Jim had. Each time I got out of bed, Jim's body tensed beside me. He asked me if I was okay, but he kept his distance. I did not ask him for help because he was having a hard enough time looking after himself. As I hunched over the toilet, I longed for the "old Jim," who would have held my hair back and out of the vomit and rubbed my back.

The next night, I woke up to Jim's whimpering. He yelled so loudly that he woke himself up. I put my hand on his arm and asked, "Are you okay?"

"Bad dream." He pulled the covers up around his neck. I wrapped my body around him and tried to absorb the pain.

As we both struggled, the void between us intensified. One evening Jim and I sat on opposite sides of my living room, and I asked him to let me in, to help him with his grieving. Jim gazed past me and said, "I don't think it's fair to ask you to carry the burden of the risk I have taken. It wasn't your choice to climb k2, it was mine, and you shouldn't be asked to share the cost."

I sat up at the clarity and practised nature of his words. As I leaned forward to assure him I wanted to share the burden, he looked at me with dull eyes and continued, "Sue, I'm having trouble finding my feelings for you."

I gulped and held my breath. A few tears trickled down my cheeks, but Jim remained on the other side of the room.

"I think it would be best for me to go and stay at Eric's place." Eric lived in Squamish, an hour's drive away.

"Please don't go," I pleaded. Without another word, he went to the door. We didn't hug. My sobs echoed in my ears until I noticed the silence surrounding me and caught my breath. It was so dark.

The reality of Jim breaking up with me clashed with my plan of being the supportive girlfriend. I continued my summer routine of exercise and socializing but avoided close friends and family. Patti called to ask whether Jim had one of Dan's ice axes. I said I would ask him but that he was at Eric's place. I asked her how she was coping, and she said day by day. She paused and asked, "How are the two of you doing?"

"Oh, fine. You know, it's an adjustment." My voice quavered. There was silence.

"You don't sound fine," she said softly. I told her everything, how Jim had left. She invited me for dinner. I couldn't believe she had the strength to listen to my problems, but she did.

"Try to be patient with Jim," she advised. "He's going through a lot."

A week later, when I was biking to my softball practice, Jim drove up in front of me. We had not seen or spoken to each other since he left my apartment. I pulled up, straddling my bike as he approached wearing a toothy grin.

"Hi," Jim began.

"Hi," I replied into my baseball mitt.

"How's it goin'?" He stood right in front of me.

"Fine," I lied and hoped my voice wouldn't crack.

"Where are you headed?"

"Softball," I whispered.

"Hm. Well. Take care of yourself." And he popped back to his car. How could he be happy? Jerk. I'd worked hard in my life to avoid rejection, often by being who others wanted me to be. Now I'd been rejected and I didn't know what to do. Anger festered deep inside of me. Anger at Jim for ignoring my pain. Anger at myself for not calling him on it. But confrontation frightened me.

Within a few days, a card arrived at my apartment:

Dearest Sue,

Of all the women in my life, you have most filled my desires and ideals for a mate. Hearts, however, are things over which we often have little control. I hope your life is treating you well and love is just around the corner. Patience is one of your many virtues and with it you will find happiness. You are one in a million. Take care of yourself, it's important. Thanks.

Love, Jim

I interpreted his card as an invitation to stay connected, which is what I wanted. I didn't feel quite so rejected anymore. With renewed hope, I began my reply, but it took me many attempts to create an acceptable first paragraph. The next day, my writing was interrupted by his phone call. My heart beat faster as we both stuttered out greetings and pleasantries. I wanted to say the right thing so that he would fall in love with me again. I wanted it to be like it was before. He needed space and time. He missed me. I needed more certainty of his feelings for me. I told him I loved him, said goodbye and sat down to rewrite my letter.

Dear Jim,

I think and dream about you a lot and am trying to make sense of this whole thing. I knew it would be difficult when you returned from K2. But I guess I had my own expectations of how you would deal with the trauma you've experienced and that included me being there to comfort you. Although it has been difficult, I have now let go of any control I wished to have over your healing process. You'll figure out what you need. In the meantime, in my eyes, you have gone on another expedition. Just as with K2, I will hold my confidence and my love for you until you return. I've made this decision consciously, although it scares me to death because there are no guarantees how you will feel about us when you return. But there are no guarantees in life and I have gone with my gut feeling here. Whatever happens, this will have been one helluva learning experience for both of us.

You asked me if I had any ideas how to recover your lost emotions. It's normal to feel numb when grieving. Counselling and allowing time to grieve are my only suggestions. An organization called Living Through Loss comes highly recommended. I've enclosed information. I've decided that I should talk to someone too, although the idea of exploring the pain terrifies me. But forgetting something we wish were not true is only too easy.

I still feel in a daze about all of this. I remember the time we've spent together with a smile. Those memories will be an integral part of getting me through these tough times. I've always had so much confidence in you and I know you'll work through the pain and be stronger for it. I can't wait for you to come home, but until then, know that I'm loving you and supporting you from afar. You are such a special person, Jimbo.
Love, Sue
P.S. I ate that whole tub of Häagen Dazs you left for me. It was great!

A week later, we met for dinner at the Naam Restaurant. I babbled away about whatever new came to mind. When I took a breath, he looked shyly at the table and commented, "That was quite a letter, Sue. I don't know what to say. Thanks."

I averted my eyes and responded with a quiet "you're welcome." He described how he met a reporter at the beach for an interview. They sat on a bench while she listened intently to his story. Looking at the table again, Jim said that this woman invited him to go for tea or a drink, whenever he wanted.

My head raced. "Why did you tell me that? We're having enough trouble as it is. Why would you say that?"

"I dunno, I dunno," he shook his head.

What did he want from me? I stuck by him even though he couldn't commit, and now he said this. Why? To give me more reason to doubt? To push me away? To build his own self-esteem? This last reason made me angry. Would he hurt me just to feel better?

His eyes were wet when he looked up at me. In a low voice he said, "I'm going away." My blouse clung to my underarms, and words stuck in my throat.

"Right," I croaked.

"It's a construction project in the Northwest Territories with Geoff. It'll be good to spend time with my buddy. I'll be gone for six weeks." My eyes sank to the table and I caved inward. He was leaving me again. This was not the plan. He had been home for two months and now he was going again. I had nothing to say. I realized that my letter was naive. I was not willing to wait for Jim if he didn't love me. I finished my meal as quickly as I could and motioned to the waiter to bring the bill.

Jim phoned most nights while he was gone. With each conversation, fear pulled my heartstrings taut like a bow. I wondered why I rejected a proposal for a date from a pleasant fellow I met by chance.

Six weeks later my body sagged as I stood in the arrivals area, waiting for Jim's flight. I cringed when he bounced over beaming a warm smile. Although his clothes hung on him and stubble shadowed his face, he looked cuter than I remembered. My legs and arms went forward out of habit and we embraced stiffly, but my body repelled his as if we were magnets similarly charged. Jim's words faltered, "Hey, how are you?" But he didn't press forward.

"Fine. You?"

It was a quiet drive back to my place. Jim gazed forward with worried eyes, and my knuckles were white from gripping the wheel. I hung up my jacket, sat on the couch and folded my hands in my lap. Jim lowered himself beside me. Through pursed lips I lamented, "This is not working for me. I've had enough. I have no idea what you want." My face stayed stiff and my gaze was steady.

Jim fidgeted with his hands and murmured, "Okay. I felt a change in you over the phone. I guess I knew what was coming. Okay." He pulled himself to his feet, shuffled to the door and left. I covered my face with my hands and cried.

Dear Sue,
Here is the inevitable letter. I can't just let you walk away without some thoughts.

Cold turkey is a bit hard on me, though I keep telling my-self that it is for the best. I miss the comfort of knowing I can call you, share my thoughts with you and feel your exciting and tender warmth – I guess that fits my unrealistic pattern of actions and emotions that don't jive with your definition of a relationship.

Next Monday (the 25th) I am on my way to Nevada to meet Eric for a 10-day stint of rock climbing (should help to clean the mental slate). I think about you often. Not with any bitterness or anger, mostly warm thoughts, disappointment and a few questions. I don't wonder why it went the way it did; that was clearly laid out. I sometimes wonder if my life is unrealistic for a relationship or whether someone could "hack" putting up with who I am. And who am I? I wonder if my lifestyle would change as a result of a relationship like I used to tell you it would. Questions. I have many of the answers to my life but not all of them! I guess that would make life a bit too easy. I certainly appreciate the energy, dedication and patience you showed with me. I think you ran into one of the toughest years of my life. I was constantly tired and my emotions rode the big roller coaster. Not the greatest im-pression. On top of that, you shared your amazing ability to excite, your love, warmth and your energy for life. You like to have fun; keep that quality in your life.

I have only one regret – our inability to jump to the next level.

Believe it or not, I know I learned from our time together. In some ways I am more determined than ever to maintain cer-tain aspects of what makes me Jim. I don't think I will waffle on that one again. At the same time, I know in the right en-vironment, I will make the changes necessary to achieve some of the goals in life that both you and I talked about and are striving for.

Sometimes I may sound a little mixed up or immature to

your ears, partly my wimp-like personality that cringes at the thought of confrontation or hurting someone. Yet I know these thoughts have to be voiced or the big hurt eventually comes and little is gained by "holding on" to emotions. See, I am learning! Regardless, I feel quite clear about the subjects we spoke about last Saturday. To be completely honest, my heart was still growing for you (in my slow way) but I sense your heart has been closed, partly by your brain to protect yourself and your ideals, and is moving in another direction.

Fair enough. Ultimately, we have to listen to our hearts.

I hope you feel comfortable enough to give me a call some day, if you feel like throwing a football around or just to shoot the breeze. We had some great walks on the beach. If you need a favour, please don't hesitate to ask. At the very least, I hope that you know I support you, continue to admire your way and am your very true friend.

Thanks for everything, Sue. We were close.

Love, Jim XO

I cried at his sweetness and wondered what he meant by "we were close." Did he mean that we knew and understood each other or that we were close to taking that next step?

When Jim returned from his climbing trip to Red Rocks, Nevada, he came over with a gift. He explained, "I can't give it to anyone else because I made it especially for you, before we split up. I'd like you to have it." I peeled away the plain brown paper and gazed at a sunrise photo of the Tantalus Range, between Vancouver and Whistler, my favourite mountains. Jim had risen at 4:30 a.m., several mornings in a row, to take the photo. I hung it in the living room, where the morning sun lit up the soft pinks and oranges.

As he told me about his trip, his voice trembled.

"We were in Red Rocks canyon doing a pretty hard route, moderate anyway. Eric took the first lead, and I was going to lead the crux. And I'm up there, a ways out from my last piece of gear, and my legs start to shake. I get the sewing machine thing happening. My hands are all greasy, and I start to think about falling. It would be seven metres at least; a pretty big fall. I back off and tell Eric I don't feel quite right. I have to talk my way through it. 'Come on, Jim, get it together,' I repeat over and over."

I sat stiffly on the couch, fists clenched, and rooted silently for Jim.

"I finished the route but, man, I was shaky. I was secretly relieved when it rained the next few days and we couldn't climb."

I lowered my gaze and forced my breath to be steady and quiet so as not to expose Jim any further. He looked like a wounded animal. After several minutes, Jim rose to his feet and fumbled in the closet for his jacket. At the door, I lurched forward into his stiff arms, and we rattled together longer than a friendship hug permits until nervous laughter broke us apart. My hand rested on his arm. When he looked at me, my eyes grew hot with tears, and he pulled me to him and kissed me.

We started seeing each other again. Maybe we never really stopped.

FOUR
BEGINNING AGAIN

(DECEMBER 1993–AUGUST 1995)

Jim and I couldn't go back to our romantic, innocent, fledgling relationship. So much had happened in a very short time; such strong experiences. Jim confided, "I think maybe the intensity of me climbing K2 pushed our relationship to a higher level too quickly." He settled in at Eric's place in Squamish and spent a lot of time at my condo in Kitsilano. We began again, but from a place of pain and love.

After his slideshow at John Oliver, several people suggested to Jim that he write a book. He wrote an article for the *Canadian Alpine Journal* and called it "Dan, K2." The CAJ awarded it best climbing article of the year. Jim began writing in earnest. After 11 weeks, he had completed a rough draft of his story. Together, we went to a desktop publishing company and they laid out the text and photos. Jim's parents put up a bond as collateral for a $30,000 loan Jim received from the bank to finance the project.

Jim and I decided to do a big trip together beginning January 1995, so I requested a leave of absence from teaching for six months. Before we left, we both wanted to finish up projects: Jim's goal was to finish his book, and mine was to finish my thesis. In August 1994 Jim and my friend Marla watched as I defended my thesis, and on December 31, 1994, I submitted the final bound copy to the University of British Columbia library.

In October 1994 Jim's first self-published book, *K2: Dreams and Reality*, was on bookstore shelves. Between October and

December Jim promoted his book by presenting a slideshow to over 20,000 people in British Columbia, Calgary, Ottawa and Toronto, and at the same time raised over $25,000 for different charities. His book became a Canadian bestseller. I attended one of the shows and, as the audience filed out, I heard one woman lament, "They just don't make men like that anymore." My chest puffed out with pride, and I quelled the urge to tap her on the shoulder and say, "That's my guy."

In January Jim and I boarded a plane to East Africa. As we navigated the small dusty airport in Nairobi, burdened with skis, climbing equipment, camping equipment and clothes for six months, a local tugged my sleeve gently and breathlessly pleaded, his eyebrows raised, "Please, where will you ski?"

I stopped, "In India, in the Himalaya."

"Ah," he nodded.

We travelled for two months in East Africa, went on safari, snorkelled in the blue waters off Zanzibar, ate fresh seafood and climbed Mounts Kenya and Kilimanjaro.

Mount Kilimanjaro is the highest peak in Africa and the highest freestanding mountain in the world, exploding from the muted plains of Tanzania like an exquisite blemish. On each side of the mountain, vast calderas, Shira and Mawenzi, step up to the main massif, Kibo. Sparkling glaciers tumble from this broad cone Hemingway described as "wide as all the world, great, high and unbelievably white." The magic of ice and snow in a crackly brown land mesmerizes.

At the trailhead, Jim and I shouldered our 20-kilogram packs while our local guides, Dismas and Meddi, balanced their bundles on their heads. We climbed "the hard way," meaning we carried our own gear and cooked our own food. With each step, our hiking boots smoked fine volcanic dust. I tongued grit against my teeth. Women wrapped in flowing, bright-orange, blue, yellow and green *kangas* craned their necks under their loads to get a look at us, followed by children holding hands who giggled when we said "*Jambo*." A flash of black and white high up in the green canopy caught my eye. I stopped and gazed upward, mouth gaping. There it was again, a flowing mass of black and white hair sailing from tree to tree.

"Colobus monkey," Dismas said and waited as we watched.

Jim and I rushed from one discovery to the next.

"Look at this beautiful orange-red flower." I lifted the delicate trunk-like appendage of a species of impatiens found only on Kilimanjaro.

"And this one." Jim focused on a mass of orange and yellow tube-like petals called lion's paw.

Kilimanjaro represents eight climatic zones ranging from desert to alpine. The lush montane forest zone, where bananas, coffee and corn grow in the fertile soil, reminds me of coastal British Columbia. Water runs from pipes connected to the main streams draining the glaciers. Higher up, the towering green vines and pine trees morph into giant heather trees up to 30 metres tall. Fissures run through the earth, and chunky black volcanic rocks are strewn everywhere as water becomes scarcer in the heath chaparral zone. Four glaciers jostle and crack their way over the crater rim of the summit.

In spite of our loads, we made good time. At altitude it is important to go slowly – *pole, pole* (pronounced "polay"), as the Tanzanians say. The body then has time to acclimatize to the lack of pressure in the air by exchanging oxygen in the lungs and getting rid of waste products more efficiently. If you go up too quickly, waste products build up in the body and the pH balance of the blood changes, causing nausea and vomiting. Fluid accumulates in the lungs, causing shortness of breath, and in the brain, causing disorientation. The body reacts like a car that is given high viscosity oil in the winter. Bodily fluids move like sludge.

Jim and I climbed as if we were in North America at sea level. I didn't know any better, and I wanted to keep up my first time at altitude because I am competitive and because I wanted to impress Jim. I tried to be perfect, to always succeed, so that I would be worthy of his love.

He asked me how I was doing at each rest stop, and I assured him that I was doing great. I felt great. Later I would learn the Swahili phrase *haraka haraka haina baraka*, meaning "great haste has no blessing."

After five hours of ascending through tropical forest, we reached our first "special" campsite at 3000 metres, a small clearing dominated by an aluminum hut with a round dirt floor: Machame Hut. All campsites off the main route were considered "special." Encased by forest, we strained to glimpse Kilimanjaro's majestic snowy summit. I thought of the first woman who climbed Kilimanjaro.

In 1927, when Shelagh MacDonald, an Australian, stepped off the train in the village of Moshi, her climbing partner remarked, "Oh, you can see the summit." Shelagh could only see cloud.

"You're not looking high enough." Her partner motioned to the sky with his hand.

Shelagh said she very nearly passed out. Kilimanjaro was tremendous, rising nearly 6000 metres from the plains. She was terrified. If there was a way to get out of climbing the mountain, she said, she would have done it, but it was too late.

Italians, Danes and Austrians arrived at our camp later that evening. I was the only female. Silently, I vowed to make it to the top.

In the dark, I crept to Dismas's and Meddi's shelter to say goodnight.

"*Jambo,*" I warned of my arrival.

"*Jambo,*" echoed a symphony of voices. I took a step back. When I did poke my head inside, at least ten bodies lay like matchsticks on the dirt floor and wide white smiles broke the darkness.

"*Lala salama.*"

"*Lala salama*," they chorused.

During the night, I stepped gingerly several times through the outdoor latrine area, a minefield, to relieve my churning gut. It's just a bug, I told myself. Nothing to worry about. But my immune system struggled at altitude.

The next day, I leaned into the long steep ridge ahead with enthusiastic strides and ignored the occasional cramp in my stomach. I pulled my hat down against the sun as the giant heather trees gave way to sage bushes jammed between the black volcanic craggy rocks. Hairy groundsel plants opened their arms in welcome. Heat wafted like smoke through the thin dry air. In this place, plants and animals must endure summer every day and winter every night.

After two hours of climbing, I sat on a rock to catch my breath. I had to push up hard to get going again. A tingly feeling sank down through my stomach and into my legs. I felt thin like the air, transparent. By early afternoon, I wobbled into camp on the Shira Plateau at 3840 metres. After filtering drinking water, I collapsed inside the tent. I wondered if I would make it to the top.

Jim prodded, "Let's go for a walk. You'll feel better." I forced myself up, and after 20 minutes of ambling around camp my lethargy and nausea eased. I spent the late afternoon reading, writing and talking to the Italian group. When the sun settled below the plains, we pulled on woollen hats and gloves. I ogled the Southern Cross blinking in the sky and felt the power of nature lift my spirits.

The next morning, we climbed into the tropical alpine zone, home to many wildflowers. Papery white everlasting fluttered on scraggly branches: happy faces in a desert scattered with shiny black rock and giant grass tussocks. Before certificates were awarded for reaching the summit, the park warden crowned successful trekkers with the hardy flowers of everlasting. We sped up the meandering trail. Above us, the 1400-metre rock wall of the Western Breach led to the crater rim of Kilimanjaro.

At 4300 metres, nausea overcame me and I sat down on a rock. Our next campsite, Lava Tower, also known as Shark's Tooth, pierced the sky in front of me. I fixed my eyes on the monolith and forced myself up the final steep slope. My body shivered and ached as if I had the flu. I looked down at my blue hands and stopped to put on gloves. What was wrong? Why did I feel so feeble? I didn't want to be the weak link and I didn't want to ask for help. Jim would know I wasn't perfect then, and he might not love me.

I plodded into camp behind Jim. "It looks like there's too much ice and snow on the breach." Jim remarked. We had planned to climb the Western Breach, the most difficult non-technical route on the mountain.

"So, now what?" I tried to sound disappointed.

"I don't know. We could go around the south side." Jim lowered his pack to the ground.

As soon as I stopped moving, I leaned over to curb the nausea. I groaned from the pressure in my skull and gagged from the scratching deep in my throat. Helpless, hopeless and miserable, I crawled inside our tent. I had never felt worse. But if I admitted that I was sick I would have to descend.

Jim snuggled in beside me with a bowl of tomato soup. I managed one mouthful before I retched.

"What hurts?" Jim was gentle.

"I dunno. I think I ate something or maybe it was the water."

"Do you have a headache?"

"Yes, and my stomach hurts, and I'm so cold. What the hell is going on?" I let go and cried.

"Let's try to get you warm." We walked around camp, but I could not generate enough heat to reverse the effects of the altitude. I shook violently as I leaned on Jim's arm. *Haraka haraka haina baraka.* Dismas sidled up, his belongings packed on his back, "We must go down, Mr. Jim." Meddi looked at his shoes.

I followed mutely, leaning on Jim like a drunken teenager,

while Dismas carried my pack and Meddi ran ahead to set up camp.

Within 15 minutes I was walking upright. Within 20 minutes I slurred a chuckle and felt foolish for causing such a fuss. After just 300 metres of descent, my nausea and headache faded to half their intensity. We made camp at Barranco Hut, perched on the shoulder of Kilimanjaro, and watched the orange glow of the setting sun set fire to the breach wall. The acute pain had subsided, but my body felt like a sack of dirt: sucked dry. I sank onto my sleeping pad.

The next morning, we decided to contour around the south side of the mountain and take an extra day to summit. Meddi and I switched loads for a laugh. He put my pack on his back while I balanced his bag on my head. With my pack on, Meddi swayed backward as if someone pulled him from behind, and my neck ached. Neither of us made it more than 10 minutes.

For seven hours we climbed over lava flows and up steep, rocky cliffs until we reached Barafu Hut at 4600 metres, the same height as Lava Tower. I braced for the onslaught, but nothing happened. I felt fine. By 3:30 p.m. we were in our sleeping bags so that we could get some rest before our start for the summit at midnight.

"Why do we start at midnight, Dismas?" I'd asked earlier in the day.

"You must be on the summit very early to get the views before the clouds rise up from the plains. And also, maybe if you saw the way, you would not go."

For several hours, I squirmed in my down cocoon, scrunched my eyes closed, listened to Jim's irregular breathing and entertained every one of my fears. The pressure in my chest began to build. The nylon roof of the tent seemed to droop closer to my face. Breathe. In. Out. Don't panic. You're fine. I shot upright and zipped open the door.

"Are you okay?" Jim rubbed his eyes.

"I don't know. I don't feel like I can breathe and my head hurts again."

"I think you should take a Decadron." Dexamethasone, branded Decadron, is a drug used for cerebral edema – fluid build-up in the brain. I pulled the sleeping bag around me and shivered.

"Don't I have to go down then?"

"No, not if you don't get any worse. And it will help you sleep, which will make you feel better."

"I don't know. What about side effects?" How many brain cells would I kill? Maybe the medication would mask my symptoms and I'd die because I didn't descend in time. As a rule, I avoided medication.

"You'll be fine. I think 90 per cent of altitude symptoms are psychological." Jim rummaged in the first aid kit. I shot him a hard look and clenched my fists in my lap.

"What do you mean?"

"Headaches are headaches. Nausea is nausea. If you overreact, I think it makes the symptoms worse. Emotion has its place, but it must not interfere with taking the appropriate action." Jim handed me the small white pill. I tried to swallow my frustration with it. My inner dialogue raged. This pain is real. I'm not imagining it. Psychological? Right.

Now, 17 years later, after I have guided people from all walks of life up and down Kilimanjaro 14 times, I understand what Jim was saying. Life is 10 per cent what happens to you and 90 per cent how you react to it. There is a point, of course, when you must have the sense to turn back.

The dexamethasone eased the pressure in my head, and I slept for one hour before the alarm went at 11:30 p.m. Jim had managed to sleep six hours. I fumbled for my clothes. Five layers on top and four on the bottom. Winter every night. With the wind chill, the temperature could plummet to –30°C.

The moon burned through the clouds to light the rubble-scree path, so we didn't need to use headlamps. For the first couple of hours, we fell into a meditative step and chatted. Then it got cold, and my legs dragged. Our pace slowed and I was breathing as if a fat cat were sitting on my chest. In my head I had conversations with my good friends Andrea and Marla back home and further occupied my mind by planning a travel language course. The words slurred and tripped in my head until I could focus only on putting one foot in front of the other. After 5.5 hours of slogging, we reached Stella's Point on the crater rim, 5800 metres. Dismas and Meddi smiled and shook my limp hand.

"Congratulations," they shouted over the wind. "You were very fast."

Jim led me to a large black boulder, where we huddled.

"Do you want to go on?" Jim yelled over the wind.

Uhuru Peak, the top, was 45 minutes away; 150 metres in elevation gain and one kilometre. My whole body screamed, "Turn back now, you've done enough!"

"I think you'll regret it if you don't go to the true summit." Jim stared at me. I wondered if he wanted me to make it more than I did. If Jim had said, "Let's go down," I'd have gone down.

"Okay," I replied meekly. He grasped my right arm as I fumbled over the rocky terrain in the dark toward the summit. At 6 a.m. we stood on the top of the highest mountain in Africa, 5895 metres, arm in arm. It is the highest I have ever been.

"Welcome to my office." Dismas beamed and swept his arms 360 degrees. Blues, yellows and oranges formed on the horizon as Kilimanjaro came to life. Below, the plains of Tanzania and Kenya stretched and curved away like the soft mound of a woman's belly. We were high enough to see the curvature of Earth. I barely moved. Great walls, several metres high, of blue ice and white snow, ran the rim of the crater and stopped us from toppling off the mountain. Nothing green. Just rock, snow and ice. I felt so small and barely tolerated.

On the way down, Jim snapped photos. My orange jacket

glowed in the rising sun. I walked on the moon, an orange moon. No smile. Arms dangling at my sides.

I gripped my stomach and forced my legs to go faster. Get down. Every 10 minutes I slumped onto a boulder, head hung low, swaying. The head lolls, I called them. Jim chatted and took photos while I phased in and out of consciousness. I thought, "I could lay down here and sleep, right here, forever." I had never been more tired or out of it. I'll have brain damage for sure and maybe just die right here, I thought.

In three hours we were back at Barafu. Meddi and Dismas sat down with their packs on. I slumped to the ground. "I can't go any farther. I need to sleep." Jim set up the tent and I collapsed fully clothed onto my sleeping bag. Dismas woke me up after two hours. I peeled my tongue away from the roof of my mouth and downed a litre of water. During the three-hour hike down to low camp, where we could sleep without worrying about succumbing further to the effects of altitude, my gait quickened and Jim and I chatted about the future: his book, finding a place to live in the mountains together. I wanted to hold that feeling of certainty forever. Jim and Sue.

Walking through the village the next day, people passed us and said, "*Poleni.*"

"What does *poleni* mean, Dismas?" I asked.

"They are sorry for your tiredness." I grinned at Jim. He was right. I was proud I'd gone to the summit. But more than anything, sharing this experience with Jim, my senses alive with the sounds, smells and tastes of this gigantic mountain, made my heart feel connected to him in a way that grounded me to the centre of Earth.

After Kilimanjaro we flew to India and braved an 18-hour overnight bus ride from Delhi to Manali in the north. Jim and I ski toured on our own to acclimatize and then hooked up with another Canadian guide, Rob, to do a seven-day ski traverse. On day three we were tent-bound on a glacier at 5000 metres for 48 hours while a storm deposited over a metre of snow on us. We took turns during the night digging out the tents. The new snow was so overwhelming that it was too hazardous to attempt our planned climb of Hanuman Tibba. Instead, we built a snow cave and snuggled in.

A whiteout greeted us the next day, and Jim led blindly up a bowl as snow cascaded from the steep cliffs around us. He chose a place to set up camp, and I asked him if we were safe from avalanches. "I think so." I slept lightly, poised to abandon camp if the roar of the falling snow came too close. In the morning, the sun hit the tent and after we dug ourselves out, we saw that we were camped on the only raised knoll in the whole basin, somewhat protected from the avalanches.

The 600-vertical-metre ski down the Beas Kund, our only ski run of the trip, was heavy with new snow. With a rope, Jim lowered Rob down the steep gully entrance to check the stability, and we followed. There was so much snow and so many hazards above us that we traversed back and forth across the slope all the way to the bottom.

From Manali we travelled south and visited the Taj Mahal and rode elephants in Corbet Park looking for tigers. In Nepal we trekked in the beautiful Langtang Valley, home of the monster rhododendrons. Jagged snow-covered peaks speared the sky. Before heading back to Canada, we rafted Nepal's Karnali River.

Neither of us were water experts, so we decided to hire a company. A 20-hour bus ride and two days of trekking later, we arrived at the put-in for the Karnali River. The lead raft guide took one look at the river level and said, "Holy shit, I've never seen the water so high. It's really pushy."

As the guides worked to prepare the rafts, they noticed we were short one life jacket. The Nepalese fellow who would steer the gear raft drew the short straw, and the rest of the crew wrapped him in a foam sleeping pad and some duct tape, hoping that would keep him afloat if an accident occurred.

The guides piled the gear in the middle of the rafts. Seven clients sank into the sponsons around the edge of each boat, toes hooked under a rope to keep from falling backwards. There was only room for six people, but we crammed in.

We began the trip with three strikes against us: heavy boats, one man without a life jacket and an abnormally high, fast-flowing river. We would be on the river for 10 days and navigate 20 rapids, some as difficult as Class IV plus. The international scale of river difficulty describes Class IV using words such as "dangerous," "boiling" and "violent." Ignorance was bliss for me. It didn't occur to me that an established rafting company recommended by a North American guide would put its clients at risk. At the time, I did not know that liability is less stringent in Nepal than in Canada and that companies do not rely on return clientele.

On the first day, we stopped at the only village we would see for the next several days. The guides bought a live chicken and strapped it face down, clucking, to the front of the gear raft.

The Karnali ripped 20 of us from our rafts that day. Some people floundered in the pumping, grey-brown river for more than three kilometres before a guide caught up to them and pulled them out. The metallic taste of the silt water lingered in my mouth until after dinner.

On our second day on the river, the group crouched around the sandy campsite listening to the lead guide.

"The river is down 1.5 metres this morning, so it won't be as pushy or as fast. We are going to stay closer together today and be more careful."

People murmured. We knew what lay ahead: a snaking canyon four kilometres long whose vertical rock walls blocked the sun and strangled the river into frothing whitewater areas called God's House, Flip 'n' Strip, and Juicer.

"I know there is talk going around. People are scared about

what happened yesterday. But we've got everything under control. Today will be better."

People spoke in hushed voices as we boarded the rafts and pushed off into the current. Downriver we heard what sounded like the roar of a waterfall. Rounding a corner, the water picked up speed. Our raft plunged first into the boiling rapids and a wave higher than the length of our five-metre boat reared up in front of us.

"Paddle!" the guide yelled as we hit a wall of water. The wave pushed our raft vertical to the sky and we stalled. In that second, I saw the cavernous black hole on the backside of the wave. I groped at air with my paddle. And then I plummeted.

Our raft went end over end. All I could see were bubbles and black. When I surfaced and opened my mouth for air, another wave slammed me back under. I thrashed. My life jacket fought against the sucking action of the river and pulled me to the surface in what seemed like slow motion. I remembered the instructions the guides gave us in case we tipped: "Hold on to your paddle. Try to grab hold of the side of the boat and then try to get on top of the boat to help the guide flip it back over." I grabbed the side of our overturned raft and the guide pulled me on top, along with one other rafter. Water streamed from his face and hair as he shouted, "Reach down and hold onto the cord alongside the boat!" We mimicked his actions and squatted to grab the elastic cord. "Okay, now on the count of three, pull up and lean back hard!" he commanded. We obeyed, and by the time I realized what was going on, it was too late. We catapulted back into the river. I squeezed my paddle and lunged for the side of the raft again. The guide was already inside and hauled me up by the life jacket. Instinctively, I scanned the waves for others who needed rescue. Within five minutes we had the whole team aboard and were plunging our paddles into the water.

A dozen strokes later our guide pushed his whole weight into the rudder and shouted for the people on the left to paddle hard.

The raft was too heavy for a last-minute change in direction. The river swept us toward a "hole," a "keeper," a whirlpool that sucks things in and swirls them around underwater like a washing machine and spits them out or, sometimes, keeps circulating them.

The hole vacuumed the left side of our raft and dragged me underwater. Kicking with my legs and beating my arms, I surfaced underneath the raft. I gulped some air and forced myself underwater again and groped my way out. I hung on to the cord on the side of the raft and tried to catch my breath as water crashed against my face. There were two people beside me and three across from me. One woman's face was ashen. "It's going to be okay!" I yelled at her but she barely nodded.

A wave tore at our cold, tightly curled fingers. I clung to the stretched cord as the water bent me backward, gushed over my closed mouth and eyes and pulled at my hair before releasing me back to the side of the boat. When I opened my eyes, I was the only one left clinging to the raft. I gasped for air through chattering teeth as water bottles, Teva sandals and paddles cruised by. Two rafters marooned on a log mid-river called for help. I surveyed the angry water. One, two, three, four, five overturned rafts. Even the gear boat was stuck on the rocks.

Our guide's arms cut through the frothy water. He manteled himself onto the raft in one swift motion, told me to look out, righted the raft by himself and climbed back in within seconds. He hauled me in along with four others. We had three paddles for six people. I paddled as hard as I could to shore. Just before we landed, I peppered the guide, "Did you see Jim?"

He looked everywhere but at me and mumbled, "He went in the hole." My mouth went dry.

As the rest of the boats limped in one by one, I asked if anyone had seen Jim. I craned my neck and saw him slumped in the last raft. Jim's features were blank, as if he had seen a ghost. I hugged him but his body moved away restlessly, and he muttered something about a warm jacket. I draped my fleece over his shoulders as he sat down and started to whittle a piece of driftwood. I sat beside him.

"Are you okay?" I whispered.

He focused on the piece of wood as he spoke in almost a childlike voice, "Yeah, yeah, um, I went into the hole."

I leaned closer so that we were touching and asked, "What happened?"

He pushed the knife rhythmically down the driftwood and explained, "At first I tried to fight to the surface but that seemed to plunge me deeper, so I made myself go limp. The river played with me, swirled me around and around for what seemed like at least five minutes. Just when I felt my lungs would burst, that I couldn't hold on any longer, the river let me go and I floated to the surface."

Jim turned his head slowly to look into my eyes and shuddered. "It's the closest I've ever felt to dying." I bit my lip and squeezed him closer to me. My body sagged. We were not safe. I had almost lost him.

Over the next five days we flipped five more times. On the final day, as the river widened into a lazy flow with not a ripple in sight, we splashed each other to ease the intense heat and the tension of the trip. Several people dove in and when one woman was inadvertently jostled overboard, she began to shake and scream. Her husband bent quickly to haul her out. Jim would later submit an article about the trip to an outdoor magazine, but they responded that the story was not believable.

After five months on the road, we touched down on Canadian soil and heaved a sigh. Clean air, mountains that beckoned and a language our brains could compute effortlessly. But we weren't home long before we headed off on another adventure. Two months remained before my teaching term began.

We drove 22 hours north in our own province of British Columbia to the Spatsizi River. We rented a canoe and drove to the put-in where we began our 10-day trip. The most difficult rapid we ran was Class III, but the consequences of an accident were severe given the remoteness of our location. Our only link to the outside world was a hunters' lodge halfway down the river, but it was early in the season and we did not expect anyone to be there. The sun shone every day and a chill in the air kept the bugs at bay. Each morning we loaded the canoe and covered our gear with a green tarp to protect it from waves. The first few days were mellow and we dipped our paddles lazily. Caribou wandered close to the shore to drink, and we marvelled at their fuzzy antlers. We camped on sandbars to avoid the bears and wolves. In the evenings, we sat on our fold-up chairs and watched the sunset. I was exactly where I wanted to be with exactly the right person.

One afternoon we stopped to have lunch and I disappeared into the tangled alder to go to the bathroom. Jim's yell pierced the silence: "Sue! Sue! Bear!" I waddled as quickly as I could back into the open, pulling up my pants as I went, and met Jim, who was backing away from the brush toward the river.

"What happened?" I panted. Jim's face was a chalky white. He kept his eyes riveted to the same spot in the trees, directly behind our picnic area.

"I heard this rustle right behind me and at first I thought it was you, so I didn't do anything. But then the sound was getting closer and I thought that it was weird that you would go to the bathroom right behind me, so I turned around. And he was right there, this black bear. He raised his big furry head, and we were almost nose-to-nose. That's when I leaped up and called to you. The bear turned tail and ran. I think he was pretty scared too!" The bear must have swum over from the mainland. We made a mental note to be on the lookout for animals, even on the sandbars.

Our guidebook indicated we would encounter a Class II plus rapid on day three. As we navigated a bubbly rocky section, we saw up ahead that the river widened and turned a 90° bend. The

waves stood up at this point and a wall of striated rock blocked
the river's course. I spread my knees wide on the scratchy floor of
the fibreglass canoe to balance against the roll of the waves, and
I raised my voice to compete with the roaring water.

"Rock river right!" I yelled.

"Got it," Jim replied. Faster and faster the river pulled us toward the rock wall, where it rushed up the sides before heading right. We fought the current to avoid being sucked against
the wall. "Draw," Jim commanded. "Draw!" Jim yelled more
insistently.

"I am!" I yelled back as the water splashed over the gunwales
of the canoe.

"I mean cross-bow draw," Jim corrected himself. We drew
closer to the wall. "Paddle harder, Sue!" We both dug in, but the
boat seemed to stall for a few very long seconds before edging
forward away from the wall. My shoulders relaxed. If something
happened to Jim and me out here, it would be days before anyone even thought to look for us.

The river widened and meandered through marsh, sandbars
and forested banks. I leaned back against the mound of gear and
dangled my legs over either side of the canoe, dipping my paddle
with one hand. Jim chuckled behind me, "I guess that's why they
call it the divorce boat!"

On the contrary, my relationship with Jim matured when we
faced discomfort and fear together. I learned that I could depend
on him under pressure. I learned that he loved me when I was
not at my best; when I was scared and withdrew and put the
responsibility on others. When I was not perfect. I had felt so
vulnerable and imperfect on Kilimanjaro, trying to keep up with
Jim. I knew now that being vulnerable allowed our love to grow.

After our river trip, we ate and slept for 24 hours at our bed
and breakfast before boarding a floatplane to the foothills of
Mount Edziza.

Rainwater funnelled down the sleeve of my jacket as I pushed through the dense salal, head lowered and doing my best to ignore the wet squelching sound of my socks inside my leather hiking boots. Under my breath I counted out 30-second intervals punctuated by a shocking toot of my air horn. Around each corner, my steps faltered and my head whipped from side to side in search of dark masses among the thick, shoulder-high brush. I stopped short in front of a steaming pile of bear scat and crinkled my nose at the acrid smell of wet fur and urine hanging in the air. If we surprised a grizzly on this narrow trail, hugged on both sides by tangled brush, there would be no escape.

After six hours of trudging uphill in a downpour, we broke out above treeline onto a moonscape of volcanic rock decorated with intermittent tufts of dry grasses. The black, grey and green striations flowed upward to the striking white snow of Mount Edziza. Brown fuzzy caribou shapes dotted the snow-covered gullies. We set up the tent and cooked dinner over the gas stove, mesmerized by the gentle movements of the caribou in the soft orange glow of the setting sun. Before bed I poked a needle into the bases of two bulging blisters on my heels.

The rain eased, and for nine days we crossed swollen glacier-fed streams, wandered over crushed black rock, and crunched on snow to the summit of Mount Edziza. We did not see another person. At our first water crossing, Jim crouched momentarily before leaping a metre over rushing water, fully loaded under a 27-kilogram pack. I edged forward on the wet, slanted, launching spot, knees bent, one arm ready to swing, puffing madly, gaze alternating between the muddy landing on the opposite bank and the bubbling water below. Breathe, bend the knees, swing the arms and jump! But my feet stayed firmly planted. What if I fall? Get wet? Twist my ankle? Come on! Get it together! Breathe, bend the knees, swing the arms and jump! But the more I thought about it, the more I couldn't move. What if? My heart sped up with the ever-increasing list of things that could go wrong. I could take off my shoes and socks and wade through, but the rocks would cut my feet, it was freezing cold and the current still might pull me over. And my blisters would get waterlogged.

"Come on, Sue, you can do it," Jim coached from the other side.

"I know. Okay, okay!" I barked. I didn't like to be left behind. I blew two short breaths through my nose, inhaled deeply, swung my arms back and then threw them forward with my leading leg. Airborne. I watched my foot sink into the mud many inches from the edge of the water and exhaled. Once I readjusted my pack, I grinned at Jim. For me, having to be self-reliant was part of the appeal of these wilderness adventures. I ventured out of my comfort zone to learn about courage, my strengths and my weaknesses, to trust myself.

The next morning, I winced as I pushed my feet into my hiking boots. The open blisters on my heels burned in spite of the padded dressing surrounding them. I tied my boots to my pack and wore woollen socks and Tevas for the rest of the trip.

The next stream crossing was too wide to jump. Water pushed against Jim's knees as he ferried our packs across. Jim returned for a third time and piggybacked me so that my blisters would stay dry.

On the final day, bugs of all shapes and sizes assaulted us as we descended through the forest. We walked briskly, at least four kilometres per hour, so that the biters were hard pressed to land. Sweat plastered the tightly woven cotton of our bug shirts to our skin. The mesh in front of my face drew strands of hair like a magnet, forcing me to continually blow at the clammy mess. At lunchtime we walked on the spot to discuss our options, slapping at miniature enemies on our hands.

"They'll eat us alive if we unzip our bug shirts to eat."

"Right. We could set up the tent," Jim offered.

"Let's do it."

As we yanked the tent from my pack, spread the pieces on

the ground and fumbled to put them together, I growled, "Now I know what people mean when they say 'she went crazy and ran screaming from the woods.' Argh! It's too much!" My hands were covered in red welts, and anywhere the mesh of my bug shirt stuck to my skin, black flies had left little bloody craters. We dived into the nylon asylum, boots and all, zipped up and thrashed about killing any bugs unlucky enough to have made it in. Satisfied we were safe, we unzipped our mesh hoods and breathed new air.

"I like how if there is something that needs to get done, you do it, even if it's uncomfortable," Jim said.

"Thanks. That's nice of you to say." I stored the compliment for safekeeping. I watched Jim eating happily, covered in welts and stinky bug repellent and thought, he just doesn't get riled. He's so steady. "You're great. I love you." I returned his compliment although he didn't need reassurance like I did.

Jim urged us to get going again. We lurched along for the last two hours, half walking, half running under our hefty packs. At the side of our pickup lake, we heaved our loads to the ground but remained standing to avoid contact with our clammy rain gear. The floatplane pilot loaded us in with a cheery, "Pretty wet, hey?" Jim and I laughed.

FIVE
TAKING THE
NEXT STEP

(SEPTEMBER 1995–MAY 1997)

Back in Vancouver, after seven months of travelling, we invited my parents out for dinner to reconnect. Over dessert, my step-mom looked at me expectantly and asked, "So, is there a special reason why you invited us out?"

"No, not really." I raised my eyebrows trying to guess her meaning.

"No special announcement?" she pressed.

"Oh. I get it. Ha. No." I laughed uncomfortably.

The next day, Jim and I enjoyed a picnic at the beach in the sun. Several curt comments escaped my lips before I mustered the courage to broach the subject on which I had been ruminating for more than a year.

"So, I was wondering where we're at," I started.

"What do you mean?"

"We've been together for three years. It seems like we could take the next step," I ventured.

"Like what?" Jim persisted with his oblivion.

Impatiently I retorted, "We could move in together."

I wanted Jim to take the lead when it came to our relationship, to take the chances, to be vulnerable, just as he did when he was in the outdoors, but he made me ask. Jim moved into my place but was only there for a few months before the ski season began.

He took a heli-ski job in Whistler instead of in the BC interior, to be closer to me, happily settling into my parents' cabin for the winter. We fell into a pattern of me driving up to Whistler on the weekends to see him while he came to me in Vancouver on his days off.

By early spring, I tired of having a part-time boyfriend. When I arrived for my weekend visit, Jim kissed my cheek, but I neglected to give him my usual embrace. We moved stiffly around one another preparing dinner. I went upstairs to lie on the bed while the sauce cooked, and after a few minutes Jim followed. He stretched out on top of me and said, "Let's get married." My heart raced. The day was March 2, 1996. I knew right away that I would marry him.

A few months later I questioned my decision.

On May 11, 1996, eight people, including two experienced mountain guides, were killed. It was the biggest disaster in Mount Everest's history. I leaned closer to the print of the local newspaper.

"Why?" I asked Jim. "Why?"

"It's hard to say if you weren't there. It's too easy to judge others in hindsight," Jim dug his hands deeper into his pockets.

"Yes, but why?" I insisted.

"Guiding a mountain like Everest is risky. The more people who go, the more inexperienced they are, the higher the likelihood of an accident."

"So why do they guide it?" I gestured at the newspaper article.

"Because people will pay to be guided," Jim sighed.

My mind chewed on the words.

Jim's climbing partner arrived at our apartment and laughed the words out, "Can you believe that deal on Everest?" His body was agitated, like a toddler.

Jim rocked forward, raised his eyebrows and guffawed, "I know, it's crazy!"

"Eight dead!"

"And Scott Fisher and Rob Hall!" Their bodies quivered with excitement. The room buzzed. I felt as if I were the only one at a party who was not high.

When Jim and I were alone, I questioned him.

"How can you act so psyched? I don't get it."

Jim shrugged.

I struggled on, "Mountaineering seems so selfish, such a waste of energy, and the courage and boldness that go into mountaineering could be put toward a more meaningful goal."

"But mountaineering allows us to be courageous and bold. In any other environment we would not perform. Accomplishments in mountaineering inspire others. Isn't that enough?" Jim countered.

"I just wonder if the cost is too great." I thought of the satellite phone conversation between Rob Hall dying near the top of Mount Everest and his pregnant wife back home, of her choking out her final words to him.

"And what about us, Jim?" My throat constricted with the truth. This was my real question. I judged mountaineering because I feared the repercussions in my own life. I admired the courage of mountaineers, but I did not want Jim to die.

Jim inhaled and then released his breath with his answer, "I'm not going back to the big mountains." My body relaxed. I did not want to ask Jim to stop doing something he loved, but at the same time a little voice nagged at me that it would be crazy to marry and to raise a family with a mountaineer who climbed above 8000 metres, in the "death zone." My pragmatic side lamented that life would be a whole lot easier with an accountant as a mate.

That summer, we drove 22 hours up the length of British Columbia's varied topography before cutting across the left-hand bottom corner of the Yukon. It took another two days to putter to Fairbanks, Alaska, where we boarded a plane to Bettles, followed by a floatplane into the mountains of the Brooks Range. A total of 3500 kilometres and 40 hours of driving.

Sometime during the third day, while stiffly raising my feet to the dashboard to relieve the pressure on my bum, I asked, "Why don't we do our own premarital classes? We could each talk about our five-year goals."

"Okay," Jim adjusted his grip on the steering wheel.

"I'll go first," I offered. "Well … let's see. I'd like to improve my climbing, find a home with you somewhere in the Sea to Sky corridor, have a baby and start an outdoor program for kids." I turned to Jim.

He gave me a cursory glance and fixed his eyes on the road. "Okay, great. Me, well, I'd like to lead solid 5.11 and climb 50 days in the year. I'd like to write a book about Alaska. More photography. I want to be more disciplined about taking photos. And living in the Sea to Sky sounds good. Yup, that's about it." He nodded his head.

There was silence as I waited for the ball to drop. Nothing.

"Jim, do you see anything wrong with our goals?" I blurted.

"No, what do you mean?"

"I'm going to have a baby and you're not." My voice lilted with the irony.

"I guess that's just where we are at," Jim clamped his lips together, staring ahead.

"That's not good enough for me, Jim. I'm 30 years old and I'd like to have a baby before I'm 35. Risk increases after 35. We need to be on the same page about this."

"It has to be the right time, and I don't know if I'm ready for a family. I know other guys who have regretted having a family."

"You're 38 years old! When are you going to be ready?" I raised my voice in frustration. Silence filled the car for the next hour and 45 minutes as we both stewed in the possibility of not getting our way. I broke the stalemate with a cautious, "So, what would make you feel more comfortable about having a baby?"

"I guess being more financially stable would help," Jim continued to stare ahead. I caught the dismissive reaction in my throat before it escaped. For me, whether or not we had a baby did not depend on finances, but I realized that Jim felt differently. And people feel the way they feel.

"What does that look like to you, being more financially stable?" My voice softened as I turned to him.

"I'd like to diversify, not to have to rely on guiding income, do more writing and sell more photographs." Jim glanced at me.

"Okay, so how about we work on that for the next few years and then see how you feel? I am very clear, though, Jim: I want to have a baby."

"Okay." Jim cleared his throat. My hand crept back into his.

For six weeks, we explored the wilds of Alaska as far north as the Brooks Range. Rain pounded down for six days straight, carving waterways beneath our tent. Grizzlies with cubs wandered through our campsite, unearthing mounds of dirt. On a boat near Seward, we clutched the railing as the wave from a calving glacier rocked us. At the end of the summer, we journeyed back to Vancouver, where I prepared for my teaching and Jim resumed guiding and writing.

In the fall, we secured the opportunity to build a house in Whistler. Over Christmas, in a backcountry ski hut where the thermometer dived to −30°C inside, Jim and I scribbled on graph paper the house we would build. Our first real home. The rest of the winter was busy as we prepared for our June wedding.

"Oh, phooey, it doesn't matter if you're not religious, you can still get married in a church!" Jim's mom swatted the air with her hand. The skin around her eyes crinkled from her laughter, and I knew she would love me regardless.

Jim and I exchanged vows in the gardens of a heritage house in Vancouver in front of 80 of our friends and family. Before the ceremony, I stood in my simple white gown and brushed my sister's hand away when she tried to fluff my hair and offer me a glass of red wine. Someone knocked at the door and pressed a card into my hand. It was a photo of a young boy whispering to a young girl. Jim had filled in the caption, "Psst, hey, guess what? We're gonna get married and it's gonna be great!" I sighed and held the card to my heart.

At the top of the stone steps, I asked my father to say something reassuring. He nodded, "You're doing the right thing."

I followed the dark-green footprints of my sisters, my oldest friend, my nieces and nephews down the grass aisle past my closest friends and family, my lips locked in a concrete smile. Jim sucked sharp, shallow breaths through the tight line of his mouth, his brow furrowed. As I drew closer, I reached for his clammy trembling fingers.

The fluffy-white-haired Justice of the Peace raised her eyebrows to peer at me over her spectacles, which glinted in the late afternoon sun. I inflated my chest and locked onto Jim's blue eyes. Tears slid down his cheeks as I spoke my vows from memory.

Jim cradled my hands, cocked his head back and held his breath.

The JP leaned forward slightly, glanced at the paper in her hand and prompted, "From the…"

Jim snapped his head around toward her and pleaded, "I know, I know!" He pulled his chin against his chest, inhaled and choked out his vows. I cried.

At the reception, Dad made the first speech. "I think everyone here will agree that Jim and Sue make a good couple. And mountaineers are a good sort, don't you think? We are drawn to them in a way. Perhaps because they dare to live closer to the line of chaos and they challenge the illusion most of us have bought into: that we are in control of our lives. They make us feel more alive. I am personally very fond of Jim and am very pleased that he is joining our family."

Kevin toasted the bride. "You know, when you talk to Sue, you really feel like she cares about what you are saying. She is a good listener. And she'll laugh at anyone's jokes, and I should know! Jim is a free spirit and he has found in Sue a partner who shares his sense of adventure, his love of the natural and elemental, his desire to live life on a daily basis. And she can keep up with him! Welcome, Sue, into our family."

Jim began his speech. "I feel like such a lucky guy because I have this incredible group of friends and such a supportive family. I often wonder when that luck is going to run out." The crowd murmured.

Jim turned and waved his arm in my direction but was silent. He clenched his jaw and shook his fists several times before he could continue without crying.

"Now, I feel as if I am the luckiest guy on earth because this intelligent, beautiful, honest, caring, loving woman picked me."

I felt lucky too. After more than 15 years of interrupted courtship and exploring the wilderness and the boundaries of our relationship, Jim and I vowed to share our lives forever. It was one of those beautiful moments in life.

SIX
BREAKING GROUND

(1997–1999)

After our honeymoon, Jim and I broke ground on our new house in Whistler with the help of many friends. I left my teaching job in Vancouver and worked as the building contractor. Late into the evenings, the steady whir of machinery cut through the night as Jim and I sanded beams, spray-painted walls, nailed in back-framing and vacuumed the constant piles of sawdust. In five months we moved in.

Jim was adamant about the type of home we should build, "Low maintenance, that's the way to go. Vinyl siding, metal windows … okay, maybe not vinyl siding. But we have to keep it simple so that we have the money to go on trips." We decided to maintain a reasonable mortgage, spend little other than for travel and have no pets or garden to speak of. Soon after Jim had finished his heli-ski season in the spring, we packed for a three-week backcountry ski mountaineering trip to the Wrangell–St. Elias mountains in eastern Alaska with friends Keith and Julia.

After several hours of driving in a heated rental car from Anchorage, we arrived in the quiet town of Chitina and my body braced against the cold Alaska air. Rubbing my forearms, I glanced about at the grey, weathered buildings, the gravel road and the wind pushing puffs of dust into the air. Even the scant greenery appeared slate coloured. I smelled wet rock, and a gritty mineral taste lingered on my tongue. Chitina reminded me of a Wild West town, without the heat, people or animals.

It was hard to imagine that dance halls, movie theatres and hotels used to line the streets. Chitina had become a ghost town overnight in 1938, when the local mill and mine closed and gave their employees two hours to catch the last departing train. Now, it was home to one hundred hardy residents; the end of the pavement and the last stop for gas before the long, dusty drive to McCarthy. I shivered.

Jim waved his arm downriver in the direction of a distant droning sound, and we knew it would not be long before the bush plane landed. Keith wrenched open the door of a storage shed in which we had organized our gear, placing it out of the wind, and we changed into down jackets and snow boots. The bush plane got bigger and louder as it approached and skidded onto the gravel runway. Paul Claus reached out his callused hand to each of us and welcomed us to Alaska. While he refuelled, we loaded our gear.

We flew along the Chitina River to the Ultima Thule Lodge, run by Paul and his family, surrounded by over five million hectares of parkland and preserve. Huskies barked from their perches on top of doghouses as our Beaver plane tottered its way to the ground. A dozen log cabins dotted the gravel along the riverbank leading to the main lodge. To one side, glaciated mountains rose 4900 metres into the clouds, while on the other side the Chitina River stretched out across the valley in a way that pulled my gaze. I felt hemmed in and drawn out at the same time, deafened by the vastness.

The next day, we bumped through the clouds over a 4300-metre pass to land on the Klutlan Glacier, a massive runway of ice stretching 64 kilometres into Canada's Yukon Territory. Behind us, at the head of the Klutlan, an amphitheatre of ice, like giant blocks of LEGO, tumbled down the highest volcano in the United States, Mount Bona, elevation 5000 metres, our climbing objective.

The wind was howling across the mile-wide glacier, so we spent the day building a snow wall around our tents, a roofless igloo. As the sun dipped behind Mount Bona, my fingers and toes froze. I felt familiar vise-grips on my temples: altitude sickness, which remained a mystery to me. I prepared mentally for it but still felt overwhelmed by headache, nausea and lethargy.

I moved slowly and took deep, even breaths, in through the nose, out through the mouth. Relax. I gulped a bowl of soup, which seemed to hit my stomach and bounce back halfway. I rocked on my knees, cradled my head and willed the internal pressure to ease. I forced a smile at Jim who rubbed my back and held a bag while I dry heaved. For better or for worse. I felt in limbo for one hour, out of control, before I escaped into sleep.

During the night, mummified in a down jacket, long johns, down booties and a toque, I wrestled to turn over in my sleeping bag to relieve my aching hips and shoulders. In the morning, I felt wet on the front of my jacket and thought, I'm losing it; I'm drooling. My breath had condensed. Crystals sparkled on the inside walls of the tent.

After several days of ski touring at 3400 metres to acclimatize, we strapped on our packs for a three-day ascent of Mount Bona. I swayed under my load, and Jim looked like a giant frankfurter on a stick.

"If you can't carry on a conversation, then you're going too quickly," Julia reminded us. I fell in behind Jim and matched his trademark shuffle gait. The sun beat down and we stripped to long-sleeved shirts and baseball hats. Peaks rose regally, looking like snow-covered old-growth trees. Séracs, columns of ice formed by intersecting crevasses, were massive ice cubes. I scanned left to right and jabbed my pole into the snow in front of me as I wove in between crevasses that gashed the glacier like forked lightning.

Every 50 metres, Jim or Keith drove a bamboo stake into the

snow that was topped with fluorescent orange tape to mark our route in the event of a whiteout. At the top of the south face, we sat down for lunch, engulfed by a sea of summits, the most impressive being University Peak.

We turned west onto a steeper, bowl-like glacier and I shortened my glides. I timed my breaths. In for two seconds, out for two. I adopted a mantra of one breath, two steps, repeat. However icy, steep or unlikely a slope appeared, however thin the air, I was confident I could keep going if I took slow, small steps. My fingers and toes felt thick. I willed my quads to drag my legs faster to create more heat. After five hours of uphill slogging, we reached high camp at 4100 metres. We worked for two hours to level ice platforms for our tents. I wolfed a frozen Mars bar, dove into the tent and tossed and turned most of the night.

The next morning, I squinted through puffy eyes at the back of Jim as we ascended the ridge toward the summit of Mount Bona. My legs wobbled like wet noodles. As the grade increased, the skins on the bottom of our skis began to slip on the steep slope, so we carried our skis and kicked steps. We took 2.5 hours to gain 370 metres of elevation, and I cursed as my energy reserves drained.

A plateau stretched like a slab of white chocolate to the base of Mount Bona, one hour away. I stopped for a snack.

With several hours of climbing ahead, I felt an urge to soak in a hot tub, eat a couple of loaded burgers and drink a beer. I dropped behind. The group waited for me, and when I caught up we discussed our options. It was 2 p.m. We had half an hour to get to the base, followed by the climb to the summit. A lenticular cloud draped over the peak, hinting at bad weather. I offered to wait while they went to the summit.

"It wouldn't be the same if the whole team didn't go up. It wouldn't seem right." Julia shook her head.

The four of us turned back to high camp. I fell behind in the whiteout and Jim slowed to check on me, "How's it going?"

"I feel bad about letting the team down, about letting myself down, and more than anything I am exhausted." I snowplowed.

By 3:30 p.m. I was dozing in our tent. Four and a half hours up and one hour to ski down. I popped a Tylenol and did not stir for 14 hours.

In the morning, we photographed the birthing sun on the highest peak in Canada, Mount Logan. We skied up to the base of Bona in three hours via a shortcut we'd found. En route to the summit, our crampons bit into the Styrofoam-like snow on the 460-metre-steep snow cone. I walked bowlegged to avoid catching my crampons on my pant legs. Plant ice axe, left bowleg step, right bowleg step, repeat. Only crevasse crossings and ice interrupted my rhythm. Jim led me by a climbing rope so that I did not topple off the ridge down the steep face. When the slope angled off, we unroped and I plodded, my mind on tropical places. Six hours after leaving high camp, we hugged on the summit. Mountaineers are one of the few groups to celebrate before the finish line. More mountaineers die on the descent than on the ascent.

On the way down, I concentrated for 1.5 hours, placing my boots purposefully as if nothing were certain. At the base of the cone, I collapsed and Jim removed my crampons. We had another 1.5 hours of skiing back to high camp. The early morning clouds had risen and even rose-coloured goggles afforded my eyes no definition in the snow. I snowplowed, neck strained to pick up clues in the terrain, knocked off balance with each plastic-like ripple in the snow. Every 10 minutes, I leaned on my poles and tried to suck energy from the ground.

Jim grinned, "How's it going?"

"I feel the shits," I snarled.

Back at high camp, 10 hours after leaving in the morning, I crawled into my sleeping bag.

"Yeah, you're really wasted. I can smell the ketones on your breath." Jim propped himself up on his elbow beside me.

I popped two Tylenols, and we watched the barometer drop.

I woke to wind snapping and drumming the tent walls and Keith yelling, "I can't even see our first bamboo wand." The storm swallowed his words.

The barometer continued to drop, but we stuffed gear into our packs to descend to base camp. The gale hurled tiny daggers of snow, so we donned goggles and face masks and slathered wind cream on all exposed skin. We developed a system of movement whereby Jim headed out into the storm and raised his pole when he found the bamboo marker. Voices were useless in the wind. The second and third person followed. The fourth person waited until Jim had found the next marker so that we could see our direction of travel. If Jim disappeared in the swirling snow, Keith ventured out until he made contact.

When we reached the south slope, the wind exploded. I lurched when I stopped, thinking I was still skiing. The ground and air were in perpetual motion. Ice built up under our goggles, on our noses and cheeks. Jim removed his glove and cupped his hand over my nose, saying, "The flesh is turning white." Like meat in the freezer. I clenched my jaw.

Julia and I huddled while Jim and Keith searched for bamboo wands. We inched our way down until we levelled out on the Klutlan Glacier, a sea of white. Jim trudged, head down, a compass in his outstretched hand, and followed a bearing to our base camp. We missed it by six metres, but Jim doubled back when he sensed we had gone too far. We dove into the tents fully clothed, warmed our faces with our hands and cracked off our frozen GORE-TEX.

"What's the point?" I buried my face in down.

"What do you mean?" Jim set up the stove in the vestibule.

"The risk/reward ratio is way out of whack for me. I thrashed my body with the altitude, had minimal skiing, had to descend in a whiteout, and, oh yeah, now I can say I climbed the fourth highest peak in Alaska. It just doesn't seem worth it." I warmed my hands on my belly.

"I can understand what you're saying, but I love our trips together. I think they make us stronger." Jim reached for some tea.

"I guess."

They scare me, I thought.

Do I dislike being on the edge because I am weak, mentally and physically? Because I do not have the energy to feel strong? Because I have little to fall back on in hard times? Why do I not desire the summit the way others do? A workout, laughs with friends, powder snow and sun are the rewards for me. But I wanted to be strong, dependable and self-reliant, and I wanted Jim to be proud of me.

Keith said extreme conditions offer more of a challenge. Julia added that these experiences reveal how much you can tolerate, and that makes you stronger.

But I did not survive on my own steam. Jim guided me. I missed that sense of self-reliance.

The storm raged on, for days. The wind ripped through the col, gathered momentum and whatever loose snow it could find, and screamed down the glacier like a river. At first I stayed in the tent for 36 hours. But I had to get out to help shovel or we would be buried.

Every day, we dug for hours to free our tents and reinforce the break walls until they were three metres high; the wind-driven snow and glacier ingested us. We melted snow for water, cooked, read, played cards and groomed. At first, the days passed quickly.

On the eighth day, the weather was so fierce that Jim and I didn't leave the tent to shovel until after dinner. The tent was submerged. We yelped as the hundred-kilometre-per-hour wind pushed us off balance. I battled to keep my shovel on the ground. Gusts drove us to our knees, where we waited for respite. Two hours later we crawled back into the tent and peeled crusty gloves, hats and GORE-TEX from our bodies. Jim did the eggbeater in his sleeping bag to get warm. I remembered the survival

Rule of Three: a human being cannot survive more than three hours exposed to severe low temperatures, more than three days without water and more than three weeks without food. I wondered how long we would be stuck on the glacier and if our supply of food and fuel would last.

At 2 a.m. Julia's voice bounced around in our vestibule, "Hey, guys, our tent collapsed. Can I come in with you?" She snuggled in between Jim and me. Keith stayed in the battered tent and braced his legs on the roof to keep it standing for the rest of the night. The storm roared like a train through a tunnel.

On day nine I brushed my hair and shuddered at the dead skin collected on the tent floor. Jim was shovelling when the lawnmower whine carried through the clearing skies. I grabbed the radio and confirmed it was Paul. We jumped into action, packed gear, put on warm clothes. In 10 minutes he landed and sauntered over, his face creased.

"Hi, guys. I can take one of you and personal gear. That's it."

"You look tired," I said.

"Yup, I've been flying non-stop, trying to get everyone out."

We decided Julia would go.

Paul looked up at the col. "Maybe I can take two." My heart flipped. As I ran to get my pack from the tent, Paul received a weather update on his radio and yelled, "Just one! I can take one, let's go. Now!" He ran to the Super Cub.

Keith, Jim and I gaped as the tiny plane took off and climbed. Before reaching the high point at the col, the plane dropped 30 metres.

"Did you see that?" Keith's eyes opened wide.

"Yeah. Oh my God." I fixed my gaze on the plane.

The plane regained altitude and flew over the pass and out of sight.

It was 9:30 a.m. Paul would take 1.5 hours to return. We packed up the rest of our camp, except for one tent, and hauled it to the landing site. We waited until a buzzing sound broke the silence, and Paul's voice crackled over the radio. The wind picked up. He backed off.

At 3:30 p.m. we were eating peanut butter and jam on crackers when the buzzing returned. We jumped up and grabbed the radio. No good. He would try again that evening. Our shoulders sagged. Keith and Jim worked on the snow walls, and I worked on the stove. We pulled necessities from our packed bags.

By 7:30 p.m. we had given up hope of Paul returning that night and slurped soup while warming our toes in our sleeping bags. When the droning sound of the plane came, we leaped into action, stuffed sleeping bags, rolled sleeping pads and packed away the stove. Our two-way radio had died, so we had no way of contacting Paul with a local wind report. He hovered on the other side of the ridge, then the col and then the pass, for what seemed like hours.

We stamped our feet on the snow to keep warm as Paul circled above at 4572 metres. Maybe he was waiting for us to take down the final tent. With numb fingers, we fumbled to break down the tent poles and shoved the rigid fabric into a garbage bag.

The plane grew smaller.

I stared at the dark sky for several moments and strained my ears. While Jim and Keith set up the tent again, I dragged our gear back to the dugout. We had no control over when we would get out.

Our situation was tedious but not dire. We had food, fuel and shelter. Paul could drop supplies to us even if he couldn't land. Failing that, we could melt snow using body heat. All of us had been tent-bound before, so we knew the score. Stay calm, keep busy, stay positive and make rational decisions. Fear, anxiety, anger and loss of will are normal reactions to high-stress survival situations, but, as Jim had told me on Mount Kilimanjaro, emotion must not interfere with taking appropriate action.

Two days later, Paul flew back in to get us. He raced the

weather. With little space in the Super Cub, and even less time, Keith, Jim and I squeezed into the plane, leaving our tents and gear behind. I felt relieved and safe inside the cramped plane. We were not going to starve or be buried by the storm, and soon we would have a hot shower.

As the Super Cub careened faster along the ice, closer and closer to a 300-metre vertical rock wall at the end of the glacier, Paul murmured, "C'mon, baby, c'mon, lift."

My gaze fixed on the rock while my hands squeezed Jim's waist. Lift, I pleaded silently. Faster and closer until I held my breath.

"Yahoo!" Paul whooped, and I felt my stomach leave the ground. He kept circling until we had gained enough elevation to soar over the rock wall. "Ha, ha!"

Once the adrenaline surge had subsided, we craned our necks to view the snowy peaks lining the glacier. "There it is!" Keith pointed.

"Yup, she's a beauty." Jim nodded in the direction of the classic-looking University Peak.

"I think I see a route on the..." And the climbing banter was lost in the drone of the engine. But I distinctly heard, "Yeah ... next year ... great."

Back in Whistler, Jim continued to diversify his work through writing and photography.

At a slideshow to promote his new book, *Risking Adventure*, a man in the audience asked Jim how his wife felt about him taking such risks. Jim replied, "Why don't you ask her?" and swung his arm my way.

When the laughter subsided, I took a breath and explained, "I would not marry Jim, or raise a family with him, if he continued to climb in the death zone, above 8000 metres. Jim decided that the big mountains are not for him anymore. We share as many outdoor adventures as we can so that I have a better idea of how skilled he is, how much risk is involved, and so that our relationship will be stronger. He works locally as a heli-ski guide so that he can be home at night, and we are only apart two weeks a year. Being in the mountains is a big part of who he is, and I accept that."

The man nodded his head up and down and took his seat. Jim grinned at me, full of love.

PART 2
AFTER

Life is pain…. Anyone who says differently is selling something.
—WILLIAM GOLDMAN, *THE PRINCESS BRIDE*

SEVEN
DAY ONE

FRIDAY, APRIL 30, 1999

I jolt awake at the sudden resonating chime of the doorbell. I lie still, listening. The piercing sound hits me again. I am not dreaming. I glance at the alarm clock: 1:30 a.m. Violent pounding on the front door rattles the window glass. I sweep aside the covers. My feet thud onto the carpet, and within seconds I am in the bathroom. My toes curl on the cold slate tiles. I wrestle with the floppy sleeve of my bathrobe.

Maybe the tenant forgot her key.

I grasp the handrail and thump down the first flight of carpeted stairs. My feet slap across the hardwood of the main floor and onto the next set of stairs. I cling tightly to the railing and swing my body around the final corner, flick on the light and freeze on the landing.

I see Jim's younger brother Kevin and Jim's best friend Eric pressed close to the glass. Kevin's blue eyes seem magnified. Eric's broad, strong, Norwegian face is set in worry. It's 1:30 in the morning and they live an hour's drive from Whistler. I search frantically for a less obvious reason why they would be here. I focus on Kevin's childlike face for the truth. Our eyes connect. His are open wide, wet. Mine plead for him to prove me wrong. He holds my gaze for a second and then slowly lowers his head.

"No," I gasp.

I stumble down the last few stairs before my knees buckle. Fear rushes into my lungs faster than I can breathe, as if I have been kicked in the stomach. I am on my hands and knees, head hung low, fingers braced against the cold slate.

Banging. Door rattling. I turn my head to Eric's worried face, reach up to swipe at the lock. There is a rush of cold air and a battery of panicked footsteps.

Eric crouches to encircle my shoulders with one hard muscular arm, clutches my forearm with his other callused hand, "I'm so sorry, Sue."

Kevin cups my elbow with one stubby hand, circles my waist with his other arm and coaxes me to my feet. I feel the dampness of my fear under his grip. As I stumble upstairs, I swallow my tears long enough to ask the question: "Is he dead?"

Kevin lowers his gaze and whispers, "Yes." I lurch forward, my mouth falls open but no sound comes out. Fear snakes around my neck and squeezes my throat. I gag. It slides into my stomach and grips my guts. Slowly it climbs its way into my thoughts.

I search for an escape. Ripped from my anchor, I tumble until I am sick and dizzy. I do not recognize myself.

I slump into the bay window seat and wipe my nose with my sleeve. Eric holds a bunch of toilet paper in front of me. Within minutes, it is a soggy wad in my hand. Kevin pats my arm and rocks back and forth on the edge of the wooden kitchen chair. "Terri and Susan will be here soon," he says. They are on their way from Vancouver.

My insides churn. I mutter, "I've got to see Jim." Kevin extends his hand to me as I stumble to the rolltop desk to pull out the wedding album. Yes, I need to see him. Where is he? The book splays open in my lap, and I let out a sigh as Jim's face smiles back at me. Crying, I trace his glossy smooth features with my fingers, the strong turn of his square jaw, the thin line of his lips. I ache to feel the soft warm give of his flesh. Oh, my sweetie.

I wonder if Jim would still have considered himself lucky if he had known he was going to be killed less than two years after our wedding?

I don't feel lucky now. I feel scared.

I hear soft voices downstairs. Someone kneels in front of me, hands on my thighs. "Oh, Susie, I'm so sorry."

I raise my gaze to Terri's big brown, glistening eyes, pull apart the wet tissue in my hand and wordlessly plead to her for help, like a wild animal caught in a leghold trap.

Kevin paces, "I wonder why I'm not crying…" His eyebrows arch. "Maybe it's because I was the closest to Jim and so have already accepted his death." I tilt my wet, gaping face to him but say nothing. Stuck. A radio on the wrong frequency.

Should I call family and friends to tell them?

Kevin has broken the news to the Haberl family so thinks I should not wake anyone else up given that it will not change anything. Wide-eyed, he recounts how the news of Jim's death spread. It was 8 p.m. when Graeme called Kevin. Vicki, Kevin's wife, was away so he gathered his two children to break the news without her. Seven-year-old Jaslyn burst into tears. Five-year-old Connor's face went still. Turning his gaze away thoughtfully, grief creasing his brow, he said softly, "Auntie Sue must be so sad."

When Kevin called his mom to tell her, he first asked whether his dad was there. She replied that he would be home any minute from his meeting. Kevin decided to tell her that Jim had been killed but learned later that his dad had not come home for another hour.

For me, time passes in a void. Finally, at 5 a.m., I call my parents in Vancouver. Eric squeezes my hand as the phone rings.

"Hullo?"

As soon as I hear Dad's deep, sleepy, suspicious voice, my throat constricts.

"Dad, it's Sue." I dig my nails into Eric's palm.

"Oh, hullo, Sue."

I take a few gulps of air, hold my breath for a moment, then, "Dad … Jim was killed." I do not recognize the voice echoing in my ears. I sit up still and straight, shocked at what I have said.

"Oh dear, oh Sue."

I hear my stepmom, Glenda, say groggily in the background, "What happened?"

"Jim was killed."

Again I hear those words.

"Oh, no. We'll be right there."

There are more calls to make.

"Hi, Marla, it's me, Sue." I rest my forehead on my hand.

"Oh hi, Sue," she says.

"Um, I have some bad news." I gnaw at my thumbnail.

"What?" she barks.

"Jim was killed." I close my eyes.

"What? No! No!" she yells.

"Yes, he was." I trace her name on the paper in front of me and put a check mark beside it.

Ken's voice in the background: "What happened?"

Marla tells him Jim was killed.

I keep hearing those words, "Jim was killed." First from Kevin, then from my own mouth, then from family and friends. Jim was killed.

It is like learning to speak a foreign language. I repeat the words but am unclear on their meaning; the conversation is going too quickly. I keep hearing the same words for weeks.

It is light outside. Incredibly, the sun has risen.

Susan leads me upstairs to shower. As I pull the flannel nightgown over my head, the reek of fear stings my nostrils. The hot water pelts my body, but I shiver. I caress my belly and plead, "Please, oh, please let me be pregnant."

Downstairs, Eric takes phone messages.

"Condolences." "All my love to Sue." The news of Jim's death spreads through word of mouth and over CBC Radio. One friend calls to say she and her fiancé were driving when the announcement aired: "A well-known Canadian mountaineer has been killed in Alaska." They pulled over to the side of the road and held their breath. The announcer continued: "Jim Haberl, the first Canadian to summit K2, was killed in an avalanche at approximately 10:30 a.m. on Thursday, April 29, in the Wrangell–St. Elias mountain range of Alaska." They burst into tears.

Where was I at 10:30 a.m.? I was giving a student some extra help in English during recess. I felt relaxed and content. No lightning bolt hit me at 10:30 a.m. I did not collapse into tears. There was no indication that the man I loved, the man around whom I had moulded my future, was dead. No sense that the heart that had beat next to mine for the past seven years as we slept was still. Nothing.

Flowers arrive. A colleague of Jim's brings pizza. A friend sits on the couch beside me holding my hand. More friends bring food.

Dad and Glenda arrive to take me to Vancouver, to Jim's parents and the rest of the family. I shift the bouquets of flowers before manoeuvring stiffly into their car. Balanced on the edge of the leather seat, I crane my neck to keep sight of our modest brown and green home, as we turn left out of the cul-de-sac and right out of the subdivision. Then it is gone. Jim and Sue's place. I pull my gaze away. It's like raw flesh ripping from the bone.

I shift forward and back, to the right and to the left, like a caged animal. I open my mouth to speak and shut it without saying a word. My father is there in the car, driving, but I feel separated from him by an entire universe. I am being kidnapped.

When we arrive at Mom and Dad Haberl's three-level retirement townhouse on the west side of Vancouver, the front door is open. I hesitate on the threshold and remember the last time I was here, exactly one week earlier, before Jim left for Alaska. The last time I would ever see him.

Two months before our second wedding anniversary, Jim prepared for a trip to Alaska to climb University Peak with fellow

Whistler guides Keith and Graeme. He printed off the usual equipment list from his computer and organized his sleeping bag, tent, fuel, stove, rope, crampons, ice axes, skis, two-way radio, warm outdoor clothing and two weeks of individually packaged dried meals into an 80-litre backpack.

Their flight left early from Seattle on Saturday, April 24, so Jim and I decided, uncharacteristically, to drive down to Vancouver the day before and stay with Jim's parents so we could connect with friends and family. Since building our home in Whistler – a two-hour drive from Vancouver – we had been coveting time with loved ones.

Mom and Dad Haberl were used to receiving Jim's postcards from Africa, the Alps, South America and Alaska. He had begun rock climbing and mountaineering when he was 14, and had recruited his brother Kevin for many of his adventures. When Jim still lived at the old five-bedroom family home, his expedition gear was often sprawled over the basement or family living-room floor. I asked Mom Haberl if she worried about Jim when he was in the mountains. She shrugged her shoulders and laughed, "Why worry? I mean it doesn't do a lick of good. It doesn't change anything." Her lips and eyes almost disappear when she laughs, which makes me want to hug her.

Every Tuesday evening Mom Haberl goes to meditation group. Every Thursday she has aquafit class. She attends Catholic church and plays bridge with friends. She and Dad Haberl travel to the United States to watch baseball games, and they travel in Canada to family reunions. Mom Haberl remembers the birthdays of each of her 12 grandchildren, her six children and their spouses. She is a retired nurse and wears a small gold pin of the tiniest pair of feet you have ever seen in support of the pro-life movement.

I stood in their living room one day when Mom and Dad Haberl had a disagreement. Her hands waved in the air and her face was set. He did not concede. She threw her arms in the air, and with a downturned mouth and creases around her eyes, she said, "Peace be with you." And she walked away.

Later that evening, Mom Haberl told me the story of how she and Dad Haberl had met in Montreal. She spread her fingers wide and positioned her hands in front of her as if she were holding the sides of a shoebox and exclaimed, "One thing that really attracted me to Bill was the fact that he takes charge. I like that." Me too, I thought. I like that in a man. She cradled one hand inside the other and shook them up and down and confided, "But you know, he always thinks that his way is the best way ... and the problem is that he's often right!" The last part of her sentence tumbled out with her laughter. She pointed her finger at me and, in a surprisingly stern voice, said, "But don't ever let anyone tell you that you cannot have an opinion."

Dad Haberl is not an outdoorsman. He loves to play golf and watch baseball and is still working at 84 years of age. He is an avid Gyro Club member and is always up for a family reunion. As young men, Kevin and Jim called their dad from northern Canada for more money to pay for extra baggage, only hours after leaving home on an expedition. He chided them, laughed and sent the money. When Jim discontinued his English studies at university after one year, his dad said he would support him to take formal guide training. At a family gathering before Jim and I were married, I confided to two of the daughters-in-law that I felt a bit intimidated around Dad Haberl. They assured me that he had really softened up in the past 10 years. Jim told me he had a lot of respect for his dad for all that he had accomplished.

We chatted with Mom and Dad Haberl that Friday night before Jim headed to Alaska, and as we said good night, his dad dropped his chin, shook Jim's hand and, with a twinkle in his bright blue eyes, barked, "You know the rules, son."

Jim nodded his head once and said, "Yup."

"Good man," his dad grunted.

I knew Jim's rules by heart:

- The summit is optional, descent is not.
- You don't conquer mountains: they let you climb them or they don't.
- Take care of your climbing partners.
- Know when to turn back.
- Be precise, be prepared, hone your skills and minimize the risk.

His mom hugged Jim and said, "See you in the morning."

I raised my eyebrows and asked Jim if she was going to get up to see him off at 3 a.m. "Yup, she's a good one," replied Jim. Jim and I curled up together and fell asleep.

Just before he left, Jim bent down over the bed in the dark and kissed me gently on the cheek. I wrapped my arms around his neck, kissed him on the mouth and mumbled, "Be careful. I love you."

After a four-hour drive to Seattle, a four-hour flight to Anchorage and a four-hour drive in a rental car to Chitina, on the boundary of Wrangell–St. Elias National Park, Jim called that evening from a payphone. My heart raced when I heard his voice, "Hey, sweetie, it's me."

It was too windy for the bush plane to fly them in to the Ultima Thule Lodge, so they would bunk down in the tool shed. I pictured the three-by-three-metre weather-beaten shelter on the west bank of the Copper River, remembering it from our trip there the previous year, in May 1998. I smelled the oil and gas that stained the wooden floorboards, and shivered at the memory of the wind filtering through the cracks. I pictured Jim pulling his jacket tightly around him as he walked the grey, windy, deserted streets to the payphone.

Jim chattered on about the spectacular flight to Anchorage. "The Chugatch Mountains look incredible. We should do a ski tour there."

I laughed because I had suggested that trip the year before but Jim had preferred a bigger objective, and we'd gone to Mount

Bona instead. I knew we'd do it now that Jim was ready. I teased him, "Why does it always have to be your idea?"

There was a pause. "I dunno. I sure wish you were here so that we could snuggle in our sleeping bags," Jim mused.

"Me too," I sighed. "I love you."

"Me too."

Those were our last words.

During that first week of Jim's absence, I busied myself with teaching, tutoring and some guiding. I was surprised to find that the time passed quickly. That Thursday night, I went to bed and complimented myself on doing well while Jim was gone.

My parents and I push through the screen door, step out of the darkness and into the light of the hallway. People move around the living room. Mom Haberl hurries toward me with her arms open wide. "Oh, Sue," she squeezes out between tears, and skin bunches around her eyes like a drawstring. I sink into her embrace, crying the sort of tears that don't make you feel any better.

I hear voices. "I'm so sorry, Sue."

I feel warm arms holding me. But I am underwater, floating in slow motion. Someone puts a chair behind me and I plunk down. Jim's sister brings me a cup of tea, but my taste buds recoil at the first touch of liquid and my stomach clenches into a ball. I cannot function in this foreign world.

Mom Haberl gathers us around the television to watch the late-evening news. The lead story is about Jim, and there is a photo of him that fills half the screen. I tense. He wears his barnyard red and royal blue one-piece GORE-TEX climbing suit with the hood pulled over his climbing helmet. His head tilts back, his blue eyes shine and his smile opens wide.

My throat aches as it squeezes down on my breath. There he is, as real as day, yet people keep telling me he is dead. I pick up a few words: "well-known Canadian mountaineer ... first

Canadian to summit K2, second highest mountain in the world …
killed … Alaska." The screen goes dark and people turn away.

Matt, Jim's long-time friend and climbing buddy, rocks forward slightly and expresses in a velvety voice his wonder at how
lucky he feels. He feels so lucky because just two weeks earlier,
Matt and Jim and Jim's brothers Pat and Kevin met in Squamish
to do a very rare day of climbing together. It had been more than
15 years since they had done that, and it was not unusual for
them to go months without seeing one another. I was there too.
I'd met them for the afternoon and we did a multiple-pitch climb
that took several hours. They bubbled like schoolboys, happy to
be together.

Dad Haberl's deep, confident voice fills the room as he discusses the logistics of retrieving Jim's body. Jim's brother Pat,
a lawyer, confirms that the travel insurance money – about
$1,500 – will pay for flying Jim's body home. I stare at the floor
and wish myself away. I feel queasy thinking of Jim's body in a
box in the cold, noisy cargo hold of a plane.

My face goes rigid and I jerk up my head in panic.

"What will happen to Jim's body?" I blurt.

"It will go to Kearney's funeral home in Vancouver and they
will arrange for the cremation," Dad Haberl explains.

"I want to see him," I demand.

Dad Haberl shifts from foot to foot, leans in and confides
under his breath, "I've heard he's pretty beaten up, Sue. I don't
think you want to see him."

I lower my head but then fix my gaze on his and implore, "I
need to see him."

Dad Haberl nods his head and turns away.

Jim's sister crouches beside my chair to show me a piece of
paper and says, "This is the obituary we've written for the newspaper. We'd like to know what you think."

HABERL – James Edward A.C.M.G., M.S.M.

A man of incredible grace, beauty and humility, Jim has left us, killed tragically by an avalanche while climbing in Alaska on April 29, 1999. Jim is survived by his loving wife Sue Oakey, parents Bill and Margaret, siblings Susan, Herb, Kevin, Patrick, Mike, their families and all the people whose lives Jim touched. Jim's bereaved family and invited guests will participate in a mass on Tuesday morning. Jim's friends are welcomed to gather at a Celebration of Jim's Life on Wednesday, May 5, at 6 P.M. at the Chan Centre for the Performing Arts at UBC. In lieu of flowers, a memorial fund is being established.

I turn to her and whisper, "It's beautiful." And it is. But I plead silently with my eyes, Why did you write that? Jim is not dead. He can't be. I love him. Why did you write that? The pieces of the puzzle are sharp like razors.

Dad and Glenda drive me to their home and make up the guest room. Dad hands me a glass of water and places a light blue pill the size of a peppercorn in my palm. "It will help you sleep," he says heavily, and he kisses my forehead. I lie in the strange single bed staring into the darkness.

EIGHT
DAY TWO

The next evening, I drive to a friend's house where Jim's immediate family gathers to hear the details of the accident from his climbing partners, Keith and Graeme.

Mom and Dad Haberl, as well as Jim's three younger brothers and his older sister, sit on the edges of the light-coloured couches. Jim is missing. I force my mind to focus on this strange world where Jim should be but is not. I force myself because I have to find him. All heads incline slightly away from the stark lights. We wait.

Before the door opens, at the first jiggle of the doorknob, people are on their feet. Keith and Graeme have driven straight from the Seattle airport. Their faces are shadowed with stubble and their clothes crumple into the crevasses of their bodies. My legs are still catching up when I bump up against Keith's chest, encircle him with my arms. "Welcome home." I step back. Keith's gaze darts above and below me and to the left and to the right.

Keith and Graeme sit down stiffly and take turns unravelling the tragedy.

Questions – why? and how? – burn in our brains. No one wants to place blame, but we all want answers: Why weren't they roped up in case of a fall? Wearing transceivers in case of an avalanche? Helmets in case of rock or ice fall? How could Jim, such an experienced, wise and talented mountaineer, die in the mountains? Why him when Keith and Graeme survived? And my irrational silent questions: Where is Jim? Why did you leave him there? How do we fix this? How do we get him back?

Jim, Keith and Graeme had planned to climb University Peak, but the pilot could not land the plane there because of poor snow conditions. So they decided to climb an unnamed peak, known locally as Ultima Thule. They discussed how the unusually low snowpack had increased avalanche hazard. As a result, they decided to ski down the glacier and access the ridge to the summit via a 50° chute that was as steep as a double-black-diamond ski run and as high as the Eiffel Tower. The chute had been pummelled by previous snowfall, and so they surmised that it had avalanched and would be a safer route. As they moved along the route, they were laughing, really enjoying being out there with one another.

"I figure," says Keith, "we were all wondering about the snow stability, but nobody wanted to break the spell."

At the top of the chute, Keith was leading and began to cut across to the other side. Their boots sank easily into the snow and then stopped suddenly at a harder slab layer deeper down. When they tapped gently on the slab with their boots, it sounded hollow, like banging on a drum. Mountaineers refer to these snow conditions as "bricks over Rice Krispies" because the snow beneath the slab layer is lighter, less dense. On the 50° slope, the harder, heavier layer over the less consolidated one could slide at any time, especially with the added pressure of a human's weight.

Without saying a word, Jim began to cut another line at less of an angle.

As Keith joined Jim's new route, the hard snow layer settled beneath them with a "whumph" sound. They froze.

When Jim moved on, he walked as if doing giant tippy toes: one slow high step to clear the snow, then he gently placed his foot down, sank slowly to thigh level and used his plastic mountaineering boot to pat the snow down gingerly. He did this over and over, agonizingly slowly, for 15 minutes. No one spoke.

As they reached the other side of the chute, they dropped their packs on a small knob of snow and began to chat again. The slope angled off to a moderate 20°, and they were out of the chute on a slightly raised feature a few hundred metres from the ridge. The hard part was over. While Keith and Graeme had a drink, Jim resumed breaking trail, pushing through the thigh-deep snow.

Minutes later there was a loud crack. Keith and Graeme looked up in Jim's direction and heard him call, "Whoa, boys!" A slab of snow the width of a small house and half the height of Jim's body fractured and rushed toward them, breaking up as it crashed into rocks and ice.

Keith and Graeme fought to stay on their feet as refrigerator-sized blocks of snow, carried along by a river of powdery snow, pushed them toward the rock cliff. As Keith waded uphill against the current, he saw Jim slide by him, fighting to get a purchase with his ice axe.

The room is silent as we stare at Keith. He raises his chin to Jim's family, and I see his eyes now as he says, "Jim came really close to me, really close ... If I had reached out, I could have touched him."

The room freezes for an instant. I stifle my immediate response: Why didn't you grab him? Why didn't you grab him?

I say nothing. I clench my teeth, lower my gaze and fiddle with the bottom of my shirt.

After a pause, Dad Haberl nods his head decisively, raises himself slightly out of his chair, opens his arms and says, "Of course, we know you did everything you could." And he lowers himself back into his chair.

I gape at Dad Haberl, as if he has switched sides and now plays for the opposing team.

His words are generous, but I am not ready to believe that Jim cannot be saved. I guard my house of cards.

Keith slowly lowers his gaze and continues talking.

When the snow settled, Graeme had hurt his knee and one pack was gone. And so was Jim. Keith and Graeme strapped on crampons to climb down the steep icy chute they had just so carefully ascended. A little voice was saying to them, "You're lucky to be alive, so stay that way." Jim had gone over a four-hundred-metre cliff, and Keith knew that there was no chance of survival. But he called to Jim over and over for 45 minutes, "We're coming, Jim. Hang on, we're coming."

When he reached the bottom of the cliff, Keith spotted a patch of snow stained brownish red. His metal probe made a soft thud as it hit something spongy buried less than half an arm's length down. He dug down with his shovel and found Jim's wrist, bent at an odd angle.

I think to myself nervously, that's not right. Jim has always been very fit and healthy. His arms were warm and alive when he held me a week ago. No, Keith must be mistaken.

Keith and Graeme uncovered the rest of Jim's body and knew he was dead before they saw the head injury. They cried.

They debated whether or not to activate the emergency locator beacon they carried. The device would inform Search and Rescue of their location. Their situation was no longer an emergency. Jim was dead. Nothing would reverse that. Yet, a man had been killed. They decided to pull the yellow plug. Then they cocooned Jim in his dark forest-green sleeping bag and left him on the snow.

On the four-kilometre ski back up the glacier to their tents, Keith fell to his knees sobbing over and over. By chance, Paul flew over to check on them and Keith exhaled into the radio that Jim was dead. Paul landed and picked up Keith and Graeme, but because Paul's young children were at the lodge and would be upset by a corpse, Jim spent the night on the glacier, alone. Search and Rescue contacted the lodge to confirm that their assistance was not needed.

I picture Jim lying there in the cold. My mind races. How can

I get to him and hold him so he won't be alone? How can I hold his hand as he falls over the cliff? How can I save him? I would die for him.

Back at the lodge, Graeme made the hardest phone call of his life to Kevin, and then Keith and Graeme drank tequila until they were numb.

The next morning, Paul's father, Grandpa John, flew back to the glacier with Keith and Graeme to pick up Jim. Then they flew to the town of Glennallen and loaded Jim's body with all of their mountaineering gear into the back of an open pickup truck. "It seemed fitting," Keith mused, "to have Jim with us, in the truck, with all the gear, as opposed to in an ambulance."

Grandpa John drove them two hours to the nearest funeral home in Anchorage. The coroner pronounced the cause of death as severe head injuries.

Keith sighs as he recounts the final facts of Jim's accident. The tension connecting the group sitting around the living room breaks; people relax back into their seats quietly, and their eyes glass over. Gradually, soft voices fill the void and a few people get up. Kevin stands in front of me shaking his head and slamming the back of his hand into his other palm, "It's such a simple thing. You throw on a rope. Jim knew better." I say nothing and search for Keith.

I guide Keith to the privacy of the bathroom and close the door. I need more information so that I will be prepared. I shift around frenetically. I put one hand on Keith's arm and stutter, "I wan… I want to see Jim's body…" I study my shoes and try to muster courage. "Ha," I laugh uncomfortably. "Um, you see, I need to know what he looks like, you know?" Keith nods eagerly and gazes at me softly.

"He suffered a head injury, a basal skull fracture. Part of his skull was missing and there was blood pooling in his face around his eyes." I try to smile in appreciation as tears drip down my cheeks.

"Okay, thanks."

I am heading to my car to drive back to Dad's house when Pat places his hand gently on my arm from behind. "There were no regrets, Sue, nothing was left unsaid."

I turn quickly and agree, "Yes." I hug him tightly. An undercurrent of truth tugs at my wishful thinking. So much living was left undone, and I think of the words I did not say to Jim: "Please don't go. Please don't leave me. Please don't die."

NINE
DAY THREE

Dad Haberl phones to say that Jim's body has arrived at Kearney's funeral home and that the director will arrange a viewing for me at 3 p.m. I sigh and hold my breath almost in the same instant.

I choke out my plans to Terri, and she says, "Oh, Susie, I understand why you would want to see him. You need closure. But ... I don't feel the same need. My last memory of Jim is the two of you walking hand in hand in the setting sun at English Bay, you remember, when we all met for dinner the night before he left? You looked so happy. That's the memory I want to keep."

Yes, I remember that evening with our friends. I hear the laughter. I smell the charbroiled hamburgers, the french fries. I feel Jim's hand resting on my thigh, the lightness in my chest.

But even if no one else wants to see Jim, I do. I need proof. I need to know that he isn't waiting for me somewhere. Injured. Dying. Waiting for me to save him. Jim would understand. He was plagued by nightmares that Dan waited for him on K2. He never had the option of seeing Dan's body.

Dad and my older sister Sharron drive me to Kearney's.

Sunrays splinter through the lace curtains, creating a strobe effect on the people half filling the reception room. I want to open a window to let the heavy air escape. A faint smell of cleaner lingers, but the scent of death cannot be completely scrubbed out.

I pause.

Dad Haberl hurries toward me, "The family decided to come and see Jim, too."

"Oh," I answer numbly. It doesn't matter who is here, but I need to have time alone with Jim with no distractions. I don't want to miss any clue that he is still alive. And I want to feel that magic of being alone with him.

The funeral home director steers me to a chair and motions to a book on the table. "We have many beautiful urns to choose from." The prices glare back at me.

"The plain box is fine." My hand shakes as I write my name beside "widow" on the form and give the authorization to have Jim's body burned.

The material of the director's suit stretches across his back as he slides open the doors to an adjoining room and invites us inside with a gesture of his arms. I scan the pews, the podium and the rectangular cardboard coffin at the front of the room. The cardboard does not surprise me. The family chose the most practical option, given that Jim is to be cremated. It makes no difference to me.

Dad and Sharron sit on either side of me in one of the pews near the back. Kevin and his wife Vicki lead their children, Jaslyn and Connor, down the aisle. Connor holds on to Vicki's arm with both of his hands and casts his big blue eyes her way several times. His eyes open wider as they reach the long box.

Connor's little hands grip the side as he peers over. With a very still face, he gazes up at his mom and whispers. Vicki nods gently and Connor's little arm reaches out tentatively and disappears into the coffin. He pulls it back sharply and turns to his mom with a sheepish grin, holding the offending finger.

When the family has viewed Jim's body and has left the room, I tell Sharron and Dad that I am ready. Stiffly, step by step, closer we creep, arms linked until I can just see Jim's hand resting on his stomach. I stop abruptly, "Okay. I'm good now."

Dad and Sharron leave me.

Dad Haberl nods to me, "They were kind to us by covering part of Jim's face." He lowers his gaze and slides the doors closed. I am alone with Jim. No heart beating save my own. The fear in my body surges, and my breath rushes in and out like boiling surf. Focus on breathing. I let out a slow breath through trembling lips. I take a step, breathe, then another step. I reach forward to grip the edge of the cardboard box and drag my feet forward.

My muscles relax when I see Jim's face. He looks peaceful. Not in pain. There is his familiar square jaw, his thin-lipped mouth with the tiny scar from a needle of ice, his symmetrical nose and then a white cloth that covers the upper half of his face. No eyes. His steel-blue eyes.

I picture the purple and blue discoloration and swelling under the bandage. How bad would it be? Would he be so hurt that I wouldn't recognize him? Would I have nightmares of his injured face?

My fingers play with the edge of the white bandage. I think of pulling it up. But I don't. I try to visualize the face I love, but I cannot rid my mind of images of bruises and blood, and I panic. I can't see him ... Oh God, I forget already. The room feels cold and cavernous. I don't know what else to do. I want Jim to say something. It is as if I am a child opening a much-anticipated gift, only to find that the box contains every monster in my closet.

Suddenly, I feel him somewhere in the room. The warmth of his relaxed, wide-open smile.

I look down at Jim again. At the request of the funeral home director, I had sent one of Jim's favourite outfits: T-shirt and jeans. The T-shirt is placed on top of his upper body. I guess they couldn't get it over his head wound. I brush his cold finger, venture up his muscled forearm, then trace a familiar line up his chest, lightly, so as not to hurt him. I search for bruises and broken bones. I exhale deeply. Perhaps he hit his head right away and went limp.

I lean over, kiss his dry lips, rest my wet cheek against his and whisper my goodbyes. My Jim. My sweet Jim.

But Jim is not there.

TEN
DAY FOUR

Horns blare as vehicles blast by me over double-yellow lines. I risk a glance at the angry faces of the drivers but grip the wheel. Ten and two. Ten and two. Focus. Concentrate. Why are they going so fast? Don't they know? Don't they know we all hang by a thread? More blaring. My gaze darts to the rear-view mirror and I sob, "I can't go any faster!" I just can't. The highway speed limit is 80 kilometres an hour and my speedometer reads 60.

I am going home to Whistler. Halfway there, I stop by Kevin and Vicki's place in Squamish to pick up Jim's pack that Keith and Graeme have brought back from Alaska. Kevin and I sit against a log in the sun eating sandwiches.

"I went through Jim's pack and pulled out the food so it wouldn't go bad. Hope you don't mind," Kevin informs me. He adds, "Yup, actually this cheese came from his pack. Didn't think there was any point in wasting it." The food lodges in my throat. I swallow hard to get it down, as if I'm swallowing a part of Jim, a part that I will never be able to get back. But Kevin's pragmatism grounds me in the real world, the world in which Jim is dead.

Kevin and Vicki convoy with me the rest of the way home to Whistler.

I stride through our front door and am halfway up our stairs before I realize that Jim is not coming down to greet me with a hug. Grief sucks out my energy like a vacuum and I crumple. I reach my hand up to the solid cool wall. "How the hell am I going to live without you, Jim?"

The memorial service is in two days. There will be a slideshow about Jim's life and a display of his accomplishments. I have returned home to gather memories, to look through the binders and binders of slides, to put Jim's life in a box.

Vicki finds the large colour proofs of the two books Jim wrote, and her eyes light up. "I'd love to make a display of these, Sue. What do you think?"

What do I think? I want to keep everything remotely attached to Jim locked away forever so that I don't lose anything else in my life.

"That would be fine, but please bring them back," I reply.

I rifle through boxes in the garage and find the five by seven photograph of Jim dressed in a suit, tie and polished shoes. He shakes the Governor General's hand and accepts a medal. The Meritorious Service Medal recognizes individuals who have performed an exceptional deed or an activity that brought honour to their community or to Canada. Memories swim through my brain and I float away.

One evening, almost a year after Jim returned from K2, he received an official-looking envelope in the mail. He gawked at me with wide eyes. I feigned innocence.

"Wow! I've won the Governor General's Meritorious Service Medal!" Jim exploded.

"Really?"

He leaned forward and guffawed like a child not able to contain his enthusiasm. "The ceremony is in Quebec City!"

"I love Quebec City!"

He sucked in a breath and stopped. "You knew."

"Yes. I nominated you and Dan."

That September, Jim and I travelled to Quebec City with Dan's wife Patti and her son Ryan. The trees radiated deep burnt reds, oranges and yellows so that entire hillsides glowed. We walked the cobbled streets and stopped to admire the work of artists.

Patti accepted Dan's award posthumously. Jim grinned and received his medal for being the first Canadian to summit K2. I was proud.

I lay the photo on the pile to take to Vancouver and turn my attention to the slides. Kevin hunches over the light table, sorting the square pieces as if figuring out a jigsaw puzzle. More than 20 years of Jim's adventures: Alaska, South America, Africa, India, Nepal and North America. Ice climbing, skiing, mountaineering, climbing, sailing … the memories dance like fireflies. Which ones to choose? I peer at the raft crashing through the vertical waves of the Karnali River in Nepal and I remember that I almost lost Jim before, four years earlier.

I jerk my head up at the sound of the doorbell. My eyes refocus and I hear Kevin breathing beside me.

"I'll get it." I need a break.

"Hi, Keith, hey, Julia." I hug them and Keith smiles at me, but his eyes stay sad. Julia joins the others in the office to look at slides, but Keith lags behind and turns to me in the dark hallway.

"I brought these for you." He holds up a gold chain, spinning on the end of which is a gold ring. I put my hand out instinctively, but when the cool of the metal hits my flesh I cover my mouth with my other hand and pitch forward as if I am going to throw up.

"Oh, God."

"Oh, man, I didn't want to upset you," Keith turns away and then turns back. There is nowhere for him to go.

"Thank you for bringing them," I manage to say, and I slip the chain over my neck so that Jim's wedding ring nestles near my heart.

Keith fidgets. "You know it wasn't the first time that Jim walked close to the line."

"Yeah, I know." I had walked there with him. But Jim always came home. He promised he would. He had "too much to live for." Our love was special and he would never jeopardize it. I trusted him. I lived by this truth.

I had to.

Jim's true lover, the one he wooed and caressed, was the line between life and death. Each time he came safely home after stepping so close to that line, a life force surged inside of him. He always acknowledged his luck but at the same time grew more and more confident that perhaps he would escape the basic rules of life.

Jim said that driving the mountain highway was the most dangerous thing he did. Our society tolerates the risk of driving because it is part of daily life and because it serves a purpose. Mountaineering is harder to justify.

Keith and I move upstairs and I change the subject. "What did you guys talk about on the trip?"

"The last night in our tent, we talked about spirituality. You know, whether or not we believe in God, what it means to us to be spiritual. When it came to Jim's turn, he mimicked wielding a light sabre, sound effects and all. 'Use the force Luke.' We all laughed."

"Did Jim say anything about the book he was reading?" I finger my bottom lip.

"Oh yeah, I saw him reading it, *Fatherhood*, the one by that comedian. He seemed to enjoy it. He laughed quite a bit and read a few passages to us."

I sigh. I was the driving force behind us having a child, and I thought maybe the pressure was too much for Jim. He wasn't able to focus properly. He'd made a mistake because he worried about having a baby …

"What about in the morning, when you woke up?"

"You know, Jim shot upright in his sleeping bag when he first woke up and grabbed for his journal. He scribbled something."

I rustle through Jim's pack to find the journal. Keith peers over my shoulder as I read, "Wash sleeping bag." We laugh.

The doorbell rings again and I hustle down the stairs. When I see Scott through the glass, he bows his head. I catch a glimpse of his dark brown eyes.

"Hi."

"Hi. Um, I just didn't feel like being alone." He shrugs.

"Come on in. Keith and Julia and Kevin and Vicki are here. You're welcome to hang out." I open the door wider.

His tall frame floats past me into the room as if he is hollow. Jim was a fellow guide, and his death ignites a fear: they are all mortal.

My eyes sting from squinting at slides. I choose photos of me and Jim together: under a waterfall in Nepal, on top of Mount Kilimanjaro in Africa, faces shining in the sun heli-skiing near Whistler, arms wrapped around one another at my parents' place, slow dancing at our wedding ... so many photos, so many trips. I want to bronze all of these memories, solidify them so that they cannot fade.

That afternoon, I beg the local photo lab to enlarge and frame half a dozen images for Jim's service. Rush job.

When darkness comes and everyone has gone home, I curl up in bed and snuggle Jim's black and red toque under my cheek like a security blanket. He was wearing it when he fell. It touched him after I did. The acrid smell of Jim's fear lingers in the soft fleece, and it does not feel like a lifeline. It smells like death. Connor's words echo, "Auntie Sue, isn't it lonely in that king-sized bed now?"

That night I hear a noise.

I creep downstairs and follow the glow of light that seeps through the cracks around the guest bedroom door. I steady myself on the wall to listen. A shuffling sound ... then another noise ... yes, there it is, a familiar sigh. My feet slide forward as if I am on a tightrope. Step by step I make my way down the hallway, brushing my hand along the wall for balance. I hold my breath, ease the door open, squint into the light and strain to see long before the door is out of the way. I spy two wheels, an armrest and the broad curve of a well-muscled back. The rest of the body rummages in the closet. I catch my breath loudly because I recognize his back. And then his blond head comes into view and I know for certain. It is Jim! He isn't dead! He is just hurt!

"Hey!" He laughs.

"Oh!" I hug him, crying and laughing. Then, with superhuman strength, I lug him in his wheelchair upstairs to our bedroom, and we giggle about how we are going to fool around.

When I wake up, I slide my hand over the space beside me. The sheets are cold.

I get into the car and drive back to Vancouver, to Jim's funeral.

ELEVEN
DAY FIVE

TUESDAY, MAY 4, 1999

Dear Jim,

Today is your funeral. I rose with the sun, to be with you, and walked to the beach. A young man balanced on a log, one leg in the air like a gymnast, and beamed, "Isn't it a beautiful day?"

"Yes." I smiled outwardly at his enthusiasm and inwardly at the irony. It was indeed a beautiful day.

A crack of thunder shook the sky. Just one. I tilted my face to the big raindrops falling from a single black cloud. A flock of birds drummed their wings against the air. A giant blue heron floated over. Dan.

I wondered what form you would take. An eagle maybe. A moment later, two eagles soared overhead. My feet rooted into the sand. You try to communicate with me. I want to touch you, to hear you, to talk to you.

Love always, Sue

My family accompanies me to the church, but I feel alone. I feel empty, as if my voice echoes inside of me. I raise my head to the morning sun, close my eyes and let the warmth caress my skin. My breaths come short and shallow, but even so, the perfume of the cherry trees snakes its way like smoke into my nostrils. Mom Haberl hurries up and pulls me right against her chest. I relax into her arms. She gently pries away the picture I clutch against my body. Jim's big grin and bright blue eyes bring the photo alive. "Oh, nice," she puts her hand to her heart. "Could we use it on top of the coffin?" She holds my arm and leans in close.

"Yes." I want to let the picture go and to hold onto it at the same time.

Jim's cardboard rectangular coffin sits on wheels at the head of the church aisle. From where I sit, I can reach out and touch it. My heart tells my hand to touch the box, to stroke it, but I stay stiff. Sharron cocoons me in her arm. As the Catholic priest approaches the pulpit, my muscles seize in anticipation of even more proof that Jim is dead.

He never met Jim, but what he says is strangely fitting. He talks about how Jim did not allow the frailty of life to scare him into living less than a full life.

After the service, Sharron is my crutch as I follow Jim's body down the aisle. Hot fluid streams from my eyes and nose. I raise my chin to breathe and notice the faces of the mourners in the pews. Some look down, some turn away from me, some lean toward me with their brows furrowed and their eyes watering, and one friend sits ramrod straight staring at me with his eyes open wide like a frightened child.

Outside, I want to cry harder but I can't. I want some sound to come out of me that will be strong enough to take the pain with it. I lean on the railing and Mom Haberl puts her arm around me. Through tears, she says, "He sure did love you." Did he know how much I loved him? Did I love him enough? She presses the Governor General's medal that they'd been keeping in their safety deposit box into my hand. "Here, you should have this."

I press the medal back into her hand, "No, you keep it, please."

Oak trees tower over us as the hearse drives off to Squamish to deliver Jim for cremation. To be burned. My body trembles. I want to run after the dark hearse, throw myself in front of it, scream … but I don't. I am frantic to do the right thing, but I don't know what the right thing is.

TWELVE
DAY SIX

WEDNESDAY, MAY 5, 1999

Before Jim's evening memorial service at the Chan Centre, eight friends join me for a walk at Jericho Beach. We amble along the fine gravel pathway, elbows linked. The late afternoon sun kisses the trees, sand and water. "I wish I had a camera, you make such a lovely picture," a middle-aged woman comments as she passes. The irony is excruciating. Love and grief, hand in hand.

The weight in my chest draws my shoulders and head down. I use my whole back to raise my head and squint into the sunlight. Is he here? Yes, there he is on his usual perch. I gaze. His wings billow and he is airborne. My eyes track him, closer and closer, until he is less than six metres above us. I hold my breath as he circles. It is him. It must be him. An eagle: mating for life, the gateway to the divine. He gains altitude as he circles, and I stop, sigh and gaze upward.

Close to a thousand people are at the memorial that evening. One friend bursts into tears when she sees the wedding picture of Jim and me by the candle in the foyer. There are several billboards and easels displaying the colourful proofs of Jim's two books and his awards for writing, his Governor General's medal.

There are speeches. Dad Haberl begins by thanking everyone for being there for Jim's mom. She knew him the longest and perhaps the best. He says that Jim taught him right from wrong, something a father should teach his son. It is a stunning confession for such a confident man.

When Eric speaks, he says he witnessed the first magic between Jim and me in the Queen Charlotte Islands in 1982. He raises his chin in my direction and says that Jim's face lit up whenever he talked about me. He admired Jim for belonging so naturally to many different groups of friends.

There is a pause as we wait for the next speaker to come from behind the stage curtain. People shuffle in their seats. And then the audience gasps as well-known motivational speaker and athlete Rick Hansen wheels into the light. He speaks of Jim's dedication to his profession and his ability to relate to and motivate people.

Graeme gives details of the accident.

Scott says he admired Jim for following his heart, for taking the time to do trips in the mountains. Pat, Jim's brother, says Jim's death helped him to find his own soul.

Kevin reads aloud a letter to Jim:

Dear Jim,

It's early morning and I finally feel like I can start a letter. I think everything's checked off – you'd be proud, oh list-meister – checked off only because so many of your friends have stepped up and taken projects. They're all going with a real sense of mission, and I think it's gonna be good tonight.

The last five days have been like a dream, Jim. Lots of hugs and tears, and some good laughs, too. Remember when? And "How about the time that..." I've been feeling a bit weird about not being a basket case. I think Vicki is a bit worried. Some people have told me how strong I've been, we both know that's not it – I think I'm just not ready to say goodbye yet. But don't worry, I will. Whatever, eh? It's the old songs that do get me going, though.

The support network has been truly awesome. Family first as always, but also so many different groups of people you were a part of over the years, Jim, Jim-Bob, Habby. In each circle, your natural way made you the guy that everyone could go to for an uncritical smile, a ready ear or an honest answer. How'd you do that? I guess they could tell you really cared – people first, right?

Some of the closest folks are pretty shattered, Jim. It's an amazing group, big bro' – some have been around forever, some just lately, but they've got good and true hearts. We're so lucky. But it's great to see everyone, there's such energy when we're together – you should be here. It's wild, too; it takes something that rubs everyone raw to make some connections work. I feel closer to some people in the last few days than I ever have.

I'm gonna miss my best teacher and my guide. You spent a lot of time breaking trail for all of us and had a ready smile when we caught up. A deep, sincere thanks for your part in making me me.

I hope nobody tries to make you out to be a god tonight. I know you always had uncertainties, doubts and questions. But the hills are a good teacher and we found a few of the answers together. We'll just try and remember your way, and carry you with us, and live it. Plain old Uncle Jim.

I'm really glad for you that you made it this far. It took you a while to realize that the path you were on was your path. And you found Sue. I loved seeing you find peace within, and I've tried to learn from that, too.

I don't think you were too scared in the slide. Probably just feeling guilty 'cause you knew how sad we'd all be. Don't worry, Jim, I don't think you left anything unsaid. We can feel your spirit here. And we'll try to be there for Sue. We'll be okay.

You always wrote the best letters. I think you'll be answering this one tonight. I can't wait. So, Jim, "Heebla," "Jacques," "Boom-Chicka-Boom."

Lots and lots of love,

Kevin.

The audience applauds loudly. Truth spoken right from the heart. So like Jim.

I sit on the edge of my seat, listening and waiting. I envision long roots extending from my body down into the earth. Patti tells me to envision light encircling my body, protecting me. I try. I try to breathe. I try to stay grounded but I am ricocheting through the universe with no compass bearing and nothing to hold me together. My hands tremble and my knuckles are white from clutching the three-hole loose-leaf pages on which I have written my farewell words. Two drafts.

I picture myself on stage, composed, reading my eulogy. People will say how strong I am, how brave. Partway through, the blood will drain out of me and I will collapse onto the floor, unconscious. People will gasp and press forward to help. But they will stop short when, from the top of the domed ceiling, an eagle will trill and dive to my side, spreading his three-metre wings protectively around me. I will rest while Jim shrieks at anyone who threatens to come near. I will wake, and, faced with his glaring amber eyes and sharp hooked bill, remain still. Haltingly, he will brush the soft feathers of his head against my cheek. I will stand, Jim perched defiantly on my arm, and we will go home.

Then Dave announces my name from the stage. My heart pounds so deeply my ears vibrate. Patti holds my elbow as we feel our way down the dark aisle. At the side of the stage she asks how I am. I turn to her and say, in someone else's composed deeper voice, "Fine, thank you." I skate on the surface of my grief, because if I go deeper, allow even one small fissure to open up, I will drown in the pain. I know it.

I climb the stairs alone to the podium. I glance out into the sea of black. It's like staring into a cave full of breathing. Pat's face is illuminated in the front row. He looks worried. Scared for me. I fix my gaze on the paper in front of me. My voice wavers: "My name is Sue and I am Jim's wife." My throat closes and it is seconds before I can breathe again. I take one long deep breath and let it out between trembling pursed lips. And I read. I stand there and I read it. There are even a couple of times when people laugh.

Today we are here to celebrate Jim's life. Everyone who knew Jim loved him.

Jim valued friendship. Alastair once said that Jim had more close friends than anyone he knew. Greetings began with a hearty hug. You'd often hear a sincere "Good man!" at the end of phone conversations with buddies. I can hear him laughing uncontrollably at Mike's jokes. There are countless stories of being tent-bound for days, of forgetting fuel, of battling pulmonary edema and of reaching summits. All of these adventures bonded Jim and his buddies. Jim opened his heart and created a safe haven for friendships to grow.

Jim was loved and supported by his family. His mom and dad believed in him. He had love in his voice when he walked through their door and said, "Hey, Mom!" and gave her a big hug. Kevin and Jim had an unspoken bond. Jim said that when they climbed together things just flowed and that there was very little need for words. He loved that. Jim was like a second father to Kevin and Vicki's kids. At the mere sight of Jim's car, Jaslyn and Connor would come running, yelling "Uncle Jim!" and beat down the door to get in the first hug. When Jim and I first started dating, my stepmom said, "Isn't it nice to be going out with someone who everyone likes?" My father sang his praises often. Once we met a client of Jim's when we were out for dinner. The man came over to say hello and said, "You know you have quite a son-in-law here." My dad replied, "I know, I'm thinking of changing my will."

Jim was passionate and full of heart and soul. He listened to his soul and lived his life accordingly. He gave people the benefit of the doubt; he took the higher ground, he looked at the positive side; he believed that things happen for a reason; he believed that it is better to give than it is to receive; and he believed that love is worth the risk. This inner strength grounded him and created something of which we are all a part. He inspired us to follow our dreams.

Now we have a big mountain to climb because we are all missing him very much. We will climb this mountain with his help, even if it takes 15 breaths for each step.

I am very fortunate because I met my soulmate and spent so many wonderful years with him. I am grateful for all of his love, kindness, understanding, passion and support ... for all of his hugs, kisses, smiles and chuckles. I am a better person for having known him. He was an extraordinary being, and I know that his spirit will live on in all of us and in everything that is good and beautiful in this world.

When I am done, I listen to the breathing. I whisper, "I love you, Jim, always."

I want Jim to see that I will be okay, but I am not convinced of this myself. I want to honour everything he and I shared. I want to shout my love for him from the top of the mountains. And more than anything, I want him to come back. I want to read the best eulogy ever so that he will come back.

The service ends with a slideshow of Jim's life: 2400 photos, music, two projectors, one image fading into the next. Climbing and mountaineering photos dominate, but there are also scenes of the ocean. In each one there is a love of being with Jim. Depending on one another in the wilderness fostered that love. Facing the unknown together with a sense of clarity and purposeful action created a respectful bond. One full section is dedicated to Jim and me. I grip my seat and gulp air as photos of Jim and me from all over the world colour the screen: under a waterfall, on top of a mountain, dancing, hugging and laughing. I smile to hold back my tears. Van Morrison belts out "Have I Told You Lately that I Love You?" I used to cup Jim's face in my hands and ask him that. Or sneak up from behind and wrap my arms around his neck and whisper in his ear. He'd laugh and say, "No." And I'd say, "I do, truly, madly and deeply." It was the song we danced to at our wedding.

I strain to hear the words of the final song, "Here in the Heart," by Daniel Lavoie:

> Here in the heart of me
> That's where you'll always be
> Deep as the deep blue sea
> Close as the air I breathe

I wipe my nose on my sleeve and hang my head and whisper, "Close as the air I breathe." Patti guides me by the elbow to the hall outside the auditorium.

"People will want to talk to you," she says and positions me front and centre. The foyer fills, and I lean against a table, chew my lip and feel like my parents have just dropped me off at my first day of kindergarten, naked. Groups form. The room buzzes. A few people talk to me, and then I slip up the stairs to the landing, crouch down and cry.

"There you are." It's my sister Sharron. I stand up, wipe my eyes and she leads me downstairs to the bubbling crowd. Kevin is right. Jim's family and friends are happy to be together.

A colleague of Jim's, a guide, rests her hand on my arm and says, "I'm so sorry, Sue. You know, Jim made me want to be a better person. And I'm going to do that. I'm going to try to be a better person, not just for me, but for Jim." I hug her, more out of habit than anything else. The room spins.

I ooze along with the crowd until we are outside in the dark.

"Hey, Sue, some of us are going to the high-school pizza haunt on Broadway. Please come." Pat's voice is charged.

"Okay." Keen not to be left behind. Keen to be anywhere Jim was. My sister drives me. Pitchers of beer, pizza, raucous laughter. I laugh at a joke and catch myself. How could I laugh when Jim is dead? I think I'm going to be sick. My body sits still, but my soul weaves across the room, tries to escape and collapses on the floor. There are shouts, people at my side, an ambulance is called, a stretcher, and my soul is whisked away. I watch it all happen and am surprised to feel the warmth of my thighs beneath my hands. My body is still here, sitting on the chair, the party goes on around me, and Jim is still dead.

THIRTEEN
DAY SEVEN

THURSDAY, MAY 6, 1999

There are bold mountaineers and there are old mountaineers.
But there are no old, bold mountaineers.

—UNKNOWN

My childhood friends Jenny and Andrea come to my parents' house the next day to visit.

"Wow, Kevin's letter at the memorial was incredible." Jenny leans forward on the couch and shakes her head.

"Yes. Everyone was saying afterward how heart-wrenching it was, and well written." Andrea agrees. I rock in my chair. No, Kevin's can't be the best. Mine has to be the best eulogy. It has to be. They chat about the memorial. I slither out of the chair and hole up in my room, face in my pillow.

"Susie?" Jen knocks on the open door. "Are you okay?"

"No." I raise my wet face to look at her.

"I don't know what to do. What can I do?" She whooshes to my side like the wind.

"Just hold me, please."

"Of course," she cries.

When they have gone, I lie down and sleep. Drained.

That afternoon I continue my task of clipping out articles about Jim's accident. The media likes a healthy, square-jawed, well-toothed, handsome young man. And there he is, smiling at me from the local, provincial and national newspapers. I scan the headlines. "Avalanche Kills First Canadian To Climb K2." "Climber's Death Eerily like Friend's." "Uncertainty of Climbs Held Powerful Appeal." I skip over the details of Jim's mountaineering career. But one article, "The Loss of Our Guide," written by a friend, Jayson Faulkner in *Pique Newsmagazine*, I read over and over:

> Nobody expects to lose a friend in the mountains. You do expect there will be a price paid if you live and play in the mountains. But not necessarily a close friend – you hope. The risks we take while mountaineering, backcountry skiing, ice climbing, kayaking and such are clear and ever present. For many of us, that is an integral part of why these activities are of value or interest. Whistler is defined by these activities and the full life they give us; the risks and, especially, the rewards.
>
> Jim was our Grand Old Man of the Mountains, putting up bold new routes since he was 18. He was the first Canadian to summit K2 and he did it in the best possible style. He was incredibly wise, strong and sensitive to everyone and everything around him. He was the only climbing partner for many of us who had the official seal of approval from our partner or spouse. Oh, you're going with Jim – then that is okay. I know you will be safe. He taught avalanche courses, trained guides and had experience and wisdom we all looked up to. He spent his professional life learning about the environment he worked and played in so that he could manage the risk. He wrote two books about the ultimate price of the game we play.
>
> One of my friends commented that he is re-evaluating mountaineering, because if Jim

could get killed, then the belief we have all signed
on to – that we can manage the risk at some level
– is pure fantasy. He wasn't sure if he could climb
again. How could he selfishly disregard the impact on his family, his children?

The loss is devastating for Jim's family, particularly for his wife Sue, as they had settled into
Whistler, built a house and become part of the
community. The future was looking very bright
indeed. We all feel mostly for Sue and Jim's family. We cannot understand why or how.

How the hell did this happen to Jim? What
went wrong? The truth is, it doesn't matter. He
was a person more defined by the mountains
than anyone I have ever known. He was the definition of a life well lived. Jim was our Guide. We
will be lost without him.

When I see my name in the article and read how Jim was
happy with me, how our life together was good, I cry with gratitude. When Jayson talks about how nobody expected Jim to die,
I feel relief. It wasn't just me who made the mistake of believing
Jim was too good to die. I save all of the newspaper articles in
a marked folder, and I send a copy of Jayson's article to Mom
Haberl. She tells me she likes it best of all.

In the evening, my half-brother performs in his high school
musical, *Grease*.

"The show must go on." Dad clears his throat. "Are you sure
you don't want to come?"

"Yes. Thanks." I swallow.

"You'll be okay by yourself, won't you?" He lumbers past, coat
in hand, his chin tucked.

"Yes." I draw my legs up under me on the couch and fiddle
with my sock. He tests me. If he coddles me too much, he fears

I will crumble. Model a stiff upper lip and I will pull through. It's his way of showing his faith in me. I stroke the weave on the cushion so that I won't raise my arms up to him like a child and wail, "Please don't go. Hold me. Rock me. Sing to me. I can't do it on my own."

The front door clicks, and my gaze darts to the darker corners of the room, half expecting ghosts to appear. I huddle inside my sweater and turn on the television. I follow a few dialogues before the noise blurs into white. I stare at nothing and sob, shoulder-shaking, aching sobs. I might not stop. I might shake myself into nothing.

Suddenly, I hear something and stop crying. There it is again in both of my ears. Loud. I straighten, jerk my head around to face whoever is there. But I am alone. Where is that breathing coming from? Like wind rushing through my ears. In. Out. Heavy. Scared. I plug my ears. Still there, with more of an echo. I realize it's my own breathing and lean my head into my hands, relieved that there isn't a stranger in the house but frightened that I am going crazy.

A book I read describes my experience as disassociation. In post-traumatic stress, a person might separate herself from her body in order to escape the pain. I do not tell a soul.

FOURTEEN
DAY EIGHT

FRIDAY, MAY 7, 1999

The eye goes blind when it only wants to see why.
— RUMI, SUFI MYSTIC

"I'd like to take you to a bookstore to buy you some books ... about grief," Andrea offers on the other end of the phone line.

"Okay." My numbness retreats for an instant to allow a dagger of fear and hope.

Andrea and I have been best friends since kindergarten. As children we spent summers at her family's cottage where she taught me to bait a hook with a live crab and to catch garter snakes. In elementary school, she was the quintessential tomboy, and the two of us would challenge the boys in our grade to a soccer game at lunchtime, and we would win. Now she is a family physician living in Victoria with her husband and two girls.

We meet in Vancouver. Andrea hooks her arm through mine as we enter the maze of bookshelves in Chapters. Normally I would head to Fiction: Elizabeth Berg, Flannery O'Connor. Or to Travel. So, the black sign with bold lettering "Grief" in the Self-help section kicks my body back. Andrea urges me forward. So many books about dying and grief.

I scan the titles for something familiar or friendly. With information comes knowledge and with knowledge comes understanding. I've relied on this mantra before. Why was Jim killed? Why? After an hour, I juggle six books and Andrea suggests two more. At the cashier, I scatter the books on the counter. Andrea grunts and spreads the titles out so she can see them. She sighs and pulls six books to her side and pushes the remaining two toward me.

"I'll pay for these ones," she waves at her pile.

The two books in my pile are *Journey of Souls*, by Dr. Michael Newton, who contacts the spirits of loved ones through hypnotism, and *Soul Mates*, by Thomas Moore.

"Okay. All right. Thanks." I glance at her and alternate looking at my shoes and checking whether the cashier is ready.

Back in our Whistler home, I pull on a pair of Jim's jeans and his fuzzy sweater and slump on the blue couch that has been in Jim's family for decades. When I look up at the clock, I am surprised that two hours have passed. Every movement echoes in the empty house. I look at the book titles on the coffee table: *On Death and Dying, Facing Death and Finding Hope, The Healing Journey through Grief, The Courage To Grieve, When Bad Things Happen to Good People, The Resilient Spirit*. I pick up one and anchor it open on my lap. My eyes water after a few minutes of reading. I read a sentence, and as soon as I pause on a word, my mind wanders so that I have to go back to the beginning. It takes me 10 minutes to read one paragraph.

The first stage of grief is shock and numbness. The shock and numbness insulate you from the intense pain until you can cope. As I read and reread, my inner dialogue pulls my train of thought: Yes, that's interesting. Shock. Okay. When is Jim coming home?

In my wilderness first aid training, I learned that one treats shock by reassuring the patient, laying her down and keeping her warm, hydrated and oxygenated. I've treated shock before.

There was that young woman, my first call when I worked ski patrol at Whistler Mountain. She was screaming when we arrived. I looked down over the side of the run, through the trees and saw her in a heap on the snow. No blood. The lead patrol crouched beside her.

"C'mon!" my ski patrol mentor ordered as he plunged into the deeper, ungroomed snow. I froze. He turned and looked at me, "Sue, come on. I need you." I followed. The radio talk sliced through the air. Young woman, about my age, maybe 23, lying almost completely flat on her back but slightly propped on one elbow, curled protectively to one side, arm reaching toward her leg and her neck muscles straining, yelling, "Help me. Ow, it hurts. Oh, help. Please." I knelt down and invited her to lean her head on my thighs. She slowly relaxed back.

"Hi, I'm Sue. What's your name? Where are you from? How long have you been here? Are you with friends or family?" Use a calm reassuring voice. Stay close so she feels your body's warmth, so she won't feel alone.

She stopped yelling to answer my questions while the patrol team scuttled around stabilizing her fractured femur, dislocated hip and broken ribs. As we lugged her in a stretcher through thigh-deep snow to the waiting helicopter, I explained that they would fly her to a hospital and the doctors would care for her.

"Are you coming with me?" She raised her eyebrows.

"No, but a patroller and a paramedic will fly with you." I patted her hand. When the machine was out of sight, my legs wobbled and I sat down on the snow.

I close the grief book, slump on the couch and encase myself in a blanket. I wish I had Jim's warm body beside me. I wish I did not feel so alone.

FIFTEEN
DAY NINE

SATURDAY, MAY 8, 1999

It is the weekend, and I know this because Susan and Terri have come to stay with me. They buy groceries and make dinner. I mash the food slowly in my mouth, like a cow chewing cud. The three of us fall asleep holding hands.

Susan and Terri snap out of bed at the first sign of sunlight to make breakfast. I move in slow motion and stay in the same sweats and T-shirt I went to bed in. I can't remember the last time I took a shower, and my hair feels heavy on my head. My eyes are half-lidded, as if I have not slept.

"Let's walk into the village," Terri suggests as she fills bowls with granola, yogurt and fruit, the same breakfast Jim and I shared each morning. I sit down at the kitchen counter, my jaw clenched.

"Why don't you two go? I'm just not up to it." My body is exhausted, and the smaller I shrink my world, the less energy I'll spend trying to contain my grief. Terri and Susan would bravely hold me up if I crumbled in the middle of the crowded village. But openly displaying such emotion terrifies me.

"Okay," Terri stammers as she pushes a bowl toward me. "Are you sure you'll be okay?"

"Oh, sure." I squeeze out a smile.

As soon as the front door clicks shut, I lumber upstairs, close the blinds, crawl into bed and draw the duvet up under my chin.

Curled in a fetal position, I cry for a few minutes and stop. I cry some more, until my insides wring dry. There is a zone between wakefulness and sleep where my mind hovers, neither thinking nor feeling. When I snap out of this no man's land two hours later, I feel more tired.

The doorbell rings and I burrow under the covers. The front door scrapes open.

"Hello? Anybody home?" I recognize Glyn's voice. Terri and Susan's husbands have arrived.

"I guess they've gone out," Ken adds. Heavy footsteps on the stairs and a pause.

"Oh, man, look at this place." They roam the main floor.

"Look at that photo of K2. Beautiful." Glyn's voice and footsteps work their way upstairs toward my bedroom. I breathe quietly and close my eyes. The footsteps stop on the stairs, followed by shuffling and heavy sighs. I picture both men sitting down.

"What is she going to do, Kenny? I mean what the hell is she going to do? This house ... what is she going to do with this house they built? She can't stay here. Too many memories."

I tense when I hear how scared they are for me.

"I don't know. Sue is a thinker. She'll think her way through it." I imagine Ken nodding his head to emphasize his opinion. Yes, I am a thinker. I think to know and I know to understand. I make decisions based on information and experience, instead of reacting instinctively, so I can avoid the unknown and feel in control. As humans we have this luxury. But now, faced with my greatest unknown, all I can think is "why?" And any answer brings me back to that same circle of why, the same black hole of uncertainty. I cannot fix death or make a different decision now to bring Jim back. I am Ayn Rand's protagonist in *Atlas Shrugged*: "He saw for the first time that he had never known fear because, against any disaster, he had held the omnipotent cure of being able to act ... not an assurance of victory – who can ever have that? – only the chance to act, which is all one needs. Now he was contemplating, impersonally and for the first time, the real heart of terror: being delivered to destruction with one's hands tied behind one's back."

But if you think too much, you don't get anything done.

My leg muscle cramps. The front door opens again.

"Hi! We're home!" Susan and Terri's high voices float up the stairs.

"Hi!" Glyn yells down and whispers to Ken, "Wait a second. That sounds like just Susan and Terri. Which means Sue is here. Which means she heard every word we said." Silence. Glyn and Ken pad downstairs to meet their wives on the main floor. Glyn confirms, "Is Sue here?"

"Yes."

I sigh and push myself out of bed, creak open the bedroom door and thump downstairs.

"Hi," Glyn moves forward to hug me. "You heard everything we said."

"Yes, it's okay." I have no energy to pretend I was asleep.

Glyn works his hands together. "I figure you're on a five-year plan, Sue."

"What do you mean?"

"It's going to take you five years to get back on track from this thing." Glyn nods his head slightly and looks right at me.

"Hmmm." Five years. I can't keep this up for five years. I'll go crazy or die of exhaustion.

SIXTEEN
DAY TEN

SUNDAY, MAY 9, 1999

"I've made an appointment for you with a counsellor I know."
Jim's close friend gives me an address over the phone. "She's a
wonderful woman. Don't feel any pressure to go, but she's there
if you want it." I stare at my handwriting on the paper: time, date
and place.

In the parking lot of the counsellor's apartment complex, I
sit in my car and breathe. When I stop crying, I open the door
and tiptoe to the pavement, half expecting a tornado to rip my
legs off. Looking over my shoulder several times, I shuffle to the
address on the paper.

The counsellor asks to see the eight-by-ten photo I clutch to
my heart. I hold it out to her as if it is a baby bird. Jim and I slow
dancing at our wedding; his eyes are closed and his lips caressing
my ear.

"This photo speaks volumes of Jim's feelings for you." She cra-
dles the frame for a second and leads me by the elbow to a soft
chair in her living room. Her townhome reminds me of being
in my grandma's apartment. Dark wood. Floral patterns. And
it smells of talcum powder. A cozy cluster. She sits opposite me
on the couch, elbows resting on her knees. The way she looks
at me with her deep brown eyes seems to say, "It's okay." I talk
about Jim and she listens. That's what I want to do: talk about
how wonderful he was.

"Would you like to tell me about Jim's accident?" She leans forward, hands clasped together.

"Okay." I fidget in my armchair and look past her at the painting on the wall. "They were in Alaska, climbing. And they went up this chute they thought had already slid."

"Hmm, hmm." She reaches out and lays her warm hand on my forehead. Her other hand hovers over my stomach. I gulp for air. My grief rushes to her hands as if they are portals. To be touched when I am in the abyss of pain, a leper to the normal world, is overwhelming. I feel human and just for a second believe that I am doing okay.

"Do you feel guilty?" She keeps her hands in place.

"I wonder whether Jim was meant to have children. It was my idea to have a baby. I wonder if he died because of that." My face contorts and I hold the edge of my chair. It must have been my fault. Please tell me it wasn't my fault.

"Survivor guilt," the experts call it. But this is also my way of keeping my world together and always has been. I make myself responsible regardless of whether I am the cause so I can pretend to be able to "fix" mistakes in life and make sure they never happen again. Be in control. If I am responsible, then I can "fix" Jim being dead.

"In the scheme of life and destiny, you are a pretty small player."

I nod and hold back sobs.

"It's so soon after Jim's death. Really, too soon for counselling. But one of the first stages of grief is denial, and I don't think you are in denial. Trust yourself. Trust your feelings."

I bite my lip and nod to let her know that I will try. I have so many doubts and fears. My biggest fear is that Jim is really dead.

SEVENTEEN
DAY ELEVEN

MONDAY, MAY 10, 1999

I get up quickly from the park bench when I see Patti approach and hug her. Her presence reassures me. The fact that she has survived gives me hope that I will too. We walk along the beach together. It has been six years since Dan was killed on K2.

I hug myself and look at Patti. "I just feel like I was on the highest, most beautiful mountain in the world, and then I came crashing down. And I'll never be able to climb that mountain again."

Patti leans around to look me in the eye. "You and Jim did share a beautiful mountain. But there are other mountains, not necessarily better or worse, just different. You'll climb other mountains."

"I don't know how to do this. Sometimes I think of how Jim would handle it if the situation were reversed, if I had been killed. He would know what to do." I feel insecure, sorry for myself.

Patti stops and grabs my arm, "Jim would have been devastated." Somehow this makes me feel better.

"It has taken me a long time to realize it, but I am angry at Dan, and at Jim. I am angry that they chose to mountaineer. They didn't have to. They could have done something else." Patti looks set in her opinion, and I have no idea how to respond nor do I want to. I don't feel angry with Jim.

That afternoon, Patti and I go to see a well-known channeller, someone who communicates with spirits, in one of the

Vancouver hotel ballrooms. I've just finished reading *Journey of Souls*, in which grief-struck people are reassured and relieved by contacting their dead loved ones through hypnotism.

There must be over a thousand people in the bright, white-walled room. We sit in foldout chairs and wait. A microphone stands in the middle of the two sections of seats, and a large platform is set up at the front of the room. When the plump middle-aged psychic with permed long blonde hair with dark roots walks onstage, the applause bounces off the ceiling and walls. I can see her mascara from where I sit near the back. She talks of life and the afterlife rather than death. The spirit prevails. Death is not to be feared. I listen. I fantasize about walking up to the audience microphone and telling her about Jim. She would cry at the depth of our love and call Jim back. His voice would resonate in the room: I love you, Sue, and I'll never leave you. I am okay.

I choke back tears at the thought.

Question time comes and the first brave soul approaches the microphone. My palms sweat. She coughs and sputters her words. I want someone to hold her hand, cheer her on. A month ago, her husband and son were killed in an automobile accident. She grips the microphone with both hands. She wants to know if they are okay. She waits, crying.

The psychic asks rhetorically, "They died of chest wounds?"

"Yes," the widow cries.

"They're fine," the psychic says, "just fine. Nothing to worry about. They've gone to the afterlife. No limbo for them. All good."

I tense and expect the psychic at any moment to say, "Next." The widow mumbles a thank you and stumbles to her seat. I don't hear the rest of the grievers. Do I feel uncomfortable because I don't believe the psychic or because she accepts death so easily? I want to believe anything that will bring Jim back to me. I want her to bring Jim back to life. Applause fills the space when she is finished. I drive quietly back to Whistler.

That night, when I watch the evening news, there is a special about the hypnotist Dr. Michael Newton, the author of *Journey of Souls*. The interviewer asks him how he contacts the deceased, and he explains. The next interview is with one of his clients who performed on his television show. The client admits he was planted in the audience and told what to say.

The final interview is with the author of the book *Why People Believe*. We believe because we are human. We need something to believe in. And sometimes we believe because we are terrified of losing who we are.

EIGHTEEN
DAY TWENTY

WEDNESDAY, MAY 19, 1999

The phone rings many times a day. Sometimes I answer it.

"Hello?"

"Hi, is Jim Haberl there please?"

I stay silent and wonder if this is a joke.

"Hello?"

"May I ask who is calling?"

"My name is Bruce, and Jim very generously agreed to talk to me about photography."

It's not a joke. He just hasn't heard. "Jim was killed in an avalanche on April 29."

"Oh, my God. I'm so sorry. I'm so sorry."

"Thank you."

After I hang up I press the button to listen to the message recording. "You have reached Jim and Sue's place. Please leave a message and we'll get right back to you." I press the button over and over to hear Jim's voice until I am bawling. I take out the cassette and put it in my drawer of memorabilia and record a new message on a different tape.

I gather my courage to drive to the post office to pick up a package that has been sent to me from my childhood friend Heather who lives in Chicago. I brush my hair, but I wear the same clothes, Jim's jeans and shirt, that I've worn for days. As I stand in line waiting, my body odour seeps through my sweater. Whistler is a small town. I wonder if everyone there knows that I am a grieving widow. When it is my turn, the clerk gives me my package and says in a hushed voice, "I've been thinking about you." I mumble a thank you and keep my head down as I leave so that people won't see me crying.

The outing has left me exhausted, so I curl up in bed with the new book Heather has sent me, *Living When a Loved One Has Died*, by Earl Grollman. The four chapters contain a series of poems with just a few words per line, and my brain is able to digest the information without feeling overwhelmed. By dinner I have read all four chapters: Shock, Denial, Recovery, A New Life. I do not feel so alone in my grief, because the author acknowledges how death has shaken my faith, how there are no answers, how I feel numb, panicked, guilty, depressed, utterly lost and that all of these emotions are normal responses to grief. For the next five years, I read the book over and over.

Some evenings I watch sad movies to unleash my tears. In *Ghost*, when Patrick Swayze's character returns from the dead to visit his widowed wife (Demi Moore), I can almost feel him caressing her skin and kissing her neck. I want more than anything to feel Jim's touch. In *Truly, Madly, Deeply*, the dead husband comes back to live with his widowed wife, and she is over the moon with happiness. But he brings his dead friends, and they stay up all night and keep the house temperature unbearably warm. His goal is to be such a pain that she will move on and let go. I don't like the ending because my dream is to have Jim back, forever. I wonder how I will recover.

One day the phone rings. "Hello." I clench my teeth and grab a pencil to finger.

"Hi, Sue, it's Marti Henzi, from Whistler Heli-Skiing. How are you?"

"Hi, Marti. Fine." I tap the pencil on the counter.

"Look, I'm so sorry about Jim. He had that very rare 'star' quality. I feel honoured to have worked with him. I wanted to tell you that our black lab, Solo, just had puppies. And you know in times of trouble, I've always had a dog, and that has really helped me. Solo has seven pups and one of them is white. The white one reminds me of Jim; he's so kind and gentle. I believe he is special. We would like you to have him."

I stop tapping the pencil. "Wow, thank you very much. I don't know, you know, I'm having a hard time just looking after myself these days. I don't know about looking after a puppy."

"There's no rush. We'll keep him until you're ready."

I hang up and lay my head on the counter.

A friend comes to stay with me and urges me to go see the puppy. When we arrive, the puppies are a mass of white, black and brown fur romping in the dirt yard, snatching at a rope dangling from a tree. Some have long, hound-like ears and others have short ears that stand up. The litter is a mix of bloodhound and Labrador retriever. The only white puppy waddles toward me. He looks like a lab. I put my hands down for him to lick and then scoop him up into my lap. His belly bulges warm and taut under my hand. He wiggles to get close enough to lick my face. I smell earth. He stares at me with amber-brown eyes.

"He's so cute! Come on, let's take him home today." My friend smiles.

"Not yet. I can't do it yet." I give the pup a kiss on the head and let him go.

NINETEEN
DAY THIRTY-FIVE

THURSDAY, JUNE 3, 1999

"Are you sleeping?" My family physician sits opposite me in her office, an arm's length away, and looks me in the eye.

"A bit. I have trouble falling asleep and then wake up in the night. Some nights I don't sleep at all." My armpits feel wet. My words are foreign. I've always been such a sound sleeper. I don't tell her that some days I don't get out of bed until 1 p.m.

"Are you eating?" She rests her pencil on her notepad.

"Sometimes. I feel nauseous. The food tastes thick." I've lost more than six kilograms since Jim was killed. I seek the twisting pain of hunger. It feels real and is a welcome change from the numbness.

"Have you thought about suicide?" She holds my gaze.

I pause. I have wondered. Sleeping pills or slit wrists in the bathtub? But too many people love me. And I worry that if there is an afterlife I won't be allowed to see Jim if I take my own life.

"Yes. But I can't do it. It makes no sense to me because I would be leaving my loved ones with the same pain I am trying to escape." I rattle off my standard answer, looking at the wall.

"I see. Are you seeing a counsellor?"

"A friend set up an appointment for me a few weeks ago. I saw the counsellor once. She said it was too soon for me to be in regular counselling."

My doctor rests her hand on the arm of my chair. "You're

strong, tough, and you'll get through this, but it won't be easy. You're too young to have to deal with this."

I am 33 years old. I have little experience with death. I take a breath and launch forth, "I feel crazy, as if I'm floating parallel to reality with a very real notion that something is terribly wrong. I feel so anxious because I believe that if I can fix this terrible wrong somehow, we will have our life back." I look up at her from downcast eyes. There, I've said it. Now she can tell me I am going crazy.

"If you keep having this feeling, I think you should see a counselor, and I would suggest seeing someone who doesn't know you and who didn't know Jim. Someone objective. A friend of mine was at Jim's memorial service, and she said how brave you were. You don't have to be superhuman, you know. You can fall apart." She nods her head and creases the skin between her eyebrows – her grief brow.

I drop my shoulders and fiddle with my jacket. My body would slide to the floor if I let it. If I let myself fall apart, how would I put myself back together again?

TWENTY
DAY FORTY-THREE

FRIDAY, JUNE 11, 1999

No life insurance. No mortgage insurance. No steady job. Back home in Whistler, I stare at the stack of bills.

When Jim and I signed the final mortgage papers, the bank representative asked whether we would like mortgage insurance. Jim faced me, eyebrows pinched. He said, "I think it's a good idea given how difficult it is for a mountain guide to get life insurance. What do you think?"

"What does it mean?" I shifted to face him.

"It means that if one of us dies, then the mortgage is paid off, no questions," he answered.

I slapped my hands on my thighs and guffawed, "We don't need that!" We had just married, built a house and planned to raise a family. Death was not in my plans.

I curse Jim for leaving me in a lurch. I chastise myself for turning down the mortgage insurance, for giving up my biweekly teacher's paycheque to move to Whistler and for becoming financially dependent on Jim.

Still, I am on leave with the Vancouver School Board, so I am eligible for a full-time position in Vancouver that pays well. There is an opening for an outdoor education teacher, a position in a program called Trek that in the past I would have coveted. I struggle, wondering whether or not to apply.

Every so often, the image of Jim's body at the funeral home

crawls into my consciousness. My brain knows he is dead, but my heart argues that he is still alive. If I teach in Vancouver, our house in Whistler will be empty during the week. What will happen if I'm not there and Jim comes home? Maybe if I am not home, Jim won't come back. I need to be here. Who will keep the house exactly as Jim left it so he will recognize it when he comes home? But if I don't get work, I might have to sell the house.

Friends help me fill in the job application.

Dad drives me to Prince of Wales High School in Vancouver, where I graduated 15 years before. We sit in those institutional chairs outside the principal's office waiting to be called for my interview. Every now and then Dad pats my leg and nods wordless encouragement. At my feet lies a sports bag full of binders exemplifying my ability to create curriculum, to lead youth in the outdoors and to teach. The former head Trek teacher, Dave, stops on his way to my interview to say hello, holds my hand for a moment and reassures me that I need not worry, they will be gentle. I feel naked and as fragile as an eggshell.

The secretary ushers me into the principal's office, where three beige leather chairs are arranged in a semicircle. The principal rises: "Hello, Sue, come in. I'm Andrew." He shakes my hand and gestures to the others, "You already know Dave, and this is Lynn." They get up, shake my hand and thank me for coming. They knew Jim. I sit on the edge of the empty chair and they take turns asking me questions.

In a cheery non-threatening voice, Lynn comments, "I see you have an incredible amount of personal experience in the outdoors, but would you tell me more about the experience you have leading youth?" I cringe at this faint challenge. I have no armour to defend myself. I have no confidence in myself and in the world around me.

I pat my sports bag as I babble, "Well, I have designed and implemented four outdoor programs for youth, and I have the curriculum here if you would like to see it. However, I do have more personal experience in the outdoors than experience leading others in the outdoors."

The principal responds in a soft voice, "Do you think you are up to the challenge of a new job?"

I take a deep shaky breath, "In the past I have worked hard. I know I can work hard. But under the circumstances, all I can promise is I will do my best."

He looks me in the eye, "That's all I can ask."

I leave the office and shelter under the warmth of my father's watchful eye. I did it.

Two days later I answer the phone and the principal offers me the Trek job. I hold my breath for a second and force out in one hard exhale: "I would like to accept your offer. Thank you." When I hang up, I stand still, shell-shocked, and wonder why I have accepted a job in Vancouver when Jim and I live in Whistler.

In just over two months, the school term begins. I have just over two months to find Jim, to prove to my brain that he is alive.

TWENTY-ONE
DAY FIFTY

FRIDAY, JUNE 18, 1999

Keith, Graeme and I are leaning over a topographical map on my kitchen counter in Whistler, going over details of Jim's accident when I blurt out, my fists clenched at my sides, "I want to go to where Jim fell."

Almost before the last word is out of my mouth, Keith says, "I'll go with you."

Graeme shakes his head slowly and lowers his gaze, opens his mouth to say something and then closes it again. Open and then close. "I'd like to go but I'm just too busy and I can't afford it," he says softly.

When I tell Jim's brother Kevin, he responds, "Yeah, yeah, Sue. I can see why you want to go. I mean, some people are saying that you're crazy, you know, that you're chasing ghosts, but I support you." We hug, but my body braces against the disapproval, and my heart trembles at the thought of more loss.

When my friend Susan offers to go to Alaska with me, she confides what another friend told her: "What? Sue wants to climb the chute where Jim died? If she dies, I'm not going to her funeral." One short laugh escapes me, and an electric current carries fear through my body. I whisper to everyone I love, "Please don't leave me. I need you to stay with me."

I have to go to Alaska, for me. To honour the place where Jim died, to absorb any remnants of his final living moments – to make sure that he is not still alive.

The risk of going pales in comparison with the risk of staying. And I know the risk of going because Jim and I ski-mountaineered in this same area of Alaska last April, one year ago.

I will return to Alaska for our second wedding anniversary, June 30, almost two months to the day after Jim was killed. I scan my list of things to do: book plane ticket, organize food, pack. Days pass. I cannot focus long enough to complete the tasks. Finally, I call Susan and explain my inertia, and she arranges the plane tickets and contacts Paul at the lodge.

Before I leave I meet Mom Haberl for tea at her townhouse in Vancouver. She greets me with the usual open arms, laughing eyes and singsong, "Hello, come in!" We sit on the floral couch, and she works a handkerchief between her hands as she speaks. "I guess I don't need to go to the mountain. I know my tears are for myself. I know that Jim is fine. I just wonder why God didn't take me instead. I've had a full life and I would have been happy to take his place. You know?" She looks at me hopefully through watery eyes. I rub her back and hold her hand, but my throat will not let any words out. I want to bring Jim back so that everyone will be happy again.

I still feel unnaturally responsible.

Mom Haberl and I hug at the door and hold on for a bit longer. She grips my forearms, looks me in the eyes, laughing, and then as if scolding a child in the most loving way, pokes at my chest. She prods a few times and makes a few false starts before the words come, laced with tears. "Now, you yell at that mountain for me, okay?" She laughs. I kiss her wet face. She stands in the doorway waving while I drive away.

The next day, Keith, Susan and I fly to Anchorage, rent a car and drive to Chitina. Paul arrives to pick us up in his six-seat bush plane. He hugs me so that the down of my jacket compresses flat against my body. "Good to see you, Sue."

When we land at the lodge, Paul's family greets us.

His wife juts out her hip to support the weight of her toddler and leans toward me, "How are Jim's parents doing?" And before I can reply, she adds, "I can't imagine anything worse than losing your own child, your own flesh and blood, you know?" I don't. I have no children and can't imagine a more heartbreaking grief than what I am experiencing.

At Jim's memorial, a friend warned me, "People will say insensitive things, and they don't mean it." People try to say the right thing. They do not try to hurt my feelings. Grief teaches me to take life less personally because, for the most part, shit happens and everyone does his or her best.

Grandma Eleanor, Paul's mom, encircles me with her arms, "We've been praying for you, and for Jim." I cannot hold on any longer and the dam breaks.

After lunch, we stack our camping and ski gear on the gravel runway beside Paul's favourite aircraft, the Super Cub, in preparation to fly to where Jim was killed, on Mount Ultima Thule. The propeller is still, but I keep a few paces back. I remember the cramped seating and the toy-like appearance of the small plane. My underarms grow damp as I recall Paul's anxious words, "C'mon, baby, lift!"

Paul flies a lighter load first with Keith to make sure the snow is hard and smooth enough for a landing. When Paul returns, Keith's seat is empty. But the landing is too soft for a heavier load, and Keith will look for a site with harder snow where Paul will land with Susan and me.

Seated on the floor of the plane, Susan and I wedge one inside the other, legs spread in front of us, directly behind Paul. As we approach the head of the glacier, Keith waves his arms to signal that he cannot find a safe landing.

Plan B. We get ready to drop an oblong, red plastic children's sled out the window so Keith can move our gear farther down the glacier to harder ice. Paul will fly Susan and me back to the lodge to get the bigger plane with wheels. The wind shoves and grabs as all three of us force open the window and wrestle the sled into launch position. Paul turns and counts loudly to over-power the rush of air: one, two, three! We push down on the sled and let it go. Paul cranes his neck to see behind him.

"Shit. We'll be all right. Hang on."

I twist my shoulders and catch sight of the red plastic sled molded around the tail rudder of the plane. "We'll be okay." I echo Paul's words. I am not scared. I am more concerned about getting to the cliff where Jim fell.

Susan braces one hand on the roof and the other on the floor. With no rudder for control, Paul throttles on and off until the plane lurches closer to the ground. The landing skis on the bottom of the plane bump hard and my chin hits the seat in front of me. The plane bounces up and down several times on the soft snow before skidding to a stop. When we scramble down to the glacier, Paul kisses us and chuckles, "I guess it wasn't our time."

Keith skis up, eyebrows raised. "That was a bit bumpy."

Paul checks the plane for damage, wishes us luck and takes off.

By the time Susan and I click into our bindings, Keith, in efficient guide style, has lashed our gear to the sled, and we ski down the glacier. Minutes later, Keith stops at a circular indent in the snow and prods at a square piece of plywood the size of a placemat with his ski pole. "This was our camp," he mumbles.

I lock my gaze onto the snow and stifle my childlike enthu-siasm. Their camp is still here. Still here. Maybe Jim is still here. Maybe. And then I see ski tracks beside me, warped from the sun. I hold my breath and place my skis in them and push off with my poles. I picture Jim shuffling along in front of me. He skied in these tracks.

Gravity pulls my skis down the slope. I lean forward against the wind pushing me back uphill. Push, pull. The spring sun has drawn a film of water to the surface of the glacier, in some places forming puddles. My skis hydroplane in short bursts sending my arms flailing like a scarecrow to regain balance.

"Yahoo!" I turn to Susan glissading beside me.

"Yahoo!" she returns.

Slushy snow splashes onto our plastic boots; rooster tails spray as we career through the deeper puddles. We fly.

My heart sings to be in the mountains, to feel Jim.

Meanwhile, the facts squat in my mind. I push my ankles out into a snowplow. My airway squeezes down until I wheeze and the back of my throat aches. Keith's jacket brushes against my arm.

"This is it," he says.

Keith leads me to a rock and sits me down. I look up as he draws a line in the air to the steep chute he, Greame and Jim climbed, to the protrusion where he and Graeme were waiting when the slab cut loose, to the crown line marking the weakness that triggered the avalanche, to the rocky cliff where Jim fell, to the snow where Jim was buried.

Keith's gaze fixes on the spot, and he says, "I'll be back in a second." He trudges closer to the cliff and picks up an ice axe and a red glove. Jim's. Two months later and the mountain spits out evidence of the accident. I cannot deny it.

As I peer up at the cliff, trying to piece it all together, to make sense of it all, a rock falls. Then snow sloughs off. The mountain sheds continually. That's just the way it is. There was no grand scheme to kill Jim. Even though Jim was so kind and good and wise in the mountains, he was still fallible. My love could not save him.

With my bare finger, I carve "I love U" in the snow where Jim was buried by the avalanche. From the top lid of my pack, I extract a limp bouquet of four roses, one sunflower and mauve wildflowers. "We love you, Jim." I don't know what else to say. It is as if I have terrible stage fright. I am in the wrong play and do not know my lines.

Back at the lodge, we eat dinner with some guests who chat excitedly about their coming adventure. They ask me why I am here. In a steady voice, I tell them that my husband was killed and that I came to say goodbye. Heads lower, condolences are murmured and a cloak of silence descends on the group. It is my first experience of feeling a sort of shame, isolation. I do not fit in. I am a reminder of mortality, and my sadness and grief make people feel unhappy and uncomfortable.

Grandpa John, Paul's father, flies us back to Chitina, to our rental car. As he hugs me he drawls, "Now you all have a very deep wound, and it will take some time to heal."

When Grandpa has gone, Keith says, "You know when I tried to settle up our bill with Paul, he wouldn't let me pay. They aren't going to charge us." I want to feel grateful for such a generous gesture, but my heart is numb.

En route to the airport, Keith, Susan and I drive to the funeral home near Anchorage where Jim's body was prepared for the flight home. They still have his mountaineering boots, clothes and sleeping bag. I explain to the young blonde woman at the desk that I am Jim Haberl's wife, and she hurries off. When she returns, she places Jim's black plastic mountaineering boots and his yellow and black, one-piece GORE-TEX climbing suit on the counter. Like a robot, I jerk forward to take the boots. I finger the suit and feel a long tear in the material. I cringe and will my mind not to imagine. I gather the remnants and go outside. Susan's arm is around me. I tell her I need to walk. My throat closes; I bend over, my hands on my knees, gasping.

As we drive away, I wonder whether they have given me everything that belonged to Jim. I need everything because I feel like I have lost everything. Several times I open my mouth to speak before the words come out. "Keith, can you turn around please? I want to go back. I think they have more of Jim's stuff."

I go in again and ask the woman for Jim's red wind stopper, his sleeping bag and long johns. His sleeping bag and underclothes had too much blood on them so they'd been destroyed. She thinks for a moment about the wind stopper and then goes into the back. She returns with Jim's favourite fleece. It is covered in dog hair and ripped at the elbow. She hands it to me and the softness of her gaze makes me feel as if she hugs me. I hold the fleece close to my chest and walk back to the car, breathing steadily.

I have gathered some of the pieces of my shattered life and think of the next place I will search, the place where Jim and I met: the Queen Charlotte Islands.

TWENTY-TWO
RETURN TO THE
QUEEN CHARLOTTES

(JULY 1999)

There's no greater blessing than a friend who
is there when good times aren't.
– MOM HABERL'S FRIDGE

"You know, Sue, when Eric went to see Jim's body at the funeral
home, he promised Jim he would look out for you," Eric's wife
Trish confides.

"Yup, that's right," Eric loops his arm around her.

I nod and force the lump back down my throat.

For years, Eric looked out for me, until he was able to pass on
the job. He is steady, dependable, honest and kind. His loyalty to
Jim made me ache sometimes.

Eric and Jim went to high school together, were climbing
buddies and best friends. When Jim and I first met on a sailboat
in the Queen Charlotte Islands 17 years ago, Eric was one of the
crew. Of the hundreds of islands that make up the archipelago
that in 2010 was renamed Haida Gwaii – to acknowledge the
history of the Haida nation – the southern portion is designat-
ed the Gwaii Haanas National Park Reserve and Haida Heritage
Site. For ten thousand years, the Haida people hunted, fished,
built their longhouses and buried their dead on these islands. As
a student, I was there to learn.

My 16-year-old body pulsed. The wide wooden floorboards of the sailboat creaked under my weight as I shifted to relieve the pressure on my seat bones. I hugged my knees and dug my chin into the sleeve of my soft Icelandic wool sweater. A curtain of my tame, long brown hair slid across my cheek marking a trail of salty residue, moss-covered earth and sweet rain. Candlelight danced with the roll of the waves, throwing angular shadows onto seamless faces. The faces talked and laughed, but I was overcome by the beating of my heart and the heat radiating from my skin.

Jim sat above me and rocked forward when he spoke so that the energy from his voice and his laugh drew me like a magnet. I wished I had made him laugh. I wished I were the funniest and most charming person in the group that night so his blue eyes were fixed on me. I wished my stomach weren't so knotted with fear so I could look at him. He was so near, and the energy between us made me dizzy.

His thigh brushed my shoulder, and I stiffened. I held my breath and sat up. At the next opportunity, I convulsed with laughter so that I could graze my shoulder against his leg. The contact left me breathless. I slid my hand down my leg and placed it flat on the floor. Each time one of my peers roared with laughter or demanded the spotlight, I inched my hand closer until the length of my little finger trembled against the instep of his stocking foot. My blood cooled and my breathing muffled the sound around me. In one motion I lifted my hand and rested it on the top of his foot. His flesh tensed beneath my touch. Then his fingers kneaded my shoulder. We did not talk or exchange a look, and that night I lay awake in my sleeping bag for hours.

The next evening, he washed dishes by moonlight on the stern. I stood in the shadows for a few minutes and then reached for the drying towel. Excited chatter bounced around in the cavernous black air as the rest of the clients boarded the inflatable boat to go swimming in a lake onshore. The inky water bubbled under the thrusting bow, and the full moon's silver light slid over the young faces like silk.

"Don't you want to go with them?" he asked me.

"No. That's okay. I'll stay and help you." I cleared my throat.

Voices skipped back to us on the water when the others splashed ashore. Their laughter faded as they pushed their way deeper into the dense, dark rainforest. The rhythmic lapping of the salt water against the side of the sailboat took over again, and the space around me expanded with the lack of human sound. An eagle called in a series of chirps and then settled into a rising scream. The wind rustled. We were anchored in the Queen Charlotte Islands, and we were alone. My skin tingled with the anticipation of romance. I stayed quiet so as not to break the spell.

When the last dish was dried, Jim looked at his watch and said, "There's still time if you want to go to the lake."

"Okay."

We canoed from the sailboat to the shore. I dug my paddle deep into the water and pulled back hard. I wanted him to feel my strength. I vaulted out to ease the bow over the rocky shoreline, and the cold ocean fingered its way up my pants to my knees. He tied the canoe to a log before we entered the tangled forest. I spread out my hands in front of me and focused on the fallen trees and slippery moss so that I did not have to slow my pace or cause him to reach out a helping hand. At the lake, I crept out along a log cantilevered over the water. He swept his hand through the fresh water and sucked in his breath from the cold. I dived in and heard his whoop as I came up gasping.

Three months after Jim was killed, Eric offers to take me back to that magical place. Along with close friends Mike, Rose, Susan and Ken, I fly to the Queen Charlotte Islands to meet Eric and Trish on their 60-foot charter sailboat to retrace the steps Jim and I took 17 years before.

The small plane bumps down onto the gravel runway in Sandspit as Kenny Loggins wails into my ear the final lyrics of his ballad, "Celebrate Me Home." I click off the Walkman. Sing me home. I wonder how the hell I will ever find home again.

Australian Aboriginals practise a tradition of navigation in the wilderness, of singing a description of landmarks along the way. If they get lost, they retrace their steps, going from singing landmark to singing landmark. They call it a "songline." My heart returns to the Queen Charlotte Islands to find a familiar landmark, to find its song, to find home.

If life were normal, I would get off the plane, squint to make out Jim jaunting toward me, grinning. In his arms I would feel whole again. He'd lead me by the hand to our kayaks loaded with food and camping gear for two weeks. We'd push off into Hecate Strait, eager to be together and alone with the eagles, mossy forests, seals and ancient totems of the islands.

But it is Eric who greets me. He feels solid as I wrap my arms around him. I look over his shoulder, just in case.

I sink into the folded sails on the bowsprit of the boat, suspended above the never-ending ripples of ocean, numbed by the sea breeze, just like the good ol' days. Dying light paints silhouettes of mountains against the sky, and the salty air coats my soul in calm. Waves slap the hull, keeping beat with the whine of the motor. Wind carries fragments of laughter, and I turn my head to watch Eric and Mike goofing around at the stern. If he were here, Jim would be with them.

As the remains of K'uuna Llnagaay village come into view, the setting sun outlines the peninsula in silver. Glistening black, long-necked cormorants torpedo into the water, hunting for fish. I strain to see the lumbering bodies of the sea lions, but they have moved on and no longer call K'uuna home. My songline is here, though. I remember.

Our canoe bobbed right below the sea lions' rock, and Jim and

I fought the waves to stay out of diving range of the huge mammals. I crinkled my nose at the combined smells of wet fur, excrement, urine, salt and fish. We shouted over the constant guttural roar. "Look out!" I squealed and grabbed the gunwales as hundreds of pounds of sea lion launched off the rock into the waves with a hoarse roar and rocked our canoe. Pfooof. Another sea lion surfaced behind Jim, making him jump. I shivered with fear and excitement. It wasn't just the sea lions. The combination of Jim's confident, strong body, his clear way of thinking, his ability to take the right action and his gentle, honest eyes drew me like a magnet. I wanted to be a part of his energy.

Eric lowers the kayaks into the water and we pair up to explore. Mike ends up in a boat with me. "Oh, Rosie," he laments to his wife, "it's our anniversary." I offer to switch so that they can be together, but Rose is set in her single kayak. I grow quiet. Mike leans over and kisses her. I struggle to breathe as if I am in a smoke-filled room.

That evening, the couples rub elbows around the dinner table, laugh and talk about future trips, plans. I float with no sense of attachment to what is going on around me. Up on deck, alone, I spin around to see which bird shrieks from shore. A seagull, I think. The noise continues, so I investigate with Jim's binoculars. On top of a tall tree, I spot the telltale white head. A bald eagle, screaming at me.

"I'm going to go for a little paddle." I stroke my throat so that my words won't sound so strangled. There is a pause.

"Do you want someone to come with you?" Rose's voice echoes from below.

"No, no. I won't be long." I balance on the stepladder and stretch one foot out to hook the cockpit of the kayak. Once settled, I push away from the sailboat toward the shoreline. I stab at the water with each stroke. Harder. Faster. I clunk the paddle down in front of me, bury my face in my crossed arms and try to cry. Get it out. The kayak bobs. Whoosh. What was that? I lift my head and jerk it around. A glistening nose disappears below the surface behind me. I scan the water like a searchlight. Whoosh. There he is again. I could touch him with my paddle. He floats up and down with the waves, but his wet eyes, like black glass marbles, fix on me.

"Hi," I whisper and smile. "Are you fishing?" He tips his head back and sinks. I grip my paddle and steer closer to shore. Every so often I hear the water break as he surfaces behind me. I look where I'm going. "You sure have a beautiful home." Rock rises steeply from the ocean in layers of colour: burnt orange, brown, ruddy green, yellow. Reflections dance on the water. I paddle for another half an hour, talking to my friend, until I no longer hear his breathing. I stretch my neck to see behind me, but he is gone.

I turn back to the sailboat and make out figures on the deck. As I get closer, I clench the paddle. So many people on deck. Everyone. What's wrong? I paddle faster. Mike leans over to catch my bow and at the same time swipes the back of his hand across his eyes like a windshield wiper. He smiles.

"Hey, Sue."

The rest of the group shuffles over to the side of the boat, shuddering, pressing their fists to their eyes and laughing. I jump from face to face and see the same thing. Red, puffy skin around their eyes. Relief.

"You know, we all just ended up on deck and we saw you out there and we looked at each other and just burst into tears." They gently lay hands on each other, smiling. "Yeah, wow, can you believe it?" They look back at me. I try to smile and be happy for them, but inside of me a voice yells, "Shit, I missed it. Shit. I wish I hadn't missed it." I missed sharing my grief. I feel so alone with my pain, and it is a relief to share it with others.

Before I fall asleep that night, Eric and Trish tiptoe to my bed, hug me and whisper, "We love you." I sob because I am fortunate to have loving friends. And I sob because I know a big part of my survival will be up to me alone; they will not be able to help, no matter how much they want to. I've seen people as brittle as fallen leaves with a vacant look in their eyes. I used to wonder what happened to them. I know now because sometimes the only way I can bear the grief is to harden my heart. I'm scared. How will I survive as a warm, loving person? How will I not become a bitter old widow?

The next day, rain pounds the aft covering. Mist veils the islands. My throat aches. Ken comes over, "Are you okay?" His concern breaks the dam holding back my tears. He holds me, and I crumble with gratitude because he does not run. The intense feelings of grief scare me, so I reason they must terrify others. Rose and Susan hurry to my side and cradle my hands. Part of me does not want them to suffer my grief, and part of me wants to grip them with all of my strength so they cannot leave. It is a relief to have a safe place to let go of the pain.

We don raingear and head to shore to walk among the remnants of the village of T'aanuu Llnagaay, whose descendants are represented by the Eagle Chief. Ghostly indents in the grass mark the outlines of longhouses. Sunlight streams through the trees and lights up the almost translucent yellow-green moss blanketing the fallen house posts. I gaze up at the cedar trees, run my fingers through the thick tickly moss and remember holding hands with Jim. Here. My feet stumble and grief pulls me to my knees. I am not religious, but I pray. "I don't know if I can make it, Jim. I try. I am grateful to have experienced this place with you. Your presence is so strong, but I want to reach out and touch you, feel you, hold you." I push my face into the moss and let it absorb my tears like a sponge might.

The next morning I wake up more fatigued. It is exhausting to hold back the pain, and it is exhausting to feel it. We cruise toward the two-thousand-year-old village of Nan Sdins on the

island of SGaang Gwaii, the southernmost point of the archipelago and the gateway to the open waters of the Pacific. SGaang
Gwaii means "Wailing Island" and is so named because of the
nine-metre waves that rush through a hollow reef beside the island, making the sound of a wailing woman.

When I was 16, I canoed around the island to hear the wailing woman. It was dark and the ocean swirled and reared up
in angry, foamy waves. I pushed as close to the reef as I dared,
held steady and listened, rising up and down with the enormous
swells, looking out at the Pacific Ocean. Whooosh. The water
forced its way through the reef with a deafening roar and retreat-
ed with a high-pitched moan. I watched, mesmerized. The wailing woman. I have no desire to hear the woman this trip. There
is enough wailing going on inside of me.

Eric nods to me as he steers the boat toward one of the islets
off SGaang Gwaii called Gordon Island. "One more stop today." I
turn away and swallow hard.

Jim led four of us on an overnight kayak trip to Gordon
Island. After setting up the tent, I explored my temporary home.
I wandered from one side of the island to the other in less than
five minutes. My toes stopped on the edge of a slab of glistening
black rock pummelled smooth by the Pacific waves that went
on forever. I closed my eyes, raised my face to the salty wind
and invited the roar of the water to bruise every part of my being into life. In the approaching darkness, I eased myself down
onto the barnacle-covered rocks. I cradled my head and gazed
at the sun disappearing into the sea. He sat down beside me.
"It's beautiful."

"Yes." When I turned to look at him, he leaned forward and
pressed his lips to mine. My eyes stayed closed and it was his
voice that brought me back.

"You know this can't go anywhere."

When my eyes flipped open, I was grateful for the darkness.
"Yes," I agreed.

But my chest ached as I hugged my knees and stared at my feet.

"It's not so bad out here because it's a bit of a fantasy land. But back home, the reality is that you are in high school and I am travelling the world. Our lives are so different and eight years separate us." He pushed a piece of driftwood into the sand, and pain plunged into my heart.

"You know, he wasn't perfect," Jim's mom's words claw at my memories.

"No, he wasn't, but he was perfect for me," I mouth to the wind. The truth is that I want to remember him as perfect. I want to remember our relationship as perfect.

This memory of Jim breaking my heart when I was 16 does not fit into my fantasy. I massage the truth until Jim promises he will return to me when I am older. He will save himself for me because we are soulmates.

Eric holds the Zodiac steady while we clamber over the sides onto the beach of Gordon Island. No one moves, and I touch the square bulge in my jacket pocket. We scatter over the sand.

I stand in one place and then scurry to another. Was it here on this knoll, or by this rock? Where was the exact place we kissed? I don't know. I should know. I drive my toe into the sandy beach and stare at nothing. Damn it. Why didn't we stay together then? We would have had eight more years.

When people ask how long Jim and I were married, I say, "Two years." If they comment on our brief time together I blurt, "We were together for more than seven years before that, and we first met when I was 16." I stretch the truth and add on the few months when we weren't officially dating. I wish I could say that we were married for 25 years and had four children.

Mike ambles up and offers me a petrified piece of seaweed, "Here, Sue, I thought you might like this, it looks like ski tracks."

Ken is behind him, "Look at this beautiful shell, too."

Susan presents me with a curled piece of driftwood.

I hold their gifts. They remind me of children who offer gifts in return for friendship or to cheer someone up.

I am lucky. My husband was killed and I am lucky to be surrounded by love. I am grateful in a way that makes me weak-kneed because I am not certain I have the courage to love again.

An eagle perches on top of a small dead tree above a grassy knoll. I creep closer and he glares at me but does not fly off. I settle below him on rocks just out of reach of the crashing waves of the Pacific Ocean. The rest of the group sidles up because they know I plan to throw some of Jim's ashes into the ocean. I light a candle and surround it with a photo of Jim and me and two good luck teddy bears. I fumble with the box in my pocket and begin to speak slowly:

> Hi, Sweetie. The Charlottes are as beautiful as I remember. But, without you, I am lost. You made life beautiful for me. It's good to be here with friends.
>
> I wish I could tell you how everyone is doing, but I don't know. Your dad cries every day. Your mom has a picture of you at the bottom of the stairs so that she can say good morning to you. She wears your favourite red fleece, the one you had on when you fell, around the house. Kevin focuses on his family and says his daily life is intact. He was really happy when I gave him your mountaineering boots. Many wonderful people carry you in their hearts. We miss you.
>
> Some days I don't know how I'll make it without you and other days I feel you holding my hand and think I will be okay. My head and heart play tug-o-war with the facts. My heart waits for you to come home and my head tells my heart that you will never come home.

I claw at the drawstring bag inside the box and sink my finger-tips into the dark, dense remains, which are like sand mixed with white crushed peppercorns, and hold Jim's body, flesh against flesh. With my eyes closed, I stroke his face, hold his hand. Without a word, I stand to face the ocean and throw Jim's ashes to the waves. The wind snatches pieces of Jim and throws them back at me. I stare at the white bone and ash sticking to my clothes and stifle a laugh. This is not how I envisioned the perfect scattering. I scold Jim. Don't make this harder than it is. I brush him away so that he settles into the crevasses of the black volcanic rock at my feet.

"We send your body back to earth, as it should be. Peace be with you."

The bag holds enough ashes for each person to scatter a hand-ful. I save the rest at home. Eric reads a poem. Rose says she never wants to wash her hand again.

I stride back to the boat, chin up and chest open.

When I return home to Whistler, I look at my calendar. A red cross marks each passing day since Jim was killed, almost three pages of them. No events. No birthdays. No reminders. I stop the ritual and throw out the calendar.

TWENTY-THREE
OUT OF THE
MOUTHS OF BABES

(AUGUST 1999)

I brace my hand on the counter and gulp into the phone. "Hello."

"Hey, Susie, it's Jen."

"Oh hi, Jenny. How are you?" I pull up the kitchen stool and slump down.

"Good. How are you?"

I cradle my forehead with my hand. "Good. Well, fine. You know. It's shitty, but I complain so much these days, talk about myself so much these days, my grief. My friends must get sick of it."

Jenny sighs. "Oh, Susie, it must be so hard. I just feel bad because I can't do anything. To be honest, when I call, part of me hopes to get the answering machine. It's difficult to hear you in pain."

"Yeah." I straighten up a bit. Honesty gets my attention. Truth is vital when my feet are on shifting ground and all is unfamiliar.

Jenny invites me to go to VanDusen Botanical Garden in Vancouver with her mom and her four-year-old son, Montgomery. She thinks the meditative garden will be healing for me. When they arrive to pick me up, I am sitting in the hallway of my parents' house, hands clasped in my lap, coat on, waiting. I follow Jen to the car, smile a hello to her mom in the driver's seat and open the rear passenger door.

"Hi, Montgomery, how are you?" I crouch to get into the back seat beside Jen's beautiful boy. His feet dangle in the air, and his palms press into the leather seat. His brown eyes are so wide open. I wait for an enthusiastic hello.

"Is Jim dead?" he asks, clearly and firmly. Jen sucks in her cheeks and flips her head to look at her mom.

I look at him. "Yes, Montgomery, Jim is dead. It's sad, isn't it?"

He nods his head slowly up and down. I sigh and sit back in my seat. Silently, I thank Montgomery for asking the question I ask every day. Is he really dead? Montgomery swings his legs and looks ahead.

The Zen meditation garden weaves through small trees, stone statues and gentle cascades. Sitting on one of the stone benches, I lose myself in the symphony of birdcalls. For a minute or two, there is nothing else. But my thoughts churn again, preparing for my trip to Mount Kilimanjaro in Africa. There is so much to do before leaving. How will I manage it all without Jim?

TWENTY-FOUR
BACK TO
KILIMANJARO

(AUGUST 1999)

You don't conquer mountains: they let
you climb them or they don't.

– JIM

In 1998 Ian Ross of the Alzheimer Society of British Columbia asked Jim if he would guide a fundraising group up Mount Kilimanjaro. Jim asked me to go as his assistant guide. The memory of my pain on the summit had faded behind the remembered brilliant colours of the African sunrise, and I agreed to go back.

Eight participants, most members of the board of the society, raised $5,000 each for the society, paid their own trip costs and attempted Kilimanjaro on behalf of the fight against Alzheimer's disease.

Jim and I led the trip in August so that we could continue to Morocco, where we would work for Eco-Challenge, a multiday competition in which teams of four race non-stop, 24 hours a day, over a gruelling 500-kilometre course using such means as trekking, canyoneering, mountaineering, camel and horseback riding, mountain biking, canoeing and kayaking.

Eager to play a defined role on Kilimanjaro beside my famous mountain-guide husband, I passed a two-week field exam to certify as a backpacking guide with the Association of Canadian Mountain Guides. From my photos, I created a book of flora and fauna found on Kilimanjaro. Jim and I met with the team and took them on a practice hike. I answered questions about Kilimanjaro and felt useful, even though Jim could have led the group without me.

We ran the trip through a local tour operator in Tanzania, Marangu Hotel. The company is family run, has organized commercial climbs of Mount Kilimanjaro since 1932 and services at least 1500 climbers a year. Seamus Brice-Bennet, one of the owners, is a soft-spoken, dry-humoured, middle-aged Brit who was raised by his mother in Marangu Village in the shadow of Mount Kilimanjaro. At the age of five he was sent away to boarding school in the foothills of Kilimanjaro while his mother ran the hotel. After boarding school Seamus went to England to become a "bobby" and met his wife Jackie. When their first-born was six months old, they returned to Africa to make Marangu Hotel their home.

The morning we prepared to leave to climb the Western Breach, the route Jim and I had abandoned, we gathered in the courtyard of the hotel in front of a line of 20 porters and five African guides.

Seamus extended his arm to an African man close to my age. "This is Frederick. He will be your lead guide." Frederick bowed slightly, lowered his gaze and held Jim's hand for an instant. "His assistant guides will be Johnny, Wilfred, Elionne and Eric." Seamus turned to Frederick and spoke in the local Chagga dialect and then turned to us. "Elionne will be your cook." Seamus introduced us to the porters who would carry our personal gear up the mountain. Porters covet this position, as they often receive more tips than regular porters. The younger porters, as young as 15, smiled. The older ones, as old as 50, nodded.

One of the team members, Bruce Allen, was a well-known Vancouver radio-show host and talent manager. A Vancouver paper published his daily journal entries from the mountain in which he described individuals on the team as "loquacious," "wry-humoured," "quiet," "a good guy," "young" and "excitable." Of Jim he said, "Jim's a pro, a hockey fan, he'll set the pace." He described me as "nice, very accommodating." His comments about me were true, but I wished he had said "smart, brave, funny and kind."

Steadily we moved up the volcano until we reached Shira Plateau, at 3749 metres, where we spent an extra day to acclimatize. Jim called it a rest day, but after we hiked for six hours to a neighbouring peak, Shira Cathedral, the team joked that it was the hardest rest day they'd ever had. As we hiked, one client asked, "So what other big peaks have you done, Sue?"

"Mostly stuff in North America, and I've done some mountaineering in Nepal and India and here in Africa."

"Have you done Everest?"

"No," I laughed. Everest was so out of my league. "No, I'm not that type of a mountaineer." Part of me wanted to say that I'd climbed K2, like Jim, to feel worthy of being their guide.

One of the other team members piped up, "Jim is our guide, but Sue is our cheerleader. We need her."

My face reddened. "Yes, I'm a pretty good cheerleader." Others in line nodded their heads.

When we returned to camp, some clients napped in their tents to relieve symptoms of mountain sickness. Bruce wrote, "Wow, for the first time a wave of nausea hit me. I thought I was going to lose it. I wake up around midnight and try to get past the point of trying to breathe. I sleep in 20 to 30 minute segments."

Clients asked my advice about medication, clothing, what to eat and how to deal with the altitude. I was snuggled in my sleeping bag before I realized that I had no mountain sickness at this altitude. Helping others was a great distraction. Jim listened patiently to my opinions as we discussed each client's needs that evening. I knew what I needed: recognition that I played an important role and accolades for a job perfectly done. When would I stop trying to prove I was perfect and worthy of love?

After two more days of hiking, we made it to Arrow Hut at 4900 metres, the jumping-off point to the summit. I did the rounds and asked each person how they were feeling and offered help. Our tents wobbled on rocky ground beside the jumbled Arrow Glacier and below the abrupt, massive, glowing-orange rock face of the Western Breach. Bruce wrote:

> Barren! Desolate! Cold! Long johns going on tonight. Everyone is moving slow. Many have headaches. Water is critical. Will leave at 1 a.m. in the dark to the summit. We are committed now. Night can't come soon enough.

The sun set after dinner, outlining our camp in silver-orange. In our tent, I outfitted my daypack with extra batteries, gloves, down jacket and first aid supplies, should clients need them. Still experiencing no symptoms, I fidgeted with excitement, poked Jim and tried to engage him in conversation. "I hope I'm being useful."

"Sure you are." Jim peeked one hand out of his sleeping bag to stroke my face. "Let's have a good climb, okay?"

"Okay." Soon I drifted to sleep, grateful for having such a loving, understanding partner. The alarm rang me out of a deep sleep.

Bruce wrote:

> At 12:30 a.m. we are up. It is dark but a half moon and a myriad of stars provide some light. With headlamps on we start up the Western Breach and can't even see the top. Eerie. Lots of scree. Two feet forward, one foot back seems to be the norm. I hate this stuff. The pace is maddeningly slow but it works and is probably what is saving

all of us. Altitude kicks in hard as we reach the rocks. Ian is the first to be sick and he passes his pack to a guide.

Four more people vomited and several had to be steadied on their feet when we stopped. At each break, Jim and I surveyed our line of soldiers, doled out hard candies, retrieved water bottles from packs to make sure people drank, and warmed stiff hands.

Bruce noted:

> Every effort produces an instant loss of breath. Back and forth. Zigzag, zigzag. My headlamp fails. The batteries can't work in this cold. People really struggling now. Every time we stop, you feel the cold. I lean on my poles and try to suck in as much air as possible.

The cold air stung my lungs, but I felt strong and alive with the unknown of the night and our adventure. Every few minutes I sipped from my drinking hose to keep hydrated and chomped at the ice forming in the plastic tube. In the dark, I strained to see some outline representing the top so I could tell the group that we were almost there. Give them hope. Black, smudged forms approached and receded, but it wasn't until we were almost there that I could see the rim of rock.

Wrote Bruce:

> Finally after about five hours, we reach the crater rim. There is little or no elation. People are just trying to cope. The sun is rising and before us lay the snow fields and, in the distance, the true summit – Uhuru Peak, 5895 metres.

People slumped on the rocks eking strength from the sun. I went around congratulating them all, high on their success and not feeling sick myself, having strength to give them instead of being the weak one. One of the clients, who had been quite sick on the way up, worried whether or not he could go on. I overheard him say, "I'd better check with my coach." He approached me and asked, "What do you think, should I go on?"

I stifled my immediate response and asked, "How do you feel?"

"Fine. Better."

"I say you go for it." I didn't have the heart to tell him he had no choice. At this point he had come far enough that the easiest way down now was up, because we would descend the opposite, less steep side.

All eight team members made it to the summit. I stayed at the back as the tail guide. Jim was the first to summit with the faster clients, and he returned to see how I was doing with the rest of them. As we walked together he confided, "Don't tell anyone, Sue, but I'm hallucinating a bit." I gawked at him. My infallible Jim.

I felt strong until I accepted tea and a cookie on the summit from the African guide Frederick. Jim raised his eyebrows as I gobbled. Within minutes I vomited.

Back at Marangu Hotel, we sat on the lawn with our 25 African guides and porters to celebrate. They sang a song about Kilimanjaro in multipart harmony.

The trip had turned out to be more than a job. The team epitomized the generosity of the human spirit in that they chose to raise money and awareness for others. And as a team, they were able to make a greater impact. They united in their fear of the unknown, their desire to reach the top and their desire to help others. I was inspired.

Back in Canada, at the beginning of April, Jim and I met with ten people, including the premier of British Columbia, Gordon Campbell, and his family, who would make up the 1999 Ascent for Alzheimer's Kilimanjaro fundraising team. Days later, Jim left for Alaska on his final trip.

On May 18, 1999, 20 days after Jim was killed, I receive a letter from Ian Ross of the Alzheimer Society:

Dear Sue,

Nice to hear your voice last Friday. I thought I should contact you with an update. Everyone sends condolences to you. All ten climbers are still committed, although they are shaken by the loss of Jim.

We would like you to consider being our guide again in Africa in August. I realize you need some time to consider this. One of the main reasons the ten climbers signed up this year was because of the job you and Jim did coordinating our climb of Mount Kilimanjaro in 1998. There is no way we can replicate that amazing journey, but I do think we can, in the spirit of Jim, try to share the experience of a team working against significant odds for something greater than each one of us.

I remember Jim scolding me (in his nice sort of way) when I suggested that after we "conquered" Kilimanjaro, we would go on safari. He suggested in his very wise and gentle manner "you don't conquer mountains – they let you climb them or they don't." The journey to Africa last August for me was a profound experience. Getting to spend time with you, Jim, and the other climbers helped push me into a more reflective state of mind and as you mentioned in your reflection of Jim, has made me a better person. Please consider joining the team in August.

Sincerely,

Ian Ross

Chair of the Alzheimer Society of British Columbia

I press my palms into the top of my desk to stop myself from grabbing the phone, dialing Ian's number and blurting, "Yes! Yes, I'll do it." My songline woos me like a lover. Kilimanjaro is another landmark for my heart, like the Queen Charlotte Islands.

I take a deep breath and reach for the phone.

Once I commit, I am momentarily shocked by the list of things to do filling my mind: get in shape, contact the team, hire an assistant, buy a plane ticket, get the equipment together, organize a training hike, pack some of Jim's ashes to take with me.

Hiring an assistant is first on the list. Who can I trust to share this journey? Someone supportive who will not judge me. Someone who will take care of the clients if I fail. Someone with first aid and experience in the mountains. Matt comes to mind: a good friend of Jim's, a first aid instructor and a mountaineer with experience at altitude. And people trust him because he seems to genuinely care. His wife is supportive and he is keen.

One of the team members works at a local television network and will film a documentary of our climb, called *A Journey to Remember*, so each meeting and training hike is recorded. The Alzheimer Society takes advantage of the Campbell family being on the team by organizing media events to raise awareness for the fundraiser. Two weeks before we leave for Africa, we meet at an indoor climbing gym in North Vancouver for a press conference.

Cameras pivot to Gordon Campbell, his wife and two grown sons, who dangle beside me on a rope. I curl my toes around the climbing hold to balance myself as I swing open to face the cameras, satellite phone in one hand, the other hand white-knuckled on the climbing wall. Click, click. Their real focus is the Campbells, but I am an interesting story too, because of Jim. When I come off the wall, a reporter floats a microphone near my mouth. "I am sorry for the loss of your husband, Jim Haberl. What made you decide to guide the ascent team by yourself this year?"

"Last year's climb with Jim was a powerful experience. It feels important to do it again. It will be an emotional journey, and I'll be taking it step by step. Jim will be at my side in spirit." I wonder if I sound detached and cold talking about my dead husband. I wonder if I really know why I am going. I am not Jim. Jim was a full mountain guide; I am a backpacking guide. Jim led the climb in 1998; I was his assistant. Jim always protected me. Now I am on my own. But the fear of failing as a guide is nothing compared to the fear driving me. What if I don't find him? What if he is dead?

I've seen his body – I've been to where he fell in Alaska – but I will not stop looking for him. I read that denial and disbelief are reactions to the stress of grief. I chase the past because thinking in the present feels unfaithful to Jim. I need more time to absorb the grim reality of his death. And it is even more than that. You would think that all of my past hurts would pale in comparison to the pain of losing Jim. But it is not true. All of my hurts hurt all over again. My parents' divorce. My estranged relationship with my mother. I felt loveable with Jim because he loved me even when I was insecure, self-focused, possessive, competitive, fearful and controlling. His death shakes the foundations of my confidence, and I am a child again who does not feel lovable. So I look for him, literally, even in places like Kilimanjaro where I know he won't be, because it is my only hope to reverse the finality of his death and to find the "lovable Sue." And to find the man I loved more than anything.

After 24 hours of flying, we land at Kilimanjaro International Airport near Arusha, Tanzania. Stepping out onto the tarmac into the black, I suck in the familiar smells of smoke, dirt, animal excrement and moist greenery. The warm evening air relaxes my skin.

A two-hour drive brings us to the Marangu Hotel. In the courtyard, surrounded by red bougainvillea, Seamus ambles up to me, eyes downcast, and hugs me.

"I'm so sorry, Sue. We get a lot of people through the hotel every year to climb Kilimanjaro, but all the staff remember the faces of Jim and Sue."

Frederick, the African guide who helped Jim and me the previous year, cups one of my hands in both of his hands, holds my gaze with his deep brown eyes and says, "*Pole sana*, Sue."

The next morning, I wake up and begin my routine. I reach for the cassette with Jim's neat square printing on it that reads "Lost Together," slot it into my Walkman and press play. Lying on my bed, I listen to the love songs Jim collected for me when we first began dating. I close my eyes and breathe deeply. I focus on relaxing each part of my body. My lips tremble and I cry. I tuck the Walkman into my pants and stand to stretch. With each extension, I breathe deeply 10 times. By the time the Walkman clicks off, I feel lighter. I finish my routine with a feeling of gratitude. Today I am grateful to have travelled in Africa with Jim. I dress and think about how I will prepare the team for the day.

The team members stroll around the extensive lawns of the hotel. The clouds part and Kibo pokes its massive head out.

"Look, there's Kilimanjaro," I point. Necks crane, eyes squint.

"Where?"

"Up there, higher." Necks tilt. Silence.

Jim and I had planned to do a new route on the mountain with the team, called the Rongai. I stick to the plan. I go through the motions of preparing the group in terms of equipment and altitude. We drive off in the huge 4WD Mercedes truck to battle the three-hour dirt road to the trailhead: 35 porters, five African guides, eight climbers and Matt and me.

I catch the eye of a porter who has been smiling at me as we bump along.

"Hello," he shouts over the diesel engine. "Do you remember Machame, with Jim? I was there." He beams.

I do remember, and my heart beats faster.

"I am Johnny."

The memories flood back ... Johnny. "It's so nice to see you," I say.

His smile widens and his eyes bore into mine. "And I am so sorry because I heard your husband passed away."

"Yes, he did. Thank you." I wonder if people around me are uncomfortable.

"He was a good guide, a very nice person," Johnny continues.

My heart rushes to meet these words, "Yes, he was."

"You are a very good guide."

I drop my head a bit, "Thank you."

Africa moves past outside and fills me up like helium. Jim fills me with life. I smile and let it be: all of Jim, all of me and all of Africa. I love Jim and feel him as I feel Africa: with all of my senses. And it is timeless.

At the trailhead, I fall into a meditative step behind Frederick and inhale the smell of hot, dry, volcanic earth. Walking feels good. In a sense I still don't know where I am going, but at least I keep forward momentum.

Briefing the team at dinner, in the morning and throughout the day helps to take my mind off my own pain. They have lots of questions and I am happy to help. Step by step we gently ascend in the thinning atmosphere. At Kikelewa Caves we are above the clouds, at 3600 metres. There are headaches and lethargy.

The next day, we gain a ridge and descend to Mawenzi Tarn, the only "lake" on the mountain. It is less than 15 metres across and ringed with green-brown algae. Mount Mawenzi towers above at 5200 metres and fingers the sky with its jagged black rock.

We are the only group at Mawenzi. As we explore the paths winding up the rubbly sides of Mount Mawenzi, I soak up the everlasting wildflowers and the view clear down to the plains of Kenya and Tanzania.

I plan to place some of Jim's ashes on Mawenzi. I ask the rest of the group to continue down to camp, and I sit among the white papery everlastings and the rough volcanic rocks to light my candle and set up against a rock a teddy bear Mom Haberl gave me. I spread Jim's ashes.

> Hi, Sweetie. It's a beautiful spot here. I thought of you as soon as I saw it. The needle-like ridges remind me of the Brooks Range. That was quite a trip. Seven days of torrential rain and the creek almost dragged our tent away with us in it. Just you and me in the wilds of Alaska. I miss just you and me.
>
> I have anticipated this moment of letting your ashes go. The pressure has been building. I focus on my responsibility to the group and try to lead them as you would have. I know I fall short. They would catch me if I crumble, but I won't. The trip goes well, but I am tired. I walk along the trail, focused on the pace, when to break, the weather, and then it will hit me ... you are dead. How can you be dead? We're supposed to be leading this trip together. I believe you are with me; that your love will always be with me. I will be okay. I am so grateful for all that we shared.

Frederick has lunch waiting for me when I get to camp. My body is limp. I have climbed my mountain. If I were on my own, I would go down.

The next day, bundled in fleece and GORE-TEX, we head across the windy saddle and settle into high camp at 4700 metres. Up at 11 p.m., we dress and pack for the summit attempt. One foot in front of the other at an agonizingly slow pace for six hours ... and then our spirits rise with the sun as the mountain glows orange.

My soul has been here before. My feet follow my heart to

catch up with the truth of my life. I am not whole, not together, not connected to myself or to others. I look up at the crater rim and tears stream down my face. He would be here.

A white-naped raven the size of an osprey skims along the ridge. He ravages the thin air, a black shimmer on a blue background. Right above me he folds his wings to his body, makes a quarter turn and flips sideways until the wind forces him back to a level plane. I fight to breathe and the raven plays on the wind. I chuckle. Nature humbles me. I hear Jim: "You don't conquer mountains…" Voices die but words live on, an African proverb.

We reach the crater rim but still have another two hours to reach Uhuru Peak.

One of the group members cannot catch her breath, even after we rest. Her lips are blue. Frederick is concerned that she has the beginning of pulmonary edema. We decide she should go down. Another client feels too ill to continue. I tell Matt that I feel weak. I have no will to go on. I reached my summit on Mawenzi.

I go down with the ailing clients, and Matt continues with the rest of the group to Uhuru Peak.

Safely down at 3700 metres, we regroup to tell our stories to the camera.

"No need to interview me, as I didn't make it," one member of the team jokes.

"Yes, maybe there can be a separate documentary for the challenged ones." The self-deprecating comments are full of disappointment. I charge to their rescue.

"Life does not play favourites. Sometimes things happen that are out of our control. Sometimes we do not make it to the summit. So, it is best to enjoy the journey." I gulp and turn away from the camera.

This time I did not need to prove I was the strongest climber. I did not try to conquer Kilimanjaro. I listened to my aching heart, followed it, to let it be whole again.

The flight home is delayed 48 hours because the plane is missing a part. When I arrive in Vancouver at midnight, a group of my friends and family are at the airport with flowers and hugs and welcome homes. Dad reaches me first with open arms. I notice Terri and raise my eyebrows. I can't believe she is here and my gaze drops to her belly. No bulge. Beside her is her 10-day-old baby, Isaak. I hug her tightly. Mom Haberl hugs me.

"Do you feel badly that you didn't make it to the top?"

"No." I look her in the eye.

I did not find Jim, but I am home.

TWENTY-FIVE
DON'T WASTE A CRISIS

(SEPTEMBER 1999)

There are only a few hours before I have to be at the first day of
my new job at Trek, teaching outdoor/environmental education
to grade 10 students at Prince of Wales Secondary School. I am
too exhausted to be nervous.

I mount the stairs to the stage and address the 90 students in
front of me. I tell them how I remember I felt when I sat in their
place, both eager and terrified of what I had signed up for. And
I tell them how excited I am for them that they were courageous
enough to step out and try something new.

We are a team of five teachers: Robyn, Lynn, Andrew, Jamie
and me. It is the first year at Trek for all of us except Lynn. Each
day, we allocate tasks and share ideas, and Lynn steers at the
helm. Jamie's laughter, Robyn's enthusiasm, Lynn's experienced
calm and Andrew's tireless compassion jell us into a supportive
team. My mind is stuffed with details of lesson plans, schedules,
trip plans, administrative tasks and deadlines. I yearn for quiet
time but hold tightly to the rope that attaches me to a sense of
the normal. The first week whizzes by.

Dad constructs a suite for me in their basement in Vancouver
so I can stay in the city during the week while teaching at Trek,
and return home to Whistler, my safe haven, on weekends. He
spends his evenings and weekends buying kitchen appliances
and hooking them up, installing a gas fireplace and painting the
walls. I leave a toothbrush and some clothes there but everything

else stays at Whistler. I feel alone and eat most of my meals upstairs with my parents. After the first week of school, however, a
ray of hope appears.

I return to my house in Whistler and go to see Marti and Lisa,
to bring the puppy, "Whitey," home. He is almost four months
old now and all legs and tongue. When he bounds over to greet
me, I laugh and let him bowl me over. I rename him "Habby,"
one of Jim's nicknames. Lisa gives me a record of Habby's shots
and a list of his needs: lots of water, putting his head in your lap
when he rides in the car, being with you (she took him to work
with her most days). Before Habby gets in the car, Lisa takes his
face in both of her hands and says goodbye. He sits beside me
in the front seat as if he had been there all of his life. That night,
I leave him in his crate and his brown eyes watch me as I go
upstairs to bed. He does not cry, bark or whimper. For the next
eight years, he is my most faithful friend.

Back at my parents' house on Monday morning I am getting
ready to go to work when it dawns on me that I have no plan for
Habby. I cannot leave him here all day. So, I arrive at work with
a blonde bundle in tow, open our office door and say to my colleagues, "I have no idea what I was thinking ... I have this puppy
and nowhere to leave him."

Robyn immediately says, "That's okay, he can stay here." And
he does, for six years.

Before and after I got to work each day, Habby and I walk in
the extensive forested University Endowment Lands just minutes from my parents' house. Twenty minutes into the walk, I
stop to stretch and to breathe. Deep breath in for four seconds,
slow breath out for eight seconds. Warrior pose. In for four seconds, out for eight seconds. Tree pose. Tension fades from my
body. The fear and doubts in my mind quiet. My inner voice
sighs and whispers 'I miss Jim. I'm so sad. Thank you for taking
the time to listen to me.' I follow this regime to stay connected to
my heart, to my pain. Before I leave the woods I tell Jim why I am

grateful. Most often I am grateful for him, but I am also grateful for Habby and my family and friends. This ritual starts and ends the day on a positive note.

Day by day, autumn seeps in and the rain softens the earth beneath my boots. The leaves explode into colour, then fall and bare the trees to the cold winter until the new growth of spring. Is it difficult to let go of all of that beauty and stay naked for so long with the uncertainty of new buds? They are brave, the trees, to face change with such diversity and creativity. I would clutch my golden, auburn and burnt-umber leaves with all of my strength. Why would I let go of such an exquisite part of my being, which I had nurtured to climax?

I gather my past life, try to reattach my leaves. But they fall so quickly and rustle at my feet. With each step, I dig them into the rich humus of the earth, where they will help to feed my new growth.

The expression "Don't waste a crisis" comes to mind. Crisis leads to transition and to change – a difficult yet exciting time. I am anxious to take some action. I want to write a book about grief. Why? Catharsis? To give some meaning to Jim's death? To hold on to Jim? Jim wrote a book after Dan died, and if I do what Jim did maybe I'll survive grief too? A friend's comment swims in my brain: "You used to be Miss Culture, Miss French Literature, Miss Art, before you met Jim. Maybe it's time for you to get back to that. It's an opportunity for growth."

I look at the trees again. So brave. And I continue to gather my leaves.

TWENTY-SIX
CHRISTMAS

(DECEMBER 1999)

My older sister Sharron hands me a soft-covered blue scrapbook.

"Now this is for you. And I'd like you to put things about your future in it, your dreams."

I nod, accept the book and, as soon as she has gone, begin to glue in the hundreds of condolence letters I have received.

Mom Haberl responds in writing to all the people who have reached out to them. She says it was cathartic. I too write a letter. It takes me a long time to finish.

December 17, 1999
Dear Friends,
I started this letter more than four months ago. It has been a tough one to write but it has been healing. I hope you can hear my heart speak through the words.

I feel like I have lost everything and I am terrified. I realize that it scares everyone else too. There is so much uncertainty. Do I send a card? Flowers? Do I call? Visit? Do I talk about Jim? We all do our best, but the pain is still there. The situation cannot be fixed. Feeling pain is part of feeling love.

The phone calls and cards came fast and furious in the first two and a half months. I still haven't caught up. I have put all of the cards and letters in a scrapbook. I read them to remind myself how much support I have. Instinctively I know that people caring about me is part of my lifeline. I am so grateful that people have reached out.

People have asked me how I feel about going into the mountains now. Some have shared their perspective on the risk of mountaineering. I am still struggling with my own perspective but I think it's clearer. Jim and I were fortunate. We spent a lot of time together and shared such beautiful moments. Travelling, working and playing in the wilderness together allowed Jim and I to accept each other and love each other at the very essence of our beings. Nature helped Jim find out who he truly was and to love wholly. The biggest risk he ever took was loving unconditionally. Somehow he figured out that love is the ultimate answer to the ultimate human question. The physical rope joining us became a permanent invisible one. The risk was higher in this environment but so was the reward. The reward being a relationship and a life together that I wouldn't trade for anything. I would do anything to get him back but I have no regrets. We embraced life and lived it fully. We realized our dreams together. My biggest dream was Jim – loving him and being loved by him.

Going into the mountains now is calming and healing. I feel Jim all around me. I breathe him in with the air and his warmth flows through my veins. He was such a skilled, wise mountaineer and I trust that he made the best decision he could under the circumstances. Jim died in a beautiful place. He died happy, at peace with himself and deeply loved.

It's been almost eight months now since Jim died but time is so circular these days, like a merry-go-round. Writing to Jim, talking to Jim, thinking about Jim and loving Jim are the only things my heart will embrace on the to-do list. People say I am doing well. I honestly don't know. I go day by day. Sometimes moment by moment. I'm treading water, feeling my way. Sometimes I am so raw it feels like I have no skin. Other times I am completely numb. My heart suffocates under a deep sadness that fills my chest, weighing me down like lead. I think about suicide. But then I would be throwing my loved ones into the same pain I am trying to escape. It doesn't make sense and it is not an option for me. Some days, I have my normal energy and I laugh right from my belly. Often I go crazy, caught between the life of happiness I had chosen and a surreal world where I have been left against my will.

I try not to get in the way of my own healing. My mind, body and soul know what's best, and I must let go and try not to judge, rationalize or hurry my process. I try to let the emotions come even though they are frightening. I try to face the pain and stay open and warm. The pain is the only thing that feels real right now. I mourn our lost future: the baby we will never have, not growing old together, never being able to touch him again. When times get dark, I imagine Jim beside me holding my hand and telling me that he wants me to be happy, that it's hard for him to see me sad. His arms encircle me, protecting me with the truth, that our hearts will always be together. It is very important for me to honour Jim's memory, our love and our relationship. Any pressure I feel to mourn the correct way is self-inflicted because Jim would want me to do whatever it takes to be happy again.

At my new job teaching outdoor education in Vancouver, the students are warm and full of life – they lift me up. My colleagues are supportive and understanding and we work as a team. It is an ideal job for me. I stay with my parents during the week and return home to Whistler on the weekends – my safe haven. My friends are getting married and having babies. Life goes on just as it should. As hard as this is, it gives me hope.

Habby, my new puppy, is seven months old. He truly lives for the moment. He is a gentle soul and he makes me laugh with his innocent antics. Spending time with family and friends brings me peace. They would do anything to take away some of my pain. When I hug people who are close to Jim, I squeeze a bit of him out. Talking about Jim and sharing tears is a relief.

Jim's death is in no way a positive thing. It is a tragedy that has left a huge hole in this world. Life will never be the same and I will never be the same. But my memories of our life together, of our love, are woven into who I am. My challenge is to find a balance between remembering yesterday and creating a tomorrow, to face the truth and to let go. My challenge is to let there be meaning in the pain, to grow from it, to become wiser, more compassionate and more loving. I want to be happy again. This is the best way for me to honour Jim's memory, our love and our life together.

I believe Jim is in a good place, whether that be heaven or within all of us and the beauty of the world. Jim always made wherever he was a good place.

There is no greater blessing than a friend who is there when good times aren't. Thank you for being there.

Love, Sue

After I mail the letter, and hand-deliver it to family, I wait. There is a tension in the house. Finally I ask Dad, "Did you read my letter?"

"Yes." Silence.

"Was it okay for you to read?"

Dad's face is tight. "It seems like a cry for help." I curl into myself. I want him to say that I am doing okay. But he is worried. I feel him looking at me as his patient. He has been a physician for 40 years.

Pain rips down my throat and I give in to the tears. Dad blankets me with his arms and leads me to the couch. "Do you see a future for yourself?"

I look down at my hands. "I see myself alone. I had my magical time."

"I want to speed up your grieving." He pauses and adds, "I'm worried you won't have a family of your own. You'd be a good mom, and I think you'd miss out by not having a family." He pats my leg. "I think you should figure out what makes you feel good and do it."

I hunker down into the couch. "Nothing feels good." But that's not true. The mountain air feels good. Running my hand through Habby's fur feels good. Hugging feels good. Just not as good as when Jim was alive.

"I don't think you should be in pain all of the time. You should have more control over it." Dad looks me in the eye.

Control. I can't think of one thing I feel in control of now, except for maybe my weight. That gnawing in my belly makes me feel alive. My body shrinks so that my pants hang on me, my collarbones stick out and my knees look knobby. I'm down to a size four. My guy friends comment on how lean I look. I've lost 10 kilograms since Jim was killed. Every time I look in the mirror and cannot pinch more than a tiny bit of flesh at my waist, I am satisfied. I keep shrinking because I want to. But the pain is something else. I cannot control the pain. It comes and goes at will.

"I've struggled with trying to control my grief and it's just not possible. I am doing my best."

At times I want to grieve like Marianne, the emotive character in Jane Austen's *Sense and Sensibility*. I want to beat my head with a rock, tear out my hair and wail until I am empty. Other times I want to grieve like Marianne's sister Elinor and get up the next morning and go to work. Sense and sensibility. I admire Elinor's selfless ability to put the feelings of others first in order to control her own. It is not that she does not feel – she feels deeply – but she does not indulge her feelings by imposing them on others. Marianne, on the other hand, lets loose with all of her anguish, with little regard for protocol. I admire her also. The books on grief say that we all grieve differently. As usual, I want to fit in.

Dad shakes his head. "I can't be emotional about Jim dying anymore."

"That's fine. I just need to know that I can cry around you," I plead.

He squeezes me and kisses the top of my head. "Okay. I love you, Sue."

"I love you too, Dad." I lean against him.

"You know I loved Jim too. I feel guilty about encouraging his risk-taking." He beats the table with his finger.

"Jim wasn't affected by what others thought. He would have done it even if you had disapproved."

"The risk isn't worth it. I've seen the pain it causes." Dad looks at me.

"It was worth it for me, Dad." I look away.

My body braces itself against the approach of Christmas as if I hold in the forces of all of the rivers on earth.

"You know, maybe this would be a good year to go to Hawaii and just forget about Christmas, not celebrate," Dad sighs. Good idea. But we always host Christmas dinner for the old folks.

I sit in the living room with Glenda. Fear lodges angular words in my throat. "What do you want to do for Christmas?" she asks.

"I don't know." Nothing. I don't want to do anything. But if I commit to a response, I open myself to judgment.

"Don't feel you have to go out and shop for presents; no one expects it."

"Thank you," I breathe out. How can I buy presents when Jim is dead?

On December 19, school finishes for the holidays. My sister Sharron is not coming home for Christmas. She wants me to drive to Edmonton to visit her before Christmas, but my homing device kicks in and I beeline to Whistler instead. Safety. Familiar territory. I surface back in Vancouver at my parents' house on

Christmas Eve. Harsh Christmas lights glare at me from the tree. I give the mound of colourful presents a wide berth. My family sits around, singing carols. I smile but cannot sing.

When there is a pause, I remind them: "So, I'll be going skiing up Cypress tomorrow morning early, for the sunrise. I'll leave about six but should be back by 10 to open presents." They nod and look sad. Nobody mentions that this is what I used to do with Jim, go for a ski first thing Christmas morning. "I guess I'll hit the hay." I get up.

Dad hoists himself up and kisses me. "Good night, Sue."

Alone in my room, I cry until my head aches.

Sleep comes in a series of short nightmares until I am too frightened to close my eyes. When it is still dark the next morning, Christmas morning, I pull on my ski clothes and ease open the front door. My younger stepsister Laura drives me to the parking lot of Cypress Mountain, where Mike, Rose and Eric meet us.

Whoosh, whoosh. The skins on the bottom of our skis sweep the snow as we climb. A plump yellow cat's eye of a moon hovers in the dark at our backs, lighting up the snow like a runway. My breath swirls in front of my face. After an hour of plodding, the stark black and whites fade to glowing greens, deep blues and oranges. My gaze locks onto the amber sun as it rises above the horizon, pulling me with it. Up. Higher. Yes. We're there. The city of Vancouver at our feet. Ocean. Mountains. Yes. The summit. Almost in the same instant as the beauty surges through me, I slump onto my poles. He would be here. At the top, he would be here.

"Merry Christmas, Sue." Rose leans forward to hug me.

"Merry Christmas, Rose. I sure do miss him." I push my face against her down jacket.

"Me too."

The snow sparkles like diamonds and we leave tracks like a snaking river as we ski back to the car.

At my parents' house, wrapping paper litters the living room floor. My younger brother discusses the pros and cons of sports. I grit my teeth at the normalcy and breathe a sigh of relief, too. I look at the ground, like a shy child hoping not to be called on in class. When my head feels stretched to breaking point, I go downstairs to let go. Christmas dinner is the usual festive affair, with 11 of us, including grandparents, around the decorative table laden with food. But I feel like an imposter wearing a purple paper crown and toasting our good health.

The next morning, I drive home where I feel no pressure to be happy.

The red light on the answering machine pulses. I slap the tape into action.

"Hey, Susie, it's Terri calling. I can't stop thinking about you. It just feels so real today. I know you feel this all the time, but it's sort of like it's Christmas and Jim's not back and he would be here for Christmas. I keep picturing your face and I feel so sad. I feel so sad for you. I wish we could bring him back. I hope you make it through the day okay. I love you so much."

Andrea visits and we ski together. Before she leaves, she stocks up the fridge. Christmas is over. I couldn't stop it from coming, but it is over.

TWENTY-SEVEN
A NEW YEAR

(JANUARY 2000)

I meet a friend to rollerblade around Stanley Park. She glides effortlessly while I jerk around bracing against the inevitable crash. When will I find my balance and confidence again? We take a break on the grass, and she hands me a piece of paper.

"This is the phone number of a counsellor I went to during my divorce. Her office is close to your parents' place in Vancouver. She works out of a big space that can take lots of energy. I still check in with her once a year to make sure I'm on the right track."

I tuck the paper in my pocket. "Thank you. It would be helpful to talk to someone. I lean on my friends a lot and they must be getting sick of my whining." My friend is confident, strong, a successful businesswoman. If she can go to a counsellor, so can I.

It's true that I am holding down a full-time job, meeting with friends and taking over fundraisers that Jim organized. I am functioning. But I feel constant angst that peaks at night and when Jim is obviously absent, when he is obviously dead, and only abates somewhat when I am in the wilderness. I am exhausted from hyper-vigilance. It's only a matter of time before the next tragedy strikes. And what if I'm not doing everything possible to get Jim back? I do not recognize myself.

I make an appointment with the counsellor.

I arrive early and wait in a small corridor for my turn. When the counsellor opens the door, her long silk blouse and skirt billow and I notice her bright eyes and warm smile. We sit opposite each other in a room that echoes. A massage table stands at one end. Large crystal bowls squat at the other end. She explains that she plays the crystal bowls with a special rubber mallet to create a sound that eases pain in cancer patients. She smiles as she talks, and her voice rides musical waves as if she is lulling me to sleep.

I tell her my story.

After an hour, she leads me to the table, settles me on my back and asks me to close my eyes and listen to her voice. She starts at my feet and works her way to my head, opening the passage for positive energy. Her hands rest for several minutes above my heart and I start to cry. Her voice melts into me.

"You are light. You are love. And you are free."

At the end of the session, she gives me a recording of our meditation together and urges me to listen to it every day.

"Feed your mind, body, heart and soul every day." We make a list together of how I will do this: breathing exercises, writing in my journal to Jim, painting, connecting with friends and family, walking Habby, exercising in the outdoors.

I make an appointment for the following week. Before I leave, she hugs me and I hug her back.

TWENTY-EIGHT
FIRST ANNIVERSARY

(APRIL 2000)

Part of me wants April 29, the anniversary of Jim's death, to sail by with no pain, no remembering. The other half knows that the pain is connected to my love and that ignoring one would be ignoring the other. So, I decide to invite family and very close friends to Whistler to let go of more of Jim's ashes at Blueberry Point, a 20-minute walk from our house, through the woods along Alta Lake. I have no idea if this is what the family wants, but I listen to my inner voice. People can join in if it feels right for them.

There is still some snow on the ground so I give Mom Haberl an old pair of Jim's boots to wear, and she grins. Jim's sister-in-law grips her husband's arm as she negotiates the roots and slopes of the trail. The point is a rocky bluff overlooking the lake. I sit down on a rock with a painted cedar box on my lap. The adults melt into the shadows of the trees, but the children cluster around me. Jessica, who is five, places her little hand on my knee. "What's in the box, Auntie Sue?"

The children's curiosity gathers in soft creases on their foreheads. I take a breath and whisper the truth so it won't hurt so much.

"It's Uncle Jim. It's his body. These are the ashes from his body." Their eyes open wider and they press closer, swaying on their feet, backs arched and bellies protruding.

"Oh," one of them whispers back.

I tell them that we are all going to take some of his ashes and find a place to let him go, to send him back to the earth. When I lift the lid, the adults inch forward. I curl back the edges of the plastic bag and these little hands reach in with great care and cup a bit of Uncle Jim. Very carefully, as if carrying water that may spill, or a baby bird, they walk to a place where they can be with Uncle Jim. My eyes fill and I want to thank these children for being so brave. When all of the hands, big and little, are gone, I sit there empty. Exhausted. I reach into the bag and sift the remaining contents slowly though my fingers. A white chunk half the size of my little finger gets caught. Bone. Jim's bone. This is what is left of Jim's body.

Amongst the trees, big people help little people to let Jim go. Vicki comes over with something metal in her hand. She holds it up. It is a large staple. I am perplexed.

"Ah, it's one of the staples from his ankle." Her mouth opens wide with the realization.

"Oh, my God," I mumble. And I remember that he fell more than once in his life.

My steps faltered as I scanned the white walls of the hospital for directions. In a hushed tone, I asked the nurse behind the desk where I might find Jim Haberl. I turned to follow the wave of her arm and there he was in the hallway. My insides jumped because I needed more time to rehearse my greeting. It was one year after Jim and I first met on the sailboat. Now I was 17 years old.

"Hey!" he nodded and grinned. Then he propelled himself toward me in his wheelchair with one definite movement. I bent over, cupped his shoulders with my hands and hugged him without our chests touching. His light-blue hospital gown billowed around his slight frame, and I thought how he looked like a little boy and how I felt like a young woman. I wondered how much weight he had lost. Jim laughed and said the nurses teased him about having so many female visitors. My heart clenched like a fist, and I remembered Jim kissing me the previous summer on that barnacled rock in the Queen Charlotte Islands. I wished I were his only visitor.

I sat very still opposite Jim as he recounted how he had fallen the equivalent of five body lengths onto rocks. He had been working as a crew member on that same sailboat where we had met off the west coast of Vancouver Island. They were anchored and Jim had kayaked alone to one of the nearby islands.

Jim explained, "I started to climb around on the cliff. But I didn't have any gear, and I was just wearing runners so I didn't plan to go too high. It was so great to get my hands on the warm rock, and to be doing something physical after so many sedentary days on the boat, you know? And my blood got pumpin' and I was cruisin'. Everything was flowing and then this bulge reared up in front of me, nudging me backwards. I slowed down and stretched wide to hang on."

Jim spread his arms and sucked in his chest to show me how he had bear-hugged the rock. I visualized the dark purple veins in his taut arms straining against his skin. My body tensed as I imagined Jim inching his way upward, clenching his stomach muscles and holding his breath from the exertion of fighting gravity. I held my breath.

"I was working it, one move at a time and it was getting harder. About halfway up I thought I was fine. But then I slid my hand over the rock feeling for the next hold. And there was nothing. I searched with the other hand. Nothing."

Jim told me how the muscles in his arms and legs trembled with fatigue. A nubbin of rock stared him in the face. He leaned his head forward and closed his teeth around the small protrusion and held on. Slowly he lowered his right arm and shook it gently to coax the blood back to the muscles. Then he gingerly raised his arm back to its hold on the rock. He did the same with his left arm. The relief was temporary, and Jim could not lower his arms in turn quickly enough to maintain strength. It became increasingly difficult to make his fingertips pinch the small holds. He peered nine metres straight down to the jagged black volcanic rock and the noisy salty surf below.

"I knew I was going to fall so I took a deep breath and pushed myself away from the rock, so that I wouldn't hit on the way down," Jim explained in a steady voice.

I gripped my seat.

Jim fell nine metres and lay still. The impact separated his pelvis, shattered his ankle and cut his head. "When I came to, I assessed my injuries and then instructed the clients, who had canoed over from the sailboat to help me, what to do in terms of first aid." Jim grinned confidently.

I sat paralyzed. How was he able to function in such a scary situation?

A helicopter transported Jim to Vancouver where surgeons pinned his ankle together with five-centimetre-long staples.

Back at our Whistler house, upstairs behind the closed door of our bedroom, Dad Haberl holds a plastic bag while I transfer some of what is left of Jim's ashes. He and Mom Haberl reserved family spots in a cremation wall in one of the local cemeteries and want to put some of Jim's ashes there.

I ask him to tell me when to stop. When his hand comes up, one third of the ashes remain. So far, Jim is scattered in the Queen Charlotte Islands, on Mount Kilimanjaro, at Whistler and in Vancouver.

"What will you do with the rest of them?" Mom Haberl gestures to the ashes left in the bag.

"I don't know."

"Just as long as you don't keep them too long. I knew someone who kept them on the mantelpiece for seven years. That's no good." She grins and clutches my arm for a second. Seven years doesn't sound like very long to me.

That evening, 80 of Jim's family and friends gather at the Brew Pub in Squamish for dinner and a slideshow. Jim's eldest brother does not come. A close friend of Jim's phones my cell to apologize and to say that he just can't be there. He prefers to be alone with his grief. I appreciate their honesty, but I miss their presence. At my request, the room is decorated with yellow roses.

I agonize over whether to show the slideshow of Jim's life from his memorial a year before. Some people request it. When I voice my indecision to my counsellor, she tells me about a First Nations tradition where one year after a person dies, his loved ones congregate and pass around his photo and say a few words and then put the photo away. His image is no longer true. He is dead. Even if he were alive, his physical appearance would have changed in a year.

So, I go through all of his beautiful slides and choose a selection to represent how he saw the world. I set these to music. Gigantic, fluted snow peaks in Pakistan, Peru, Alaska and Canada fill the screen. People ski powder so deep it sprays over their heads. Jim's two brothers Pat and Kevin, along with Matt, stand at the top of Mount Denali, harnesses and ice axes dangling. Along with Jim, they are the youngest team ever to summit the highest peak in North America. A younger Jim with thicker hair hangs upside down like Spiderman on a massive sandstone overhang. His mom laughing, sitting on driftwood on a beach in the Queen Charlottes. There are sunsets and sunrises from all over the world. When the music stops, there is a pause before people clap. I stand up and thank everyone for coming.

Vicki says, "Sue, tell us about the yellow roses."

I look around the room at the dozens and dozens of yellow roses and clear my throat. "A friend sent me a story about a woman who had recently lost her husband. She went grocery shopping and started crying when she saw the yellow roses at the checkout because her husband would always surprise her with yellow roses when they went shopping together. She went to the meat counter and couldn't find a steak small enough for one person. As she deliberated, a young woman stood beside her and picked up several packages and put them down again. Finally she turned to the widow and said, 'I don't know, this steak is just so expensive, but my husband enjoys it so much.' The widow put her hand on the young woman's arm and said, 'Buy the steak. Treasure every moment you have with him.' The young woman put the steak in her basket and said goodbye. The widow continued on. As she went down one of the aisles, she saw the younger woman striding toward her clutching a package. 'These are for you.' She offered a bouquet of yellow roses with a smile. The widow accepted them gratefully and started to cry. When the younger woman had gone, the widow whispered, 'Oh, John, you haven't forgotten me.'"

By the time I finish this story, I am crying and so is Vicki.

After dinner, Dad Haberl stands up and clinks his spoon on his glass. "I would like to invite anyone who would like to say anything about Jim to stand up. I thought we could start with Schultze, as he has some great stories." Schultze went to high school with Jim. The "high school Jim" is not the Jim I know. I want stories about Jim and me being in love, or stories about Jim with the buddies I know.

Schultze scrapes his chair back and stands up. "You might know that in high school we had some pretty exclusive clubs. The 'heebla' club for instance was one of them. And of course there was the pizza joint hangout. Lots of laughs and good times. But you know the big thing about Jim for me was how loyal he was. After high school, I disappeared for about eight years, moved away and did my own thing. I did not keep in touch with friends at all. But when I came back to Vancouver, Jim was the first one to call me." There are a few more speeches. I feel dry.

When I go to settle the bill with the owner, he says there will be no charge. Jim was one of the nicest guys he ever met.

TWENTY-NINE
MOTHER EARTH
CAN TAKE IT

(SPRING 2000)

Two more hours until the school bell rings and then I can let go at my counselling appointment. I herd my thoughts, pin them down by clamping my jaw shut.

"How are you today, Sue?" My counsellor Lou's singsong greeting, warm smile and flowing silk clothes envelop me in a hug. My jaw eases.

"I'm fine. How are you?" Years of practice lead me through the social norms. My grief readies like a loaded spring. I leave my shoes at the door, pad over to my usual armchair and sit down clutching my journal.

"What would you like to talk about today?" Her eyes sparkle with eagerness as she smoothes her skirt over her thighs. I imagine myself as her.

"How do you do it, Lou? How do you listen to people's sadness all day every day and stay so peaceful and loving?" I lean forward.

Lou chuckles deep in her throat, throws up her arms, looks at the ceiling and says, "I give it all up to the Divine."

"Oh." That sounds good. I breathe deeply, look past Lou out the window and unload. "I don't know what to do with all of the anger."

"Can you tell me more about the anger?" Her words ease out like a slow-moving river.

"I just feel angry so much of the time."

"Angry about what?"

"About life. About where I am. About what has happened."

"That's understandable. It's very unfair what has happened to you. Do you feel angry at Jim?"

I snap my head up. "What for?"

"For getting killed. For leaving you."

"No, I could never be mad at him. I mean, sometimes I feel angry with him for leaving me, but I can't stay mad long. He was such a good person. He would never hurt me intentionally." I tighten my stomach to stop the truth from exploding out of my mouth. To stop myself from stomping around and throwing things.

I saw a movie once where criminals held hostages at gunpoint in a bank. Every hour, they would shoot a hostage to speed a response to their demands. One young male hostage hid behind a pillar with an older male hostage. The young guy was hyperventilating and babbling, "What are we going to do? Shit, man, they're going to kill us." The older man calmly looked at him and launched verbally abusive comments at him. The young man came back with an equally abusive tirade.

"What did you do that for?" the young man whined.

"Well, do you feel scared anymore?"

"No," the young man admitted.

Anger trumps fear.

Lou's voice brings me back to the quiet room.

"You know, anger serves a purpose. It is there for a reason. It demands action and helps you to move forward. It is powerful. Do you have a way of expressing your anger?"

"I meditate, do yoga, write, run."

"How about an activity where you're hitting a ball, such as tennis?"

"No, not so much."

"A physical outlet is good. You know, this friend of mine arrived on my front doorstep one night, full of rage. She was going through a divorce. She asked if I had a shovel. I gave her one and followed her into my backyard where she dug a hole about 30 centimetres deep. Just as I was wondering what the neighbours would think, she plopped herself down on her stomach with her face over the hole and began to shout and scream. The wailing went on for a good 10 minutes. She pushed herself up, handed me my shovel and said, 'Mother Earth can take it.' Your anger is trying to tell you something. Let it out and listen."

When I get home to Whistler that weekend I study the back-country roads and trails book, choose Blowdown Creek and head off in my 4WD wagon. For over an hour I weave logging roads together to a small clearing at the trailhead. My backpack bounces as I hike, and at the top of a hill, my panting echoes in my ears. Meadow flowers and snowy peaks still my soul. Okay, this is it. This is a good spot. I look all around and there is no-body in sight. I fill my lungs and bare my teeth for the scream of a lifetime.

But nothing comes. I am scared of causing a disturbance. What if someone thinks I am in trouble? What will I say? I was screaming to let my anger out? What if I start screaming and can't stop? No, best to keep it inside where it is safe. I trudge on.

THIRTY
DRAWN BACK TO
KILIMANJARO

(SUMMER 2000)

"Those who bring sunshine into the lives of
others cannot keep it from themselves."
—SIR J.M. BARRIE

Jim and I had thought in 1998 that the Ascent for Alzheimer's
fundraising climb up Kilimanjaro would be a one-time thing. But
it builds momentum, and in 2000 there are two teams. I don't
want the responsibility of guiding the groups, but at the same
time I can't leave it alone. I still don't know why I am going but
something draws me there, and my feet follow my heart. I ask
Jim's younger brothers, Kevin and Pat, if they will come with me.

Of the four brothers, Pat looks most like Jim. And when he
throws back his head and laughs, I do a double take to make sure
he is not Jim. In Tanzania there is a tradition of widows marrying their husband's brother, because someone must take responsibility for them as dependants. I can see, too, that it would be familiar and reassuring for me to marry Pat. I feel hopeful around
him because I can fool myself that he is Jim, and hopeless, too,
because I know he is not Jim.

We work together to guide the team, and I feel Pat's gratitude for the opportunity to do something that Jim did. In helping these people to reach their goal of summiting the highest

mountain in Africa, we feel wanted and needed and we honour Jim's memory.

A week later, when Kevin and I arrive at the summit with the second team, he hugs me and says, "There are no ghosts here. You're a good guide, Sue. Strong." I listen, bow my head but am not able to take pleasure in his compliment. I tuck it away, though, for when I am ready to rebuild the part of me that will survive without Jim.

I have now guided over a hundred people to the summit of Kilimanjaro for the Alzheimer Society of BC. They have guided me as much as I have guided them because they allow me to help them, which takes my mind off my own pain and makes me feel stronger. And they inspire me with their courage. Each time I go to Kilimanjaro, I visit Jim at Mawenzi. One year when I returned to camp after one of these visits, a team member pressed a folded piece of paper into my hand. It was a beautiful poem.

In Memoriam – Jim

Like the red dust rising
To meet
The white clouds drifting
On this volcanic mountain
My body meets your soul
Inhale the scattered ashes
Of memories kindling still
Then exhale with the wonder
Of this peace
Upon my will
Here, on Kilima Njaro
Step with me and then
Over the plains of Tanzania
Drift free away
Again

After my climbs with Pat and Kevin, I arrive at Vancouver airport to a welcoming committee, smaller than the previous year, but just as warm. Once again I did not find Jim. I did everything right. I led everyone safely to the top, and still I did not find Jim. The harsh reality sinks into the crevasses of my mind.

THIRTY-ONE
STRESS LEAVE

(FALL 2000)

Back at Trek in the fall, I choose to do more of the administrative tasks rather than teach. During recess I walk around the school field with Habby listening to my Walkman so that my mind can have some Jim time. There is a weight on my body, an incredible feeling that I need to be doing something else. I have a full-time job and I cannot handle this grieving, which is a second full-time job. I need to grieve. Time is what I crave. Very slow time.

I once heard life described as a train and that when you suffer an incredible loss, you fall off the train. The train chugs along but grief holds me at a different speed. I cannot gain enough momentum to get back onto the train, and if I do succeed in getting pulled on for a time, the speed makes me dizzy. I cannot function. I am in a different time zone.

On the weekends, I drive home to Whistler right after work. When I enter the front door, I listen for the patter of Jim's feet as he comes down the stairs to greet me. I sit around trying to soak up the familiar. I run my hand along the couch and gaze at the photos on the wall. My palm lies open beside me, heavy with the weight of Jim's nonexistent flesh. At dinnertime I strain to hear the phone ring and Jim's voice reassuring me that they have landed safely after a day of heli-skiing and that he will be right home after his customary beer with the clients. In the morning, I lay very still with my eyes closed, breathe deeply into Jim's pillow and listen for his purposeful movement out of bed and the tinkle of his teaspoon in the kitchen.

The evening before I am scheduled to be back at work, I slowly pack my clothes and clean the house until it is too late to begin the two-hour drive. It feels as if pieces of my skin cling to the walls as I drag my body out of the house at five the next morning in order to get to work on time. There is never enough time. I never want to leave.

I ask my counsellor about taking time off. The words seem more real when spoken out loud. I need time to myself, to grieve, to nurse my very deep wound, to have no other responsibilities, to rebuild. Just as it takes time to heal a physical wound, it takes time to heal an emotional wound. The pain of losing Jim is so close to the love I feel for him that I could nurse my wound forever. But I won't. My counsellor supports my desire to be free, to have little responsibility so that I can focus on nourishing myself. She supports me taking stress leave, saying that I've kept busy for so long, and now I'm slowing down and starting to feel the deep pain.

I don't want to be a bitter old widow.

I tell Terri, Sue, Marla and Heather, most of my close friends, that I would like to take some time from work.

One day Glenda says to me that she and Dad heard that I plan to take time off. When was I going to tell them? That night I ask Dad if we can talk. The three of us sit in the living room and the air is thick. I feel like it would take an effort to reach my arm out across the room to touch my father, that it would be like feeling my way in the pitch black. I start by saying that I am not coping very well at work. His smile fades. I am overwhelmed by grief and work; it feels like I am trying to do two full-time jobs and not doing either of them well. I need time.

Glenda clenches a fist in her lap, "A lot of people come in my office wanting time. But time for what?" Her disapproval is apparent.

"I want time to heal," I say softly without looking at her. It is almost a question.

Dad frowns, "How do you know work isn't healing for you?" I think of the motto in *Little Women*, "Hope, and keep busy."

I feel cornered and look for an escape. "I don't really know but I have to trust my gut feeling."

"Your gut feeling isn't good enough for me," Dad says impatiently. "I'd like the word of a professional."

"What does that mean?" I glance at him and turn away from the challenge.

"Go and see a psychiatrist. If the psychiatrist agrees with you taking time off then I will support you, or at least I will feel better about it." He sighs deeply and sinks back into his chair. Dad proposes another way to fix me. "How about taking anti-depressants?"

"I want to avoid that." The silence is thick with unspoken words. I keep my head down.

Glenda says they have seen so many positive results from anti-depressants. I do not want to get hooked on them, and I feel I have other things in my life that give me a sense of joy: walking in the woods with Habby, writing in my journal, taking deep breaths in the outdoors, being in the mountains, visiting with friends, hugging, memories. Dad explains that after a trauma, the brain can stop producing serotonin and if the production ceases for long enough, the brain can forget how to produce it. The anti-depressants serve as a kick-start. They wonder if I need a kick-start. Dad thinks it is too long after Jim's death for me to be grieving and needing time off work. I do not look at him. I want to plead with him to trust me, to believe in me, because I need that more than anything.

My family doctor refers me to a psychiatrist.

I arrive 15 minutes early for my appointment. The waiting room feels like a white tunnel, and the only other patient glues his eyes to the pages of his book. I hope I don't see anyone I know.

I strain to hear familiar sounds: cars outside, a phone ringing. It is as if two pillows are strapped to the sides of my head. I fiddle with the pages of my journal and wonder if I will say the right thing.

"Susan Oakey?" His voice hums through the room.

"That's me." I extend my hand to him and at the same time fumble for my pen that has shot to the floor. I follow him several steps. Well dressed. Relaxed walk. I hope he's kind. He steps aside at the door to his office and gestures ahead of him. I slide into the leather IKEA chair and rest my head on the back for an instant while he shuts the door. I sit up on the edge of my chair. He lowers into his chair, crosses one ankle over the other knee and swivels to face me. He rolls a pen between the fingertips of both hands. There is a pause that seems like minutes. Should I start? No, that's ridiculous, he's the therapist.

"So, what would you like to talk about?" he enunciates slowly.

"My husband was killed just over a year and a half ago. I want to take some time off work to grieve." I use half of my lung capacity as I wait for his response.

"Hmmm." He nods his head up and down and looks at me with such heavy thought that if someone yelled "Fire!" he would still take the time to respond to me. I breathe faster and concentrate on the sound of the cars outside. Is he waiting for an explanation?

"Tell me a bit about what you have been doing since your husband was killed." He reaches for a pad of paper.

For 30 minutes I babble about going to Alaska to where Jim fell, about visiting the place where Jim and I first met in the Queen Charlotte Islands, about guiding the Alzheimer group up Mount Kilimanjaro and about my new job at Trek. He listens.

"You're most likely experiencing delayed grief. I support your taking time off." The sound of his voice envelops me like a soft blanket.

"Um," I venture, "I'm wondering if I need to take

anti-depressants. My parents think it would be a good idea." I hold my breath.

"What do you think?" He gestures with his hand at me.

"I'd rather not. I don't want to become dependent on them. But I am sensitive to the fact that my mom needed them once. So, I wonder if I do, too." I focus on the wall behind him.

"You seem to have a good sense of self. I don't think you need anti-depressants." He scribbles instructions for my health leave on a piece of paper.

I exhale and thank him.

When I relay the conversation to my good friend, she says, "Good grief, you're guiding people up mountains. I'm sure he thinks you're doing great compared to lots of normal people! Not that you're not normal … you know what I mean." We laugh.

PART 3
HEALING

Turn your face to the sun and the shadows fall behind you.
—MAORI PROVERB

THIRTY-TWO
BEGINNING A
YEAR TO HEAL

In February 2001, the first month of my health leave, the sun shines 25 of the 28 days. Habby and I cross-country ski from our front door, around frozen Alta Lake and the Rainbow Trail and back to the house. It is 90 minutes of crisp air, calming mountains, the freedom of gliding, the smell of snow and Habby romping like there will be no tomorrow. Sometimes the wind blows, and I come back with red cheeks, huffing and close to tears. I thank the universe for sending sun.

My heart feels peaceful for the first time since Jim was killed, because I have made a conscious choice to care for it. I try to make myself a meal every day, exercise, stay connected with loved ones, write, meditate and stretch. Some days I don't get up until noon. Other days I eat only chocolate. Every day I go outside, if only for a few minutes with Habby.

When I feel darkest, I let the phone ring.

I listen to the voices of my friends and family on the answering machine. Three or four calls a day. If I feel able to keep myself from crying, I answer.

"I feel that I reached my summit with Jim, I reached my highest mountain, and that the only way to go from here is down. I mean, you don't tell Romeo and Juliet to buck up because they'll find another love. I feel like that. The only way to go is down."

There is a pause on the other end of the line and then Terri sighs and says, "Let me think about that one. I'll get back to you."

I sob to my sister on the phone, "I feel completely in love with Jim. How will I ever love someone else?"

"It's safe for you to love Jim."

"What do you mean?"

"He can't hurt you anymore," she replies softly.

Oh, God, I think to myself, she's right.

I've feared what would happen if Jim fell out of love with me but it never occurred to me the repercussions of not being able to fall out of love with him.

One evening, I sit alone on the couch. A force presses against the inside of my skin and tears are not enough relief. I rock back and forth, grip my hands together and moan. My ribs ache, my lungs burn and my gut spasms. The energy presses hard to get out. My eyes and mouth open wide because I cannot hold back forever. I fall to my knees and suck in air and vomit it out. I gasp, moan and push animal sounds from deep within my belly. A hot energy rushes around my body and pushes out of every pore. I bang my fists on the table, shout. I fall back onto the couch, cradle my head and sob so hard my shoulders ache.

I lift my head and corral my breath into a strong regular rhythm. I grit my teeth, stare at nothing and clench my fists. A voice surges. You left me. How could you leave me? How could you be so selfish? I am so angry with you for dying.

The books say it is normal to feel anger. That it will pass. Is it normal to feel such strong rage that I pummel myself from the inside out?

The skin on my face relaxes and I stare at the floor. I sleep for six hours straight and in the morning get dressed at first light, have breakfast and take Habby for a walk up the trail. I spend the rest of the day writing, drawing and ticking things off of my to-do list.

I have cried every day for almost two years. But, that night in bed I wait for sleep and it strikes me that I have not cried all day. I feel guilty and relieved. It is comforting to see progress.

Friends invite me for dinner and when I arrive, Scott, one of Jim's colleagues, is there. He is a full mountain guide and lives in Whistler. He hunches his tall frame to wrap me in a hug and watches me quietly with his dark brown eyes. After dinner, I drive him to his car, which is parked at a nearby trailhead because he has just completed a solo two-day traverse from Wedge Mountain to Blackcomb Mountain. As he reaches for the door handle, he asks, "How are you doing?"

I give him my standard answer. But the reality is that I feel alone. He says goodnight, shuts the car door and I heave a sigh of relief.

That night I dream of the devil. He is tall, dark and alluring, but his features are blurred. If I give my soul to the devil, he will bring Jim back to me.

Scott invites me to ski into a backcountry hut. My jacket clings to me while I pack the car in the pouring rain. The sun rises behind bruised clouds, and I switch on the headlights to make my way to Scott's house. When he answers the door, he smiles with his eyes and says, "If it were anyone else but you, I would cancel." I chuckle, avoid his steady gaze and busy myself with transferring my gear to his car. I chew on his words. Does he mean he wouldn't cancel because I am a grieving widow and he doesn't want to hurt my feelings? Or is he really looking forward to our spending time together?

As we drive, the air between us feels light, as if my body would float through it to brush against him. I squeeze my arms against my sides.

As we ski away from the car, my skin prickles. I stop.

"I'm feeling weird," I stutter.

"What is it?" Scott stops behind me.

"This is the sort of thing that Jim and I would have done..." My voice trails off.

Scott lowers his head and then raises his deep brown gaze to mine.

"You could ski ahead a bit and just pretend that you are on your own, and I'll be here for backup," Scott offers.

"Okay." I look to the sky so that emotion won't pour out of my face.

That night at the hut, the moon is full and Scott, Habby and I go for a ski before bed. We plod uphill toward the ridge. The wind starts to howl and snow swirls around my face. I pull the drawstring on my hood and burrow into the collar. Scott's hunched frame twists to peer back at me. My lungs suck harder, my heart beats faster and my body balloons with oxygen and blood. But it isn't enough. I need more air. More. I need warmth to fill the emptiness inside of me. But the pain does not ease. I let out a cry and then crumple to one knee and sob into my gloved hands. Habby nudges his wet nose between my fingers and draws his tongue over my cheeks and nostrils.

Scott's black mass turns and gets closer. He lowers his face to where I can feel the heat of his breath.

"Are you all right?" he shouts over the wind.

I raise my wet face to his and choke, "I can't do it."

He looks at me, says nothing and leads the way back to the cabin. I wonder if he thinks I am weak. I slow my pace so that the storm veils my grief and watch Scott's figure get smaller in front of me. With each stride I throw out a fresh wail of anguish. What's wrong with me? Why can't I do this? Jim, I need your help. I feel you. Are you here? Have you sent Scott to guide me, to look after me like you did? I stoop lower with this thought. Before I enter the hut, I swipe my glove across my eyes and take a deep breath.

That night, I curl up with Habby on the main floor because dogs are not permitted in the loft sleeping area.

I call my friend Andrea and tell her about Scott.

She asks, "How do you think it will be for you getting into another relationship? Do you think you will be able to love more strongly now?"

"Yes, because my worst fear has been realized. Now I will be able to love more strongly because the fear of the unknown, what it would be like to have your mate die, is no longer unknown."

"Yeah, I think you're right."

My psychiatrist's voice echoes, "You seem to be confused about what you think you should feel and what you actually do feel."

A month later, Scott invites me to a party at a trendy club. I buy a short dress. Scott holds the door of the taxi for me.

"I'm a bit nervous." I pull my dress down to cover more of my thighs. "It's been so long since I've been on a date."

"Oh, is this a date?" Scott smirks and shifts in his seat. His expression becomes serious, "I think you're being very brave." Scott refills my wine glass promptly all night. When another fellow asks me to dance, Scott leans against the wall and watches.

After the party, I invite Scott back to my place for tea. He slumps low in the couch while I stumble around the room preparing and serving. Several times he opens his mouth to speak but all that comes out is "Um."

"What is it?" I slump down beside him and let my dress slide up my legs.

"Nothing." But he avoids my gaze. For once I do not feel responsible for the discomfort of others. The wine has thickened my skin and I am light and giggly. We talk until late and he takes a cab home.

I check my e-mail first thing the next morning and there is a message from him. He had a great time. He did want to tell me something. He is going to Brunei to visit a woman he met while working on Eco-Challenge. He worries that he gave me the wrong idea. I e-mail him back, wish him luck and reassure him. I ask him if he is bringing home a wife. He responds, "Good question."

I go back to being Jim's widow.

THIRTY-THREE
MOVING THROUGH SPRING

Today is my birthday and I hardly slept last night. My fingers drummed the same pattern over and over on my chest; my mind raced from topic to topic, from fear to fear. Fear of turning 35, fear of lying alone in my bed, fear of having a wound in my heart so grave that it will never heal, fear of spending my birthday without Jim. I miss waking up with Jim and having him say, "Happy Birthday, Susie," and giving me a kiss and one of his romantic cards.

A friend meets me on the mountain and we ski the morning away under blue skies. It was supposed to be cloudy. From bump to bump, I jump and yahoo, pushing my skis as fast as I dare, so fast my eyes tear. I choke on the air rushing past and giggle with the excitement of flying. In the afternoon Habby and I cross-country ski around the lake for two hours. Friends and family phone to wish me well. I put one foot in front of the other. I shed layers like a snake, looking for that deeper core and the deep calm of an ocean beneath a pounding surf.

My chore today is to sort through all the e-mails people sent after Jim was killed. It's difficult to delete them. Many I print out and put into the third scrapbook I have made of condolence letters. I don't know what I would have done without the compassion of others to buoy me.

Valentine's Day arrives. I ski with a bachelor friend, go out for dinner and invite him home to my place. We have sex. I lie very still afterward, shell-shocked. "These are experimental times," I tell him. "Don't take any of my reactions personally." I feel awful about who I am and try to tell myself I am light and love. It doesn't wash.

I call Terri and tell her I've had sex with someone I do not love. She says, "Shake it off." I want to go away from everyone who might judge me, go away by myself to heal and come back. And I am desperate to make love with someone the way Jim and I made love.

The next day I ski for hours up the snowy hill to the summit of Whirlwind behind Whistler. Surrounded by mountains and blue sky, Jim flows through my body and I tingle with the intimacy. I power to the top and sit on the rock, inhale deeply and pull Jim right into my core. My ski buddies are specks below. For half an hour I enjoy being with Jim alone. Being in the mountains is the closest I feel to the Divine, that and being in love. My insides settle; the world makes sense. I don't miss Jim, because I feel his sweet, gentle essence. With nothing but giant snow pillows in front of me, I ski short slalom turns until my quads ache. When I stop to catch my breath partway down, a bald eagle soars over me and glides effortlessly down the glacier. If I get any lighter, I will take off like that eagle.

Full of energy and confidence, I launch into organizing Jim's books in the office. I agonize over every decision: what to keep, what to give away, what to throw out. Within an hour, I crave the feeling of being on top of the mountain with Jim, free. I want another high. I call my bachelor friend with no strings attached. But I get cold feet and when he arrives I will not fool around with him unless he can commit. I know I ask for the impossible. He asks, "Are you lonely?" I bite my lip and look away.

"I think it's going to be really difficult for the first guy you have a relationship with." He slaps his hands on his thighs.

"Why do you say that?"

"I mean, look at this place." He swings his arm to encompass the living room and my gaze follows to the framed photos crowding every surface. "It's a shrine in here." His words try to flatten the photos as a gale bends a sapling. He pauses, "And you're still wearing your wedding ring."

I push my ring around my finger with my thumb. "Yes, hmm." The photos and my ring link together and tug at my heart, creating a circle of desire to live in the past, when Jim and I laughed and hugged and kissed and planned for the future. What's wrong with that? It's natural to want to live in the past. Why wouldn't I want to go back to where I was happy? I lower my head and cover my ring with my other hand.

I do not ask him to spend the night.

For two weeks I do not write in my journal. On Wednesday, March 21, almost two years after Jim was killed, I climb the stairs to my bedroom, wiggle my wedding ring off of my finger and lay it in a jewelry box. Like a robot, I appear back in the living room, my arms collect all of the framed pictures of Jim and me; I reappear in my bedroom where my hands place the photos on the bookshelf. I move back to the living room, almost brushing my hands together as if to say, "Well, that's that." I dare to look at the empty places left by the photos and my legs go numb and I lose peripheral vision. I grip the edge of the sideboard, sink to my knees and suck the truth into my heart in fitful sobs.

The subdivision I live in organizes a multi-house garage sale. For several hours I sort through buckets and buckets of Jim's outdoor gear: eight tents, five pairs of skis, nine backpacks. Touching his clothing makes me feel the worst.

"It would be better if someone could just do it for you. Then it would be done," my stepmom says.

But my counsellor disagrees. "I think it's an important step for you to sort through Jim's stuff yourself." I want help but I don't want it done for me. Mom Haberl comes up to sort through papers and photos with me.

Surrounded by boxes and accounts, she says, "You can't keep all of this stuff. You just can't." I am so relieved.

One day I turn on Jim's computer to try to deal with all of his files. The screen goes blank as the hard drive crashes. At first I panic that I've lost something incredibly important, and then I laugh and look to the sky and say, "Thanks, Jim."

I read Jim's journal account of his trip to ski the Haute Route in France and Switzerland and I feel restless. On the second anniversary of his death, I fly to Europe and follow the same route with other guides for six days. Mom Haberl and several friends telephone the little mountain hut where I'm staying on April 29 to send love. After the ski trip, two of us drive south in France and rock climb. Back home in May, I ice climb for the first time using Jim's tools. Then Habby and I jump in the car, drive for four days to meet Terri at a tennis camp in Utah and rock climb at Red Rocks, Nevada. On each adventure, I push myself and dare the hand of fate to snatch me. I want my old life back.

THIRTY-FOUR
SCOTT RETURNS

In May Scott returns from Brunei alone. It did not work out with the other woman.

He invites me to bike to Logger's Lake. My clothes are sticking to me by the time we reach the lake. We stretch out on the dock and heat up even more in the low-slung sun.

"Are you going to swim?" Scott dips his fingers in the dark mountain water.

"It's pretty cold. I don't think I've been in the lake this early in the season." I'll go in if he does, and maybe even if he doesn't, to show how tough I am. I turn away when Scott peels off his bike clothes and lies on his back. Sitting up, I wrestle mine off and try to dive into the water without revealing my nakedness. Scott rolls onto his stomach, crouches and dives into the water. I wonder why he all of a sudden seems bashful and then the ball drops, and I dip my face in the water to hide my smile.

"It's cold, but nice. This is the earliest I've ever swum in Logger's Lake." He spurts water my way.

Afterward, we lie on the dock beside one another, naked. I feel heat radiating from his body and lie very stiff and still. We pretend we are just friends, but the energy between us has shifted.

A short time later Scott and I go to a party together. On the way home he pulls over by the side of the road. "Would you like to come to my place?" he asks.

"Sure," I answer nonchalantly.

Lying by the fire in his living room, Scott looks at me and says, "I think we should have a serious talk."

"Okay." I sit up. I feel like I am in elementary school: there is no way I'll divulge my feelings. The best I can do is pass him a note in gym class. I get that caged animal feeling again, the urge to run with nowhere to go. I just want him to kiss me and get it over with.

"I'm single, you know, and I'm really enjoying the time we're spending together. I could easily phone you all the time and bug you to do stuff." He smiles. I feel more relaxed and stop looking at the door. I take a deep breath.

"I've been with unavailable men since Jim was killed because that's all my heart could handle. But with you I sense it would be different. I feel a connection with you. Opening my heart to you would be a real acknowledgement that Jim is dead." I look down nervously.

Scott thinks for a minute and says carefully, "I wouldn't want to do anything that makes you feel uncomfortable, and I don't want to compromise our friendship ... but I'd be all over you if you gave me the go-ahead." He grins.

I laugh. "Part of my heart aches to be connected, loved and wanted, but I need affection more than sex."

"I'll leave it up to you, then." He moves up against the wall. I want to pull him back close. But my internal voice whispers hoarsely: Do you feel I am betraying you, Jim? To open my heart to someone else, will that diminish our love at all? Jim answers: Please be happy, be in love, live your life.

The next day, I arrive at Scott's for dinner and there are a dozen long-stemmed roses on the table with a card: "Sue, For you ... just 'cause, Scott oxo." After an evening of dancing, I go back to his place and we lie on the couch. He massages my legs, and I want to be closer so I snuggle into his chest. We sleep just a few hours, and I lean into his affection like a cat. He strokes my face, whispers how beautiful I am to him and how he loves to be near me. We explore each other's bodies, and I close my eyes at the pleasure of being touched lovingly, of being wanted, of feeling special to someone again.

In the morning, he gathers me in his arms and asks how I am doing. I feel safe, relaxed and present. "I'm fine. I have no expectations." I hold his hand.

He leans back so that he can see my face and says, "You know I don't want to have kids, right?" I didn't know. I want a baby more than anything.

"Why don't we see how it goes," I say.

He neither agrees nor disagrees.

"I want you to know that there is no one else in my life. I'm chasing *you*."

I laugh nervously. "Thanks for being so honest." My heart tugs at me. Go slow, it says.

In Vancouver I visit my colleagues at work and ask them if I can come back to work in January. Jamie takes my hands and says, "What's good for you is good for me." How will I ever repay these people's generosity? In the psychiatrist's office, I reiterate my plan to return to work in January.

"I support that. You know, 25 per cent of people who are on disability for six months do not return to work and that number jumps to 45 per cent after one year." He nods his head. I will have been on leave for one year in January. "I don't think you're depressed, I think you are grieving. But I am concerned about your eating and sleeping." I exercise and feel strong, but my hipbones stick out.

My counsellor meets me at the door with her usual hug. After a few minutes of catching up she says, "You feel different. Your energy is stronger, more present." I tell her about Scott and about returning to work. She asks me to lie on the table so that she can do some bodywork.

"Look into your heart, what do you see?" I go inside and see healthy, rosy-red, bright, beating tissue and Jim's smiling energetic face. I also notice a lot of inviting space in there, a lot of light and room.

Scott leaves for three weeks in June, to scout Eco-Challenge race courses in Jordan. He sends heartfelt e-mails. When he returns from Jordan, he plans the date to end all dates. I must scout out a training hike for the Alzheimer team, so we begin by hiking to Brandywine Peak. It is a stellar day when we 4WD to the trail-head, our dogs bouncing around in the back seat. Our boots squish into the marshy meadow as we follow the mountain river to the head of the valley.

"I think this is a good spot to cross," I shout over the roar of the water.

"I'll check upstream." Scott nods to me and disappears. I lunge from boulder to boulder and squeal when I slip on the moss-covered bank, half submerging one boot in the icy water. Habby muscles past me and licks my face as I scramble to dry land. I stamp my foot, laugh and look gratefully at the bluebird sky. I feel strong.

When we gain the ridge, we can see Whistler–Blackcomb, Wedge and Black Tusk.

"Beautiful," I gasp. We lunch on the summit, boot ski partway down and reach the truck tired but giggly and ready for stage two.

As we drive down the highway, I tug off my hiking clothes and shimmy into a bikini. We stop at a lake and dive from boulders into the clear warm water. Habby belly flops after me.

"We should skinny dip." Scott grins.

"You think?"

"There's nobody around." Scott fumbles beneath the water. We toss our suits onto the rocks and luxuriate in the caresses of the water. As the sun softens in the sky, I towel off and slide into a fitted sundress. We have reservations at a fancy seafood restaurant overlooking the ocean. After a satisfying dinner, my skin tingles from too much wine. I lean forward, hoping Scott will touch me, anywhere. I quiver at the thought. Over dessert, Scott checks his watch and asks for the cheque. We go Dutch.

We bumble to the car and race to the Lion's Gate Bridge. At the turnoff, a flashing sign warns: "Bridge closed 8 p.m. to 6 a.m. Use alternate route."

"Shit. That's ridiculous." Scott looks at his watch. "It's only 10 after eight." He gears down, sets his teeth and guns the motor. "We're going for it." He whoops and swerves around the barrier onto the deserted bridge. I lock onto the safety handle and feel the adrenaline mix with the heat of the alcohol. I am excited to be breaking the rules, and scared.

In downtown Vancouver, we park at the Odeon Theatre and boogie the night away listening to the Buena Vista Social Club. It's midnight by the time we head north on the highway back to Whistler. My limbs are heavy and my head lolls back onto the seat. I wish for my bed but Scott has other plans. He pulls into the climbers' parking lot in Squamish below the granite giant known as the Chief. He collapses the backseat, sets up sleeping pads and sleeping bags in the back of the truck and waves me in.

"Your quarters, my princess." Scott checks the full moon before he snuggles in beside me. "It will be a couple of hours before the moon is high enough for us to see the route." The plan is to rock climb a multi-pitch route called Dièdre, by the light of the full moon. It will take several hours. I close my eyes and wish for a snowstorm.

My eyelids flutter to the gentle chime of Scott's alarm. He is up and rummaging around before the chimes quit. It's 2 a.m.

"Okay. Looks good. The moon is high enough to see." Scott is like a teenager sneaking out. I rub my eyes and prop myself up on one elbow.

"What's that?" I point in the direction of Dièdre.

"What? No way. I can't believe it. Those are headlamps. Someone poached our route." Scott slumps.

I laugh from my belly. It seems ridiculous that we waited hours to climb in the middle of the night and someone beat us to it. Scott's face is drawn. What a determined guy he is, full of ideas and enthusiasm.

"Thank you, Scott. You planned a great day. I've never been on a date like that before." Scott smiles shyly.

On the way home, he mutters several times about the dumb luck of being beaten to a night climb.

One afternoon, we bask beside a lake drinking beer and then bike back to my house for lunch. When it is time to go, I see him to the door. Halfway down the walkway, he quarter turns back to me, his head slightly bowed and gazes at me sideways with those big brown eyes, a shy grin … and he just keeps staring. I fidget.

What is that look? What does it mean? I look at the ground.

"I love you," he mouths. The words stun me into a tense stillness, and my heart thumps. No, I plead silently, please don't love me. Our eyes lock, he slowly turns and walks away, giving no indication that he senses my terror.

I escape to Kilimanjaro to guide the Alzheimer climb and then go on safari. It buys me time.

When I return from East Africa, Scott is busy getting ready for Eco-Challenge in New Zealand. I meet with the Alpine Club of Canada and Jim's parents, brother and a few of his friends to discuss building a memorial hut in the Tantalus Mountains near Squamish. I envision a 20-person round hut made of stone with wood beams inside. I see a fireplace in the middle, a kitchen in the back and a sleeping loft. Jim will like whatever we do. Mom Haberl walks me to the door and I tell her, "I'm going to visit Scott in New Zealand."

She raises her eyebrows and says, "Ooh, are you in love?"

"I don't know." And I don't. My heart needs time. The buildup to departure day tenses my body; I don't want to leave Habby, my home, Jim. The night before I fly out, I bang my face into my pillow and yell, "I don't want to go. I don't want to go without you."

Scott picks me up at the Queenstown Airport and I relax into his arms. It takes some time to settle into the car, as our bodies crave touch. As soon as we arrive at his little apartment, we make love. We walk hand in hand through the quiet streets, stop for Thai food and walk back in the dark along the water. Scott stops suddenly, pulls me to him and kisses me deeply on the mouth. So romantic. So charming. I am speechless.

The next day, Scott leaves for work. He is the designer and safety manager of the 500-kilometre Eco-Challenge adventure race that starts in just over a week. I hike up Ben Lomond, through the forest and into the alpine, where it snows. After a few hours of laboured breathing, a lump forms in my throat and my chest aches. My heart strains to contain its shy thoughts and fears. Finally, the tears explode. I miss you, Jim. I feel alone. Why did you leave me?

And I am scared because I have come all this way to see Scott. This is a huge acknowledgement of my feelings for him and of the truth that Jim is dead. I feel exposed, naked and vulnerable. I try to go beyond my fear, to feel my heart, and I feel nothing, which is even scarier. Am I in love with Scott? The more time I spend with him, the more I trust him. Every day he tells me he loves me; our lovemaking is passionate and his eyes look right into my soul. I take a deep breath and try to let him in.

When he gets home from work I tell him I'm struggling. He holds my hand and I feel the heat of his body beside me.

"I'm feeling very exposed," I stutter.

"Oh, Sue, I thought it would be okay. I invited you here because I thought it was the right thing."

"It's not your fault. I just need you to know that I feel vulnerable."

He relaxes and holds me while I cry.

That evening the Canadian guides arrive and Scott hosts a welcoming party. I think back to being with Jim in Morocco. Now I'm with Scott. It feels strange. Three times I head up the stairs to the party and three times I retreat to the safety of our bedroom. These people are friends who want the best for me. I coach myself. Please, Jim, give me strength and courage. When I finally surface shyly, friends hug me, bring me into the circle. One of Scott's best friends says he is so happy we are together. I heave a sigh.

It is November and in a week I will leave on another adventure.

THIRTY-FIVE
NEPAL

I fly from New Zealand to Nepal, where I guide an Ascent for Alzheimer's team up 5350-metre Gokyo-Ri, in the valley adjacent to Mount Everest.

My feet move and my heart searches.

The Twin Otter feels like a crowded delivery truck. As the pilot throttles the plane to life, I could reach out and touch his crisp white sleeve. There are 13 passengers, eight of whom are my clients, who will climb Gokyo-Ri to raise money to fight Alzheimer's disease.

It is fitting that I struggle to preserve my memories of my life with Jim as I support the Alzheimer Society's struggle to find a cure for memory loss. Dad once told me of a lovely old woman who developed Alzheimer's and eventually went into a care facility because her husband could not manage. Almost immediately, the wife fell in love with another Alzheimer's patient in the facility. Her husband visited daily but was devastated. The one who is left behind suffers. I do not want to be left behind.

The engine revs and vibrates our seats. I clutch the armrest. The pilot lurches with the plane as it fights gravity. Bump, bump, bump, smooth. Airborne. He loosens his grip on the steering wheel, so I let out my breath and ease back into my seat. Kathmandu shrinks behind us. The mountains peekaboo out of the cloud.

I press my knapsack into my lap and whisper to the team

doctor, "This is going to be great." He nods, smiles and turns to look out the tiny convex window. Yes, it is. I already feel Jim. I want my high.

The co-pilot twists in his seat.

"We should have a great view of Mount Everest."

The crowd murmurs.

"Do you have your camera?"

"I hope I don't get sick."

We climb up the Khumbu Valley toward the Himalayan giants. The wings teeter-totter, and I sit forward to see if the pilot is scared too. But he lazily flicks switches and lets his body roll with the movement of the plane, which is like a boat bobbing on the ocean. We shout to be heard above the drone of the engine and the wind thumping against the plane.

"Is that it?" one of my clients gestures and asks.

"No. Not high enough," I shout back.

Twenty minutes into the flight, the pilot points, "There it is. That's Everest." We strain against our seat belts. It is a faraway hulk. We fly at about 4000 metres, and Everest towers at 8848 metres. A cloud moves across it like a curtain. We look at one another open-mouthed as we weave up the valley between the world's most spectacular peaks. The plane banks hard left, and I turn my attention to the cockpit.

The pilot talks into his mouthpiece and nods at his co-pilot. They sit up, scan the instruments and peer over the nose of the plane, pointing down at layers of cloud. They navigate by sight, which worries me, given how much cloud there is. The pilot works the throttle, and the plane whines and shudders. Flaps clunk down. The plane dives at the side of a mountain. I hook my fingertips on the rim of the window and press my cheek to the glass. Through clouds a patchwork quilt becomes terraced hillsides. Large grey boulders turn into buildings. A postage stamp stretches into a small landing strip headed into the mountainside. I finger my bottom lip and look around to see if anyone else has noticed. How will we land on that? How will we stop before crashing into the side of the mountain?

The pilot grips a stirrup hanging from the ceiling, and I wonder if it triggers his parachute. But he seems attentive and calm, even as the ground gets closer. The postage stamp gets a bit bigger, but not much, and stops abruptly where the terraced earth rears up. The landing strip is 20 metres wide and 450 metres long. It is situated at a staggering 12 per cent incline to help the plane slow down. Moderately.

I sit on my hands and squeeze the edge of the seat. My internal dialogue attempts to soothe my fears. These pilots land here several times a day. And anyway, the situation is out of my control. Either we make it or we don't.

At the same time, I scan the interior for emergency exits and parachutes. I don't want to die. This is good. It wasn't so long ago that I was neutral about the whole idea.

Just before the wheels hit, the pilot throws the propellers into hard reverse, and I close my eyes. He works the flaps against the wind to stop the plane. I open my eyes as we careen past blurred figures of people, yaks and luggage.

Our surroundings come into focus, the plane jolts to a stop and we clap furiously like old windshield wipers. We have made it to the mountain village of Lukla at 2800 metres, the jumping-off point to Mount Everest Base Camp and our objective, Gokyo-Ri: 2500 metres to climb.

As we collect our duffle bags and backpacks, hopeful sherpas move down the hillside. Yaks tear at the short grass. Our sirdar, the head of our Nepalese support team, directs us to a nearby lodge for tea while Sherpas and porters load our gear onto yaks. I give the massive, curved-horned, long-haired beasts a wide berth. A steady stream of trekkers going to Everest Base Camp shares our route for the first few days. Buildings become scarce as we roller-coaster our way up the valley. After a brief stretch of pine forest, the trail dives to the river Thado Khola, where a humungous suspension bridge stretches to the other side. We wobble across it single file, flattening like pancakes to let yaks pass.

In the bustling town of Namche, construction is everywhere and baked goods abound. Several businesses offer Internet here at 3500 metres. Most people experience some sort of altitude sickness above 3000 metres: headaches, nausea, loss of appetite, shortness of breath. I wait for the feeling of malaise, like an experienced warrior. We spend two days here to acclimate and climb a few hundred metres up out of town to view the big mountains: Everest, Ama Dablam, Lhotse. The clients move slowly but enthusiastically, some with headaches and lethargy. A few of them are not sleeping well.

The Nepalese greet us by putting their hands together in front of their hearts, closing their eyes, bowing and saying "Namaste." My *Lonely Planet* guide offers several definitions of the salutation, and I cobble together my own meaning. The light inside me sees the light inside you and I honour the spirit in you that is also in me. There is a divine spark within each of us that is located in the heart chakra so you bring the hands together at the heart to increase the flow of divine love. Bowing the head and closing the eyes helps the mind surrender to the divine in the heart.

The next day, we climb up the other side of the village to a Tibetan monastery. I hear the tinkle of prayer wheels as we get closer. A serene-looking monk dressed in brown robes motions for us to enter the two-room sacred building. Yak butter burns in front of Tibetan statues. I pull at my long skirt and long-sleeved shirt and crouch to go through the wooden doorway. The scriptures are more than a thousand years old. I try not to breathe on them. The monk stills and looks like he is in a trance. I wonder if he is praying.

Tibetan Buddhists believe that saying the mantra *om mani padme hum* out loud or silently to oneself invokes the powerful benevolent attention and blessings of Chenrezig, the embodiment of compassion. The prayer can be translated as "Hail the jewel in the lotus." *Om* symbolizes one's impure body, speech and mind and also the pure noble body, speech and mind of the Buddha. The good and the bad. *Mani*, the jewel, symbolizes compassion and love and the altruistic intention to become enlightened. *Padme* means lotus and symbolizes the wisdom that keeps you out of contradiction. *Hum* means inseparability and can be achieved through compassion and wisdom.

The mantra is everywhere: in tin wheels that you spin by the side of the pathway, carved into rock walls, on flags poised high in the mountains. I would like to know the jewel in the lotus.

We leave Namche and hike steeply to a ridge where a stone *chorten* sits in the middle of the path, like an adobe oven with a big hat. Tibetan tradition is to pass by these sacred monuments in a clockwise manner, so we pass on the left. We climb until lunch and, heartbreakingly, must lose all of the elevation we have earned to descend the other side to the river of the Gokyo-Ri Valley.

I follow the last client, a grey-haired gentleman in his sixties, to come into our riverside camp at Phortse Tenga. He is well behind the rest of the group, struggling with the altitude.

"You did it." I hug him.

He slumps onto the first rock and leans his forehead on his hand. His body shakes, and I kneel before him, my hand on his shoulder.

"That's okay. You did great." I struggle to keep my voice from cracking. I hate to see him hurting.

He looks up with a tear-stained face, "It's just that so many people are counting on me to get to the top." I hold him while he cries.

On day seven of our journey we reach 3500 metres. After morning chai, I sit in the sun watching my breath swirl into the air. The team members move slowly around camp.

Like the yaks, we set off one behind the other up the steep

dirt trail that winds out of the valley through rhododendron forests. We pass by rock wall enclosures, *kharkas*, that look like ancient ruins but serve as summer grazing grounds for Sherpas' herds of yaks. As we climb, the sweet smell of rhododendron gives way to the nutty smell of juniper trees. Every so often I look over my shoulder at the massive snowy peaks of Khumbila (5761 metres) and Tawache (6540 metres). My mind slows to meet my pace as we traverse a hillside, up the side of the Gokyo-Ri Valley, above the largest glacier in the Himalaya, Ngozumpa, below. I think of the clients. I feel strong, with a purpose. Lead them to the top. Step by step.

As the air gets thinner, so does my armour. The layers peel away and I feel naked. Mountains are great equalizers. I cannot fight Mother Earth any more than I can fight my own heart. My heart pumps out its real purpose. Find Jim. I want my old life back. I want what is familiar. I want my old compass bearing.

The uncertainty of life is unbearable to me. I falter on the steep mountainside above the rumbling glacier and lean more heavily on my hiking poles. Suck breaths through my aching throat. Shit. Don't fall apart now. I grit my teeth. I head to the top of the pass where the prayer flags snap in the wind. The Nepalese place the flags as high as possible so they float farther on the wind and reach more people.

A flutter catches my gaze and I look up. There, at 4500 metres, an eagle soars in front of me, so close that its individual feathers shimmer in the sun. He stares ahead but keeps me in his peripheral vision. I stop and watch him glide all the way down the valley.

"Namaste," I whisper, eyes closed, head bowed and hands at my heart. The light inside me sees the light inside you.

The client behind me follows my gaze and rests his hand on my arm.

"That is amazing."

"Yes." I gulp and swipe at my tears with the back of my hand.

My mouth gapes in an awkward smile that is a cross between laughing and crying. I interpret the eagle's presence as a sign from Jim, that he is with me in spirit. I pick up the pace.

Three days later, at 5 a.m., we leave the small hamlet of Gokyo – at 4750 metres one of the highest settlements in the world – for the final push to the summit of Gokyo-Ri. For two hours we ascend in clouds and there are no views. Less than 500 metres from the top a Japanese team descends, lamenting that they saw nothing from the summit because the clouds were so thick. Several of my team members look at me. I grab the hiking poles of the most tired person and begin to tow her behind me.

"Let's go. It's going to be great. We're almost there." I am determined to get to the peak, because he will be there. An hour later, as we crest the final ridge just steps from the summit, the clouds slide down the valley to reveal a wall of towering legendary peaks: Cho Oyu, Gyachung Kang, Lhotse, Makalu, Cholatse, and Mount Everest, the highest of them all.

We made it. People reach for the sky, hug, yahoo, slump to the rocks. While I hug each person, I make a mental note of how coherent they are. We shouldn't spend too much time at the top. I take a group photo and feel my heart thumping. I walk a few steps away, sit down alone on a small ledge and contemplate the highest mountain in the world. I yank off my glove, caress the cold stone beside me and touch the warm flesh of my face. He's here. I feel him.

I push myself up and gather everyone for the descent and our return to Canada.

PART 4
RETURN

Life can only be understood backwards;
but it must be lived forwards.
—SØREN KIERKEGAARD

THIRTY-SIX
COMMITMENT

In January 2002 my year is up and it is time to return to Trek. I move back into my parents' suite in Vancouver and resume the routine of driving back to Whistler every weekend. When Scott is not guiding or scouting locations for Eco-Challenge, we spend time together. I am excited to see him but feel relieved when I am once again on my own. Before he leaves for a three-week trip to Jordan, we meet for dinner. I chat about school, the kids, Habby. Scott strokes his glass. My words begin to run together.

"Is something wrong?"

Scott takes a gulp of his wine and breathes out, "I don't want to have a baby."

I grit my teeth and look past him. No, don't leave me. I will do anything. Just don't leave me. The old Sue, the person I know and love, who loved Jim, hangs by a thread. Scott is my hope of res-urrecting the past, of reversing Jim's death, of keeping Sue alive. I bring fear to my relationship with Scott: my fear of accepting Jim's death and of losing myself. I will believe anything to calm this fear.

While Scott is away in Jordan, we e-mail and talk on the phone. He knows I will not accept a relationship where my part-ner does not want to have a child.

"We love each other. Love is the most important thing. There must be a way for us to be together." I encourage Scott to believe, too. He wants to be my knight in shining armour.

Scott and I continue to see each other. That summer, we plan an overnight mountaineering trip to climb the highest peak in the Whistler area, Wedge Mountain. As I sweat under my load and lean into the steep trail, Scott comments, "It's good to see that my girl can carry a heavy pack and keep a good pace." I flush with pride. In less than three hours, we cover the 11 kilometres and 1200 metres of elevation gain to reach the opaque turquoise waters of glacier-fed Wedgemount Lake. We set up the tent on a bed of pebbles ground smooth by the glacial ice, and the peak of Wedge towers above us.

The alarm rings at 1:30 a.m. and I feel for my headlamp in the dark. I dress without unzipping my sleeping bag but the cold air sneaks in and my teeth chatter.

Scott cocks his ear. "What's that?" Boots crunch past on the frozen ground outside of our tent. "I can't believe they got up this early!" Scott laments, referring to the other climbing party camped farther down the lake. "Let's go! Hurry."

"Okay." I fumble with my gloves and try to keep a straight face. Scott is even more competitive than I am.

I stomp down hard to get the teeth of my crampons to bite the glacier. Crystals shatter under my weight, echoing through the amphitheatre of snow, rock and ice. Crunch, crunch, crunch. The odd clink of metal dangling from my harness bounces into the black. The higher we get, the thicker the darkness feels. It envelops me like cotton wool and I fall into a meditative step.

By the time we step over the chasm where the glacier ice has pulled away from the rock of the mountain, the sun has warmed my fingers and toes. The other climbing party has taken a different route, and we reach the summit ridge well in front of them. "Yahoo!" Scott looks at the figures below us and then at the summit peak.

Scott packs down steps in the snow as he makes his way up the sharp ridge. I look down to my left at the steep snow slope and decide to keep my eyes focused straight ahead. I stretch my stride to follow Scott's long-legged prints until we are on bare rock, 50 metres from the summit. Scott steps aside and motions for me to go ahead. He follows silently and I wonder if he contemplates our route down.

At the cairn marking the top, I turn 360°.

"You can see Mount Baker!"

"Yup," Scott reclines on the rocks, squinting in the sun.

I kneel down in front of him. "It's beautiful."

His eyes well up. "Yes. This is where I was going to ask you to marry me."

"Wow," I swallow, take his hand, and then add, "so are you still going to ask me?" Scott laughs and pulls me to him and kisses me.

"Yes," he says. "Will you marry me, Sue?"

"Yes, I will."

When I tell my parents they hug me. Glenda cries. People are happy to hear the news. I am getting on with my life. I am better. But none of my friends really know Scott. He's not around much. Jim's younger brother Kevin and I climb one of the neighbourhood peaks one day. As we plunge into the deep snow, revelling in the meditative nature of our repetitive task, our senses tingling and alive, Kevin turns to me and says, "I'm happy for you with Scott. He's a good guy. I support you. But you know, some people are saying you're dishonouring Jim's memory by being with another mountain guide."

"Oh." I don't know what else to say. I feel enough guilt about carrying on without Jim.

I launch into my new fantasy.

Scott will leave for Fiji before I return from my trip to Africa with the Alzheimer Society team, so we will not see each other for three months. Scott suggests I come to Fiji in September. I arrange a 10-day leave from Trek, but my gut feels uneasy because I am committing to Scott. When he picks me up at the airport in Fiji after three months of not seeing each other, I relax into his strong arms and breathe in his familiar smell. We sail, surf, hike and horseback ride in this stunning country. Only one of his

colleagues congratulates me on our engagement and his friends
seem quiet. Something feels wrong.

THIRTY-SEVEN
LETTING GO AGAIN

I am home in Whistler for the Christmas holidays.

"I should give my tenant notice at the beginning of January if we're going to start renovating in February." I rest my chin on Scott's chest. He shifts under my body, takes a breath and clamps his lips together. I push away from him to bring his face into focus, "What is it?"

He turns away. I swivel my legs off the couch so that I balance on his belly.

"What's wrong?"

"I'm struggling." Scott lets go of his breath.

"What do you mean?"

"I can't picture having a baby." He scans my face. I slide off his body onto the couch beside him. His brow creases and he lies still as if he hopes not to get a beating.

"I don't know what to say." My heart goes into survival mode. Lock the doors. Conserve energy. Keep busy. Brace for pain.

"I need to know that I can go away and work for however long and you'll stay home and look after the baby."

"I've been clear with you that I have no desire to be a single mom. I want to share parenting with my mate. I don't understand why you need to go away."

"Purely selfish reasons." He pauses and takes a breath. "I thought you'd be mad."

I look at the floor and fiddle with my fingernails. "I'm sad." We sit side by side saying nothing. I place my hand on the side of his cheek and look at him. "You're scared."

"Yes."

"I want you to be happy." I move down the couch so we both have room to escape. Tears roll down my cheeks.

"I'm sorry for hurting you." Scott places his hand on the couch beside my leg.

I tighten my jaw and my anger builds. "I've heard that too many times for it to mean anything. I knew all along you didn't love me."

"I'm screaming inside. Maybe there are different levels of love. If I can't be there for you 100 per cent then I don't want to be there at all." He sighs, pushes himself to his feet. "I'll go." I rest my chin on my hand and look away. My crying gets louder as his footsteps fade down the stairs.

I hear Scott say, "Oh, Sue," and he thumps back up to the living room, wraps his arms around my stiff body. "Is there anything I can do?"

"I'll be okay, you know. I'll be okay without you. You don't have to worry about that. I've survived losing Jim, so I know I'll survive losing you." I purse my lips and stare at him, wanting to hurt him back.

He stands up and shrugs. "I guess I'll get going," he whispers. With each slow footstep on the stairs, a drum beats louder in my body until I vibrate with rage. Why didn't I let Scott go when he first said he didn't want to have kids? I hate him for not being like Jim. I hate him for not knowing what he wants. I hate him for being selfish and hurting me. My eyes burn.

Before Scott has opened the front door to leave, I stand up and shout with clenched fists, "Wait a second. Get back up here."

He jogs back up the stairs and stands before me, hands buried in his pockets.

"What do you mean you can't do it? You proposed to me. I've taken a leave of absence from work so we can move in together and start a life together and now you bail? How can you do that?" My arms stiffen at the shrill sound of my voice.

He mumbles at his shoes. "I know. I'm sorry."

"Go. Get out." I wave my hand and turn away from him. The front door opens and closes. A motor putters, whines, revs and fades.

Looking to the ceiling I bawl, "Jim, please come back. I tried so hard to let go and to be with Scott. I took all of the photographs of you down. I didn't go to your family's place for Christmas. Please, come back."

For two hours I sit on the couch, paralyzed. The numbness of grieving Jim returns, and I go to bed with thick, heavy limbs and dream of that night when Kevin and Eric came with the news.

The next day, in Scott's driveway, I visualize the possible scene. Perhaps Scott will open the door, gather me in his arms and say how sorry he is and that I am the one he loves more than anything. Finally, I knock.

Scott opens the door slowly.

"Hey."

"Hi. Do you want to come in?"

"Yes." Scott's dog licks my hand and wags his tail as I pass by.

I perch at the kitchen table, and Scott slouches on the couch, knees wide apart.

"I don't know what to say." I stare at my hands. "I don't know why we can't figure this out if we love each other." I slide my fingers along the wood grain of the IKEA table.

"I don't know, Sue. Given your special relationship with Jim, I didn't really feel like you accepted me for who I am." Scott deflates as these words suck his energy.

With a few steps, I kneel before him, hands on his thighs.

"Maybe you're right. Maybe I haven't done enough to let go of Jim." A sneering voice inside of me says, Yeah, you know Scott has seen the rest of Jim's ashes on your bedroom shelf and those clothes you keep in the closet. You even gave him one of Jim's old jackets to wear once. Shit, that doesn't seem fair, but I'm doing my best.

I choke out, "But I'll try harder. Why don't we just try living together? Forget about getting married and having kids. We'll just move in together and see how it goes." I breathe quickly and look at him.

His face does not soften and his mouth barely moves when he says, "I'll think about it."

I withdraw my hands to my sides and sit back on my heels. "Okay." I couldn't have begged much more than that. Completely exposed, I use the chair to help me up, feel for my keys on the table and let myself out.

Two days later I return to work in Vancouver for the month of January. My leave begins February 1, when Scott and I were supposed to move in together. When I arrive at school, I coach myself. Okay, pull yourself together. You survived before, you'll survive this. Don't let it affect your job. I open the door to our office and Robyn turns around from writing on the board.

"Hey. How's it going, Sue?" She smiles.

"Great, Robyn, how was your holiday?" I beeline to my desk and drop my bag.

"What's wrong?" She moves toward me.

My chin quivers. I stare at my desk.

"What's wrong?" She puts her hand on my arm.

I look at her concerned face and let go. "Scott bailed."

"Oh, no." Her eyes fill with tears and we lean into each other at the same time.

There are outdoor trips to plan, assignments to grade and lessons to teach, but every chance I get I seek refuge at my desk with the latest book I've bought, *Feel the Fear and Do It Anyway*. I earmark every other page and underline every other word. My insides feel like an old fuzzy television screen. Sometimes I don't want to swallow, for fear that my saliva will never hit bottom. Scott is important to me, but I've been in this prison of hollowness before. Scott goes away to work for three weeks and sends one e-mail in which he reinforces his decision and signs it "Scott."

When I am quite sure that Scott has really bailed, I venture to tell other people. One friend asks me why our relationship didn't work out. I tell her, "I guess he didn't love me." She responds sternly,

"You mean he didn't love you the way you wanted him to." I want Scott to love me the way Jim loved me.

Dad and I walk along Jericho Beach and talk.

"I wonder why I chose to be with Scott." The "it's my fault" voice chimes in.

"Because you were trying to continue your old life," Dad says confidently, walking with his hands clasped behind his back.

"Yes, that's part of it," I agree, but the rest of my response percolates in private as we walk along in silence. I try to heal old wounds. Jim's death has a cascade effect on my past hurts. I had tucked those hurts away but now they surface and demand attention. My confidence is eroded and I question my decision to leave my mother to live with my father when I was 16. I question my decision not to see my mother for eight years. I question my once-a-year relationship with my mother now. Was everything my fault?

The positive good-girl voice in me perks up. "You know, I've learned two great lessons from being with Scott: I know that my heart is able and willing to open up and love even after losing Jim, and I will not abandon myself in the name of love."

Dad nods.

Robyn teaches more of the classes so I don't have to be in front of the students as much. The month crawls by. On February 1, the end of term, I pack up and drive to Whistler for my five-month leave of absence.

I call Scott and drop by his place. He is quiet, contemplative, resigned, as if he is waiting for me to lose hope. We go on hikes and sometimes we have sex. Afterward, I feel ill. Emptier. But I will do almost anything to avoid more loss. The monkeys in my brain hoot and holler and swing maniacally.

I coach myself. Enough of Scott. Don't use him as a distraction. You have your own work to do.

Thoughts writhe in my mind like snakes, seeking a pattern and strangling one another in the process. Why am I frantic? Because I try to convince myself that I am worthy of love. Maybe letting go of Scott represents more than the relationship. I need to start fresh and stop clinging to what is familiar. Take a break from this house Jim and I built. Jump. Make a decision and embrace it. Take responsibility for my life. There's no one else to blame. Scott is no longer a part of my life, so wish him well and move on. Don't try to change the way he feels. There's nothing wrong with me. Stop wallowing. Get on with the things I want to do: art, wilderness trips, travel. Write a book; study alternative medicine.

In my journal I write pages summarizing my relationship with Scott and who is to blame for what. I come out much better than he does. My anger subsides, my pen slows and I finish with a blessing to Scott:

> I loved laughing with you, skiing with you and dreaming with you. I loved when you were tender and loving with me – when your heart was open. You are a good person: sensitive and well meaning. I'm sorry that our journey together is over. I thought we were going to grow old together. You are not a part of my life anymore and that is heartbreaking. I will try to accept that and wish you well.

I wake up the morning after writing that entry with a vivid dream about Jim and Scott fresh before my eyes and reach for my journal to write it down.

In the dream, I am at home in Whistler working on the computer. Jim and Scott are rock climbing a new route nearby that

Jim and I climbed the day before. A ghostly transparent figure of Jim appears before me. By the way he looks at me I know that something is wrong. He floats away, looking back to see if I follow. My family and friends yell after me that I don't know the way, that I will get lost. But I know the way like my own heart and climb up the rock after Jim. When I catch up, Jim turns to me and motions above him. I climb past Jim, focused on each move, worried about Scott. I see Scott's body lying flat against the rock. As I approach, he turns with a resigned look, hanging from his arm that disappears into a fissure in the rock, as if he is being swallowed. His face tells me not to worry, but he looks like a child trying to be brave. I think of options: amputation … but he is buried too deep. We look at one another and it is clear that this is it. This is as far as he can go. He tells me with his eyes to go on without him. I float back down to Jim.

It's been a long time since I dreamt of Jim. It feels like we had a visit.

THIRTY-EIGHT
DO WHAT'S GOOD
FOR SUE

One sunny day, I walk to the village on the valley trail to meet Dad for lunch at the Italian trattoria. My mind wanders to images of Tuscany and me cooking with tomatoes right from the vine and smearing sauce across my apron as I juggle several pots on the stove. While I wait to be seated at the restaurant, I notice right there in the entrance several brochures for cooking schools in Tuscany. I finger the glossy photos and ponder the serendipity. When I inquire, I find that the eight-day session is out of my price range.

A few weeks pass and the woman I spoke to at the restaurant about the classes calls back to say they have had a lot of cancellations because of the impending war in Iraq, so many that she can offer me a screamer of a deal. It takes me 15 minutes to get a flight on points and confirm my dates. I Google "art schools in Europe" and enroll in a week-long studio in medieval Anversa, Italy, after the cooking course. A week does not seem long enough, and so I find another six-week art school in Aix-en-Provence, France. I will go to Italy for two weeks and then France for July.

I arrange medical insurance, travellers' cheques, buy new clothes, pack, prepay bills and call my aunt to see if she can look after Habby. The familiar pre-trip routine eats away the days until there's one week to go. One item remains on my to-do list: Jim's ashes.

On April 29, 2003, the fourth anniversary of Jim's death, I face down the wooden Haida box on the shelf in my bedroom and hike to the lookout point on the trail behind our house. "Our" house. Jim and Sue's place. Not my house. It's been four years since Jim was killed and some of his ashes are still in my bedroom. Habby bounds ahead of me. Looking out over the lake, I hold the box against my belly and stare, silent. I've run out of meaningful things to say about grief, death and love. I am empty. I need to fill myself up. Finally I open the bag inside the box and scatter the ashes like birdseed. It takes too long and I grab handfuls and toss them so that whitish grey mounds form on the ground. Near the end, I pull out the plastic bag, upend it and shake until it is empty, like I do with the cracker bag in the sink. The last of Jim's ashes. Done.

I will go to Italy and France to learn, to do things that are good for me, good for my soul. I am proud of me for taking this step. Learning can be an effective antidote to depression, disinterest in life and loneliness. I will shed an old skin, shake free of my own chains.

This trip will be good for me. I am ready for a loving relationship with someone who is available. Keep me strong, Jim. Keep reminding me of what is genuine.

Villa Delia perches on a hill surrounded by 30 hectares of olive groves, grapevines, vegetable gardens, brilliant yellow sunflowers and luscious red poppies, delicate as lips. An authentically restored 17th-century country estate, some of its olive trees are 120 years old. Pope Pius VII exiled here during the Napoleonic Wars.

Signor Sylvano, our host, smiles with his eyes as he shows us the grounds. He gestures at an employee bent over in the vegetable garden. "Most Italians want a small plot of land where they can put their hands in the earth."

I nod and track the vineyards and sandstone villas with terracotta roofs floating in the distance in a haze of soft yellow hues.

Dark-green cypress trees outline a tapestry of rolling hills like a fringe. The soil burns red from the long-ago heat of a volcano.

I'm in the heart of rural Tuscany.

The romantic countryside makes me feel alone. I want to nudge Jim and whisper, "Isn't this beautiful?"

Dad asked me once, "Why do you want to travel? You won't find any answers, you know."

"I know but it's good for me," I laughed and changed the subject. Later I replayed the conversation and had time to prepare the response I wanted to give. Travelling gives me perspective and opens my eyes to different ways of being. It reminds me of all I have to be grateful for. And being grateful helps me to love. And be loved.

I breathe in the smell of rich Italian earth and feel the warm breeze on my skin. It's beautiful, I tell myself. Life has its magical moments even though Jim is dead. Enjoy. Self-pity will get you nowhere.

My elbows brush the walls as Sylvano leads me up a narrow, winding staircase to my dark-wooded, brightly sunlit room. He sets my small suitcase down by the door.

"*Grazie.*"

"*Prego.*"

I survey the room. Sparkling white bathroom, elegant tiling, plush towels, antique washstand. Double bed. Too romantic for a widow. I picture myself snuggled under the white duvet with Jim, watching the yellow-orange sun through the oblong windows. I stand paralyzed. I'm afraid of being alone. I want to go home to the familiar. But I'm too frugal, too sensitive to what others will think, too scared of failure to bail. And on some level I know there is not much to go home to.

I slink into a dress and join four Canadian couples and one American couple for our welcome dinner: a scene out of *Babette's Feast*. It takes an hour to get through the appetizers – prosciutto, antipasto, chicken liver, melon and a classic pasta dish rolled up like a neat hairdo. For the main meal we pass around serving platters of roast potatoes smothered in olive oil, Swiss chard, tender beef strips blanketed in parmesan and pickled vegetables. The wine and conversation flow. Mostly about food. Gerda and Eric, a jolly, rotund couple from Vancouver describe in detail the family dinners they host. I laugh, slur my words a bit and steady myself on the back of the chair when I get up to go to the bathroom.

I am the odd person out in our group of 11. Yvonne and Mario, a middle-aged Canadian couple sitting beside me, ask me about my life. Each question evokes painful answers.

"Do you have kids?"

"Are you married?"

"No. My husband was killed in an avalanche four years ago." The American woman seated across from me looks uncomfortable and turns away to begin another conversation.

There is a short silence as Mario and Yvonne glance at each other before Yvonne says, "I'm sorry. What happened?"

My lips and heart loosen with wine. Jim is a part of me. My wound is a part of me. I am a 37-year-old widow. I adored my husband. I would like someone to love again. I tell them about Jim's accident and their eyes look sad, but they don't change the subject.

I stumble to bed well after midnight, feeling lighter.

The next morning, the sun rises fiery red. The birds form a symphony of melodic whistles to ease me into the day. I stick my tongue out at the mirror. Purple. Too much wine last night. At the breakfast table, Sylvano says that today we learn the feel of cooking, which means no recipes. My face stretches into a smile to stop any quivering. How will I remember everything without a recipe? How will I know the right way to do it? I like to have a plan so that I can avoid mistakes. No recipe? It's like going into the wilderness without a map and compass.

The cooking school runs for 10 days. The stainless-steel

kitchen is about nine metres long, with individual learning stations, and pots of every size hang from the ceiling. Margareta, our teacher, instructs with a shy smile. "You don't use a garlic press because you will bruise the garlic. You must chop it." A younger woman translates while the eight of us scribble notes. Throughout the demonstrations, Margareta handles the tomatoes, chicken and fresh rosemary the size of a branch as if they are precious heirlooms.

I squish egg, flour and salt together with my bare hands to make pasta dough, roll it out and feed it through a machine to create spaghetti and tortellini. My confidence builds as I learn. After morning class, our creations are served to us for lunch on three round tables sparkling with cutlery, crystal and china in the courtyard. The open-air living suits my soul. A lemon tree climbs the wall above the brick pizza oven, mingling its tartness with the sweet smell of plump roses. I chew the spaghetti Bolognese slowly. The chicken legs stuffed with ricotta cheese, rosemary and new potatoes inspire me to close my eyes. The ratatouille melts on my tongue. Like sentinels lined up in front of me, four wine glasses of varying size reflect golds, yellows and reds meant to accompany each taste sensation. For dessert, pears float in Prosecco, Italian champagne. I roll away from the table, swim a few laps in the pool before our afternoon excursion and wonder how I am going to eat dinner.

And so the days go. Wake up. Eat breakfast. Go to class. Eat lunch. Go on an excursion. Eat dinner until midnight. Go to bed. I realize that I do not think of Jim, or death, or grief when I cook. I am alone and I am fine. Jim is in my heart. I listen to my heart.

Every day I learn to prepare and enjoy delicious food. I learn there's no such thing as extra-virgin olive oil. It's either virgin or it's not. I work the flavours around in my mouth and taste the butter, cheese and fresh herbs. My clothes cling to my curves. I let go to the pleasure of feeding my hunger.

In Siena I marvel at the domes, arches and tile mosaic floors of the Duomo, which was begun in the 13th century and took three hundred years to complete. I climb the narrow marble staircase of the tower, Il Torre, to get a bird's eye view of the cobblestone road that circles the main piazza. In front of Il Palazzo Pubblico, the town hall, the Piazza del Campo serves as a slippery race-track twice a year to those bold riders and horses competing in Il Palio. The different neighbourhoods of the city prepare jockeys all year for the races, and the names of the competing horses are drawn just days before each event. It takes several hours to settle them at the start line. In one and a half minutes, they race three laps around the square, negotiating 90° turns downhill. Horses and riders have died.

It seems nuts, but then most people consider rock climbing and mountaineering to be crazy, risk-taking stuff. I'll bet more horseback riders in Il Palio have died than rock climbers. I'm not so sure about mountaineers. I have a hard time picturing myself careening around the slippery racetrack with hundreds of other riders to contend with. The system seems overloaded. Rock climbing and mountaineering feel more comfortable.

In Florence I sit for two hours on a stone bench staring at Michelangelo's statue of David. Over five metres of smooth, rippling, white-marble muscle. David is meditative, almost worried-looking with a furrowed brow. His slingshot is over his shoulder, partly hidden, and the rock he holds in his hand is out of view. Such a strong being exuding such humility. David's characteristics remind me of Jim, of my unified goal of living with an open heart, of what's important in life. I want to run my hands all over his naked body to absorb his strength.

On the last day of school, I feel weary, melancholy and indecisive. For eight days I have fed myself well. I feel full and empty at the same time. I want to feel good like I did when Jim was alive. But feeling full does not get rid of the pain. I do not need to eat so much. I want to make the smallest footprint possible and use only what I need. Indulge once in awhile, but moderation is important and moderation takes discipline. This is who I am. I hug Yvonne and Mario goodbye and am grateful that I have learned to love food again.

THIRTY-NINE
DRAWING FROM
THE HEART

I board a slow train bound for Rome on phase two of project Do What's Good for Sue. For €100 a taxi driver takes me the remaining 120 kilometres east of Rome to the small village of Anversa degli Abruzzi, in the Sagittario River valley. The driver drops me as close as he can to the address I give him, and I stumble down the steep, cobbled alleyways lit by old London-style lanterns. Ovid, the Roman poet, resided here, and it feels as if I am stepping into a medieval play. One hundred people live in the village, and the ones I see at the main piazza outside the only bar return my greeting, "*Buon giorno*." There is no trace of tourists.

Patricia, the art teacher, meets me at my apartment wearing jeans, and I study her auburn hair as she leads me around my new home as if it is her own. In my bedroom there is nowhere to hang clothes, the bed sucks my body in like quicksand, the plaster is cracked and I wear a sweater to keep warm. This is no Villa Delia. But the view from the creaky window plummets to the valley floor and then climbs like a fighter jet straight up the mountainside. My roommate, Laurie, is an upbeat 27-year-old "corporate consultant in transition" from New York. The other three American participants cancelled because they did not want to travel, given the war in Iraq.

The first day of class, Laurie and I walk five minutes to the studio, on a path that hangs on the side of the hill. An arched, wooden double door opens into the first floor of the studio, where the cement floor is splattered with different colours of paint. A kitchen lines one side of the room and shelves of art supplies range the other. Rosa, a middle-aged Italian with a ponytail of long grey hair, wearing a stained apron covering an ample stomach, turns from the stove. "*Buon giorno*. I, Rosa, the cook." She waves a wooden spoon in the air and returns to her cooking. Patricia and her younger friend Katie, a photographer from Paris, rise from the table to do introductions.

Patricia pulls down a wooden staircase, and we climb to the second floor, the attic. Floor-to-ceiling shutters push out onto a teeny balcony. Easels stand patiently and a still life of a pewter jug, a blue-and-white patterned clay pitcher, three bunches of garlic and two ripe tomatoes nestle in the folds of a sheet draped over a table in the middle of the room. There is space for three people to create comfortably.

Our first exercise is to do a charcoal drawing of the still life, without looking at it. Patricia instructs us to observe the image for two minutes before she covers it up, then we will draw "blind." The purpose is to learn to see what is really there as opposed to being a slave to preconceived notions. This is one of the rules of survival. You can't deal with a situation effectively if you don't see it for what it really is. I am nervous about losing my reference point, just as I feel lost without Jim. But if I keep living as if Jim were alive, I will truly be lost.

Laurie laughs as she settles in to the task. I fidget and finger my notebook, chew on my pencil and look around the room for some way to memorize the objects. My brain darts from object to thought and back again until the scene is scattered in my brain. When Patricia covers the still life, I shift from leg to leg several times before I draw the first line. It's too big and I scrub it out. After five minutes we compare our memory to reality. The sizes of my objects are all off. I scoff to myself that a preschooler could have done better. I'm ready to toss mine in the garbage; Laurie is curious to see what she remembered, rather than be judgmental.

We spend an hour on a second drawing and are permitted to look at the still life but must focus on lights and darks. Patricia comes behind me as I work. "How long has it been since you drew with charcoal?"

I think back to my university art course. "Fifteen years."

"You seem to be remembering just fine."

Rosa calls us down for lunch, and we sit at a thick wooden table outside. Katie unscrews two bottles of wine and my body relaxes. The conversation rolls around to boyfriends and spouses. "How about you, Sue? Do you have someone special?" Katie nudges my arm.

I take a deep breath and brace my hands flat on the table. "I was married to a wonderful man. But he was killed in an avalanche four years ago." I pause to look up.

Katie no longer smiles as she puts her hand on my arm. Patricia leans over from her conversation with Rosa to listen. I clear my throat.

"He was mountaineering in Alaska with two other guides. He was leading. An avalanche broke above him and swept him over a cliff." Some of the words stick. "The other two survived. His name was Jim. He was a good guy." I wonder if this is the only chance I will have to talk to them about Jim and if I should cram in a few more details.

"I lost my husband too. To cancer," Patricia says in a soft voice. "When he died, I brought his body back here, to Anversa. We both loved it here so much." I cry thinking of the image of Patricia accompanying her husband back to Italy. Patricia cries.

Rosa pats her on the back. "Don't talk about sad things. Don't cry." She clears the table.

"Sometimes talking about sad things makes you happy." I smile and wipe my eyes with my hand.

"How long were you married?" Patricia asks.

"Two years." Again, I wish I could say longer.

"You're too young to have that happen." She shakes her head and we finish lunch.

That afternoon, I hike for hours on the mountain trails that extend out from Anversa. Blood pumping through my veins feels good. The only sound I hear is the high-pitched, undulating, drawn-out whistle of the wall creeper with its extraordinary crimson wings, and all I can smell are sweet grapes, tangy pine and spicy saffron. The Sagittario River supports all sorts of life amidst a backdrop of towering, grey, craggy mountains. The Oscan goddess of snakes and healing, Angitia, is thought to preside here, and I lead with a walking stick as a precaution.

I end up in a village of 10 inhabitants called Castrovalva, balanced on a steep ridge 1500 metres above the valley. The Dutch artist M.C. Escher painted this village from the very spot where I'm standing, with wildflowers, ferns in the foreground.

In the evening, Laurie and I return to the studio to work on our still-life drawings, listen to mambo and play cards. On the way home, as we cross the piazza, Laurie whispers, "That cute guy there is checking you out." I keep walking and file the compliment for a time when I feel more ready, more attractive. Right now I am enjoying the company of gentle women.

For a change of pace, Patricia drives us to the bustling town of Sulmona to paint images from the market. I buy a bunch of sunflowers that are almost as tall as I am and begin to draw them in pastel as soon as we get back to the studio. Using purple, black and brown, I painstakingly dot in the seeds in the middle of the flowers. For hours and hours I sit at the outdoor table and draw. After three days I ask Patricia for some fixative to spray on my finished drawing to stop it from smudging. She lightly traces her finger over the swooping, curvy leaves I have drawn. "I see you in these leaves more. The lovely curvy lines seem like you."

"Really?" I did the leaves more by memory, not looking up at the real thing as often. I was tired of doing so much detail in the flowers and trying to make them look perfect, so I went faster on the leaves. They don't look as much like the real leaves. I wonder why she thinks they are more like me. I am more comfortable with the way I drew the flowers.

At the end of the week, Laurie and I exchange e-mails and invite one another to visit in North America. Carefully I roll my artwork into a hard tube to carry onto the plane to France.

Being away is a good thing. It is lonely at times but I am proud that I am doing something just for me, that my heart no longer waits for Scott. I realize I am ready to love again now. I don't think I was when Scott and I first connected – which is probably what attracted me to him – but I'm ready now. I am worthy of love. I love Jim and will always love him, and whoever chooses to love me will have to accept that and realize what a gift it is. I will not second-guess my heart again. I will not compromise on true love again.

I have seen the beautiful sights of Tuscany, eaten wonderful food and drunk great wine and laughed. I am drawing again and it feels amazing – my heart is alive. I have explored the Italian wilderness. I have met interesting people, all with their own stories. Life is good. I will love again. *Via avanti*, time to move forward.

FORTY
FRANCE

If you paint long enough, you come
face to face with who you are.
—MY ART INSTRUCTOR, GRANT SMITH

"*Ouf! Trop de bagages.*" My grey-haired new landlord grunts as he hauls my duffle bag from the airport bus to the trunk of his car.

"*Oui,*" I agree with a laugh and hoist my guitar case onto the backseat.

He steers onto the grand autoroute circling the town of Aix-en-Provence, like a boat entering rapids. Darting across four lanes, he veers onto a cobblestone road barely wide enough for his economy car. I stretch my neck to comb the sandstone walls, clock towers, archways and storefronts boasting bright sunflowers and herbes de Provence. Pedestrians yield as the car squeezes past.

Monsieur chats in French about his wife, and the Tunisian who rents the first floor of their apartment building (I will be on the second floor), and how he hopes I will enjoy Aix.

"*Et voilà.*" He waves his arm triumphantly to the right. "*La cathédrale Saint-Sauveur. C'est beau, n'est-ce pas?*" He pauses for effect. Stone walls reach up to spires and statues on this national monument. The wooden entrance door looks as if it would withstand a battering ram. Cars and people stream past, but the courtyard in front of the immense door is quiet. A few people tiptoe into this 12th-century church.

"*Ah oui. C'est beau,*" I agree and make a mental note to visit.

Just one building past the Roman Catholic cathedral, on the other side of the street, Monsieur brakes, slaps on the flashers, pulls the trunk lever and jumps out.

"*On est arrivé.*" He smiles as he yanks at my duffle. A car honks behind us. Monsieur leaves me on the sidewalk with my bags while he revs off to find parking, returning a few minutes later.

The apartment building grows straight out of the edge of the sidewalk, with ornate black balconies dressing the windows on each floor. Monsieur and I bump up the narrow staircase. One floor. Two floors. He rattles the key in the lock and pushes the door open into a roomy studio, living area and bed on the left and kitchen and bathroom on the right. Monsieur invites me up for a drink later to meet his wife and leaves me with a smile. Two windows face the street. I push open the shutters and stare across at carefully carved and placed stones that have been there for more than eight hundred years. My limbs are heavy and I feel grounded in the years of human experience. The Cathédrale Saint-Sauveur.

The bells sound as I close the shutters so I push them open again to listen, watching a small stream of people enter the cathedral. Carpe diem. I jam my feet into my sandals and clip down the stairs and across the street. The walnut door is three times my height and adorned with carvings of four giant men in robes, major prophets of the Old Testament. Above them are 12 pagan fortune tellers. Framing these men are all sorts of fantastical creatures such as dragons and basilisks, symbolizing the fight between good and evil.

I follow a young family in, grasp my cardigan closed at my neck and try to stretch my skirt further over my knees. The gothic stained-glass windows at the back of the cathedral bathe the pews in coloured hues. Walking toe to heel, I ease down the corridor, reading the information pieces outside each room. The cathedral was built and rebuilt from the 12th to the 19th century. The site first housed a Roman forum in the first century, followed by a church in the sixth. I catch my breath and slide into the baptistery, which was built at the beginning of the sixth century. Roman columns encircle me, and in the middle of the room is a hole, about the size of a manhole, cordoned off by a steel rope. Peering down, I see the bases of the porticoes of the first-century Roman forum. I move slowly and deliberately as if I do not want to disturb the past. When I am outside the cathedral, I breathe deeply and stand there for five minutes, waiting for my soul to catch up. I just walked on rock from the sixth century, and I breathed dust from the first century. Old rock. Old mountains.

After unpacking, I flop spread-eagled on top of the bed covers, my hair flutters under the fan and I sleep for nine hours.

At first light, I click on my Walkman and close my eyes to the soothing voice of my meditation tape. You have no one to please or to satisfy. Focus on your breath. Let your body relax. You are light, you are love and you are free. For several minutes I lie still after the tape has finished. Today I am grateful for the opportunity to paint. I am worthy of love. I will let go to being in Aix, let life unfold instead of forcing it. I will face the truth even when it is difficult. I will take care of myself. My fears today: I won't be able to express myself in my art. I will be judged for who I really am and come up short. I will never love again. As I get out of bed, I remind myself that only 10 per cent of one's fears come to fruition. Aix is only scary because it is different. Relax. Learn. Make mistakes. You have nothing to prove.

There is no need for an alarm clock. At 7 a.m. the bells of the cathedral resonate in happy discord, enticing me to the open window where I do yoga in my short silk nightie. Inhale. Long exhale. Stretch. It is as if I say good morning to each cell in my body. My blood flows more easily, as with nature. Imbalance is only tolerated for so long in nature before the dam breaks, before the snow slides, and flow is once again achieved. My mind strains to jail the sadness, pain and grief within my body, but if I keep doing this, eventually these feelings will turn to disease.

When the good and bad feelings roam free, they dance wildly. I breathe them in and out so that the energy is not trapped. Letting go takes concentration and effort. The emotion scares me.

The street cleaners come and go. More window shutters open. A bald man holding a guitar unlocks the door to the charcuterie across the street. The swallows scream and dive-bomb from the sandstone towers of the sun-kissed cathedral. As the day heats up, a slight odour of garbage hangs in the air, dripping over everything. Cars buzz by more regularly. There is a rhythm to a day in Aix-en-Provence.

I slather on sunscreen, pull on a light dress, catch my hair in a ponytail to keep my back from sweating and wander the cobblestone pathways of my new neighbourhood. At the daily open market, I taste fresh goat cheese, sausage, olive oil and tartinade. A friendly madame bags deep-red Roma tomatoes for me and a long-stemmed bunch of sunflowers (called *soleil* for short). After several hours of weaving in and out of the maze of streets, I feel more comfortable getting lost. On the way back to my apartment, I look into the local rock-climbing club, buy two mountain posters, a basil plant and a chocolate éclair. Six weeks will be enough time to sample each delicacy at the patisserie.

My apartment begins to feel comfortable. Sitting on the bed, I try on several outfits and finally lie down and squeeze my eyes shut against the idea of meeting the other students in my art course in an hour. I practise answering the questions I am certain to be asked.

"So, where are you from? What do you do? Are you married? Kids?"

How do I respond to these normal questions? What is the truth? Am I married? No. My one-word answer hangs like a storm cloud.

I rehearse my reactions to their reactions, their potential discomfort. Smile. No. Keep my face relaxed. If I stay relaxed, they'll feel more relaxed. I don't want to stick out. I want to belong. But this is part of my challenge: to accept what makes me different. Twenty-two of us meet for our briefing at the famous sidewalk café Les Deux Garçons, where Zola, Cézanne, Picasso, Cocteau used to go, on the classic carriageway Le Cours Mirabeau. Great plane trees shadow the walk. One of the students, a beautiful woman who I saw at the airport, smiles at me and gestures for me to sit beside her.

"I'm Cathleen. When I saw you at the airport and found out you'd be in the art course, I said to myself, 'She has such pretty hair, I wonder if we'll be friends.'" Her smile beams and I want to stay close to her warmth.

"Thank you. I'm Sue." I smile back at her and hope we will be friends.

People introduce themselves around the table and I brace for further chit-chat. But the meeting begins right away.

The art instructor, a good-looking, charming, middle-aged artist from North Carolina who has lived here for over 30 years, outlines the learning outcomes and expectations. Our art will be graded on the basis of how much we improve. I stiffen at the impending judgment because I need a safe environment in which to shed my skin. Inside my head a personal goal formulates: take more risks in my art and express my uniqueness. If I achieve this goal by the end of six weeks, I will have earned an A. If not, maybe I need more time.

We all listen carefully to the comments about French culture: drinking until you are sick is incomprehensible; the home is a very private place; do not place your hands on your knees during a meal; reading is very important; exercise is not a priority; lunch happens after noon and dinner happens after 8 p.m.; French people work to live as opposed to many North Americans, who live to work; avoid being the smiley tourist (a smile to a stranger is an invitation); be polite and if they are rude back call them on it; begin conversations with, "*Bonjour, madame/monsieur. Comment allez-vous?*"

We move next door as a group to the art store, where I practise my cultural learnings.

"*Bonjour, madame. Comment allez-vous?*" I speak to the saleswoman. She smiles broadly and moves forward to help me. It works. I leave the store with a bag full of art supplies. Tomorrow we begin to draw.

Wake with the sun, meditate, write my journal in French, do yoga using the 15th-century cathedral as a focal point, drink my hot lemon tea, dress, visit the boulangerie downstairs to buy lunch, walk to the art studio, paint, play guitar. This is my rhythm, and day by day I feel more at home, less discombobulated.

"*Bon matin, madame. Comment allez-vous? Je voudrais une quiche aux épinards et une mille feuilles, s'il vous plaît. Merci. Au revoir, madame.*" I place the savoury and sweet goodies in my knapsack and begin the 45-minute walk through the town and along the more rural Route de Cézanne to the Marchutz art studio. Climbing the gravel driveway alongside poppies, wildflowers and flowing long grasses to the simple white building nestled against the hillside, I breathe to myself, "I may never go home."

The students sit in a semicircle around a chair draped in silky cloth and softened by pillows.

"Today you will practise observing the visible world. What do you really see? First the model will pose for five minutes at a time, and then we will move to two-minute poses." The art instructor calls to the model that we are ready and a waif of a woman, ribs sticking out all over, enters.

"This is Dorothea." We nod our heads in her direction. Some say, "*Bonjour.*" I sit with my pencil poised, waiting for the start gun. Five minutes will never be long enough to get a finished product. She assumes a pose and lead scratches on paper. I hold my pencil out in front of me and use my thumb to measure for accuracy. A body is made up of eight heads. The ears are in line with the eyes. The nature of the line of the neck to the head is revealing. Look up. Look down and draw. Look up. Look down and draw. Shade in the armpit. Leave the face for last.

"Change." The instructor orders and the model morphs into a new pose. Not finished. My pencil continues to draw the first pose. Finally I let go and move to a clean page. By the time we do two-minute poses, my whole arm moves to sweep the pencil across the page. I have drawn her torso and one arm when the call "change" comes. Ugh. Faster. Just the essential: where her hand reaches out to grasp the chair, the weight of her front foot as it supports her lean, the tilt of her head, light coming from the side. The finished drawing looks like a figure, if only just. I coach myself. Don't forget, your goal is to take risks, make mistakes and explore the limits of your imagination.

I draw through lunch.

Our seminar in the afternoon is about lines. Lines do not hold the figure separate from the environment but rather encourage a connection to the greater whole, as in nature. Light and air move through the drawing freely. This allows the drawing to be illuminated from the inside out. How does the artist achieve this effect? By letting go. I shift my eyes around the room of attentive faces and wonder if everyone notices the thick solid line encasing my body.

In theory, I agree. Human nature tends to control, cling and contain. Yet human spirit – compassion, faith, hope and love – is not bound by lines or bodies. Human spirit connects us all to something bigger as it flows from space to space, sharing its energy. When the spirit is blocked and disconnected from the greater whole, it withers and cannot illuminate. It follows that art must be connected to the greater whole. And the artist breathes life into her creations by creating with an open heart. The more the artist lets go to the process, the less she tries to control, the more energy and spirit will flow. We cannot create as islands, just as we cannot live as islands. We are here on earth to feel that connection with one another, with the universe.

That night I sleep heavily.

After my morning routine, I mosey along the streets, gazing at whatever catches my eye, lulled by the caresses of the warm air. By the time I reach the studio, my dress sticks to my back and chest. The model stands at the side of the room in a silk dressing gown.

After a warm-up five-minute pose, the instructor explains the next challenge.

"You will have three minutes to draw the next pose and then the model will cover up and you will have three minutes to draw the same pose from memory." I gulp. I try to focus on the essential but still only get half of the figure drawn. Reluctantly, I turn the page, keeping my drawing from view. Memory. I can't even remember the pose. Was her right hand up or her left? Should I peek? No. The point is not to get it exact.

"Okay, you have three minutes."

Scratching. Paper rustling. Some groans. For a few seconds my pencil hovers over the paper because I am not sure. Time is wasting and finally I think what the hell and start to draw. I get a bit of an endorphin rush. When time is up, I flip back to my original drawing and compare it to the blind one and have a good chuckle. I am learning to be brave, to be less perfect. Feel the fear and do it anyway.

The next pose is seven minutes, and I use the time to add as much detail as I can. My figure looks like a woman, and I lean back so that my drawing is in full view.

"All right, now you have another seven minutes to do the same drawing but with your opposite hand." Groans. Several minutes in, most people are laughing. I catch myself with my tongue half out of my mouth, concentrating. The instructor asks us to display both drawings on the wall side by side. I rub my earring between my thumb and forefinger as I silently compare and critique. My right-hand drawing is anatomically correct and my eye recognizes it as a naked woman reclining. I am satisfied.

My left-hand drawing does not look anatomically correct. The bum and thighs on which her weight sits are much too large. But the more I look, the more I like the left-hand drawing. It feels less sterile, more alive. The figure is distorted and by no means perfect, but I relate to it more as a human being. I stare at the drawings on the wall after the class has returned to their seats. Why is the more perfect one less appealing, less alive? Perfect is good, isn't it?

A lively discussion ensues in response to Rembrandt's statement on drawing, which is that physical likeness is recognized and appreciated by the masses because it perpetuates the illusion that we are all separate, perfect, independent beings. But one of the most important roles of art is that it reveals truth: we are all connected; we are not perfect; we are not the most important in the universe. This can be a disturbing truth. An artist distorts in order to find this truth. But first the artist must know the truth. You have to know and understand something in order to let it go.

I fill two pages of my artist journal with notes.

Voices rise and fall with the opinions of the group, and I raise my hand several times. After I reread my notes, I bow my head and slump my shoulders. You have to know and understand something in order to let it go. I knew Jim. I understood him. But can I face the truth so that I can let him be dead?

In my perfect memory, Jim was perfect and we were perfect together. Being perfect makes me lovable. If I remember the argument where Jim called me a bitch and asked, "Do we need to split for awhile?" If I include the image of Jim yanking me to my feet when he lost his temper after I'd bugged him just a bit too much. If I uncover the conversation of me crying and leaning on Jim for support when I felt insecure. If I reveal these imperfections, people will be appalled at the real me.

Jim courses through my veins, but I can only paint part of him. And so I can only let part of him be dead. And I can only paint part of me so only part of me can be alive.

People judge my recovery by how much I move on, let go of my old life, of Jim. New job, new place to live, new puppy, new relationship. I crave external praise and reinforcement so that I know I will be okay. How can I move on and take Jim with me? I will try to repaint Jim in my mind and in my heart as "dead Jim," not "alive Jim." But how the hell do I do that?

When the cathedral bells clang the next morning, I lie in bed staring at the ceiling. My irrational, deeply ingrained belief is that if I paint my imperfections, people will not love me. And what if I paint something incredible? Then what? It's almost as scary. I skip yoga and dress for a day off. No painting class today.

At the American University, one block from my apartment, an expert offers a seminar on wines from Bordeaux and the Rhône. Cathleen, Jennifer and I sit in the classroom along with 75 other students, mostly younger. The hum of chatter eases when the middle-aged Frenchman at the front of the room turns his ample nose to his audience to introduce himself. He moves with the calm enthusiasm of someone fully engaged in his job. His even tone and odd, innocent humour remind me of l'Inspecteur Jacques Clouseau in *The Pink Panther*.

He holds the foot of a glass and swirls the wine before inserting his whole nose into the glass and then gulps a mouthful and swishes it around, almost like mouthwash. You must hold it in your mouth for at least 10 seconds. The first flavour is called *l'attaque*. After four or five seconds, *l'évolution* develops. The third flavour hits after eight seconds and is labelled *la finale*. Then you swallow. The fourth and final flavour comes after you swallow and is called *la persistance*. Seventy-five novices mimic his actions: lift, smell, swirl, taste and burst into a babble of commentary.

After the fourth tasting, the lecturer raises his voice considerably to get the audience's attention. Cathleen, Jennifer and I stumble off to dinner at a Moroccan restaurant.

The maître d' shows us to an inner courtyard lit by candles, surrounded by lush greenery. Elbows on the starched white tablecloth, we gaze at the stars and giggle when the waiter comments on our beauty. My thoughts race to interlock with theirs as we talk about creativity, writing and the relationship of art to all things. Four hours pass easily as the wine makes us friendly. Jennifer talks of a potential boyfriend who will visit; Cathleen talks of her husband, who is in Spain; and I listen and ask questions. My body is warm with wine, and even though I think I know what is coming and I try to steer the conversation, the drunk part of me thinks Bring it on, I can take it.

Cathleen veers off in a surprise direction.

She leans forward and rolls the beads of her necklace between her fingers, looks both ways as if she is going to cross a street and lowers her voice. "You guys might think this is crazy, but I feel something in my apartment, a presence, and some stuff has happened."

"What do you mean?" Jennifer and I both lean forward.

"There is this covering on my skylight and it moves at night, on its own. There's no wind or anything. And I just feel as if I am not alone there." She sits up and picks up her fork.

"Are you scared?" My skin prickles and I rub my forearms.

"At first, yes. But it doesn't feel like a scary energy." She raises her eyebrows and nods her head. She is so beautiful, so openhearted, I want to believe everything she says. Jennifer adds her own ghost story. It feels risky talking about ghosts. I have my own ghosts. There is a pause as we drink and eat and ponder. Here it goes, I think to myself.

"I don't know if I believe in ghosts, but I believe in something spiritual." I look down before continuing. "I was married to a wonderful man. His name was Jim. He was killed in an avalanche four years ago." I shove these sentences out and wait as they fall with a thud on Cathleen and Jennifer. Wide eyes. Horror. Hand covers mouth in shock. I don't like to be the bearer of bad news. I shift in my seat.

"I'm so sorry. That is awful." Cathleen has tears in her eyes. Jennifer's mouth quivers.

"Thank you." I'm learning to say thank you and move on. "So, I understand when you talk of seeing ghosts, because I feel Jim, his energy. I believe when you connect with someone you share some of his or her energy. A channel opens and there's a flow, an exchange that is vital for life." I take a breath and sneak a peek at their warm, open faces. Encouraged, I keep talking. "The more you connect with people and nature, the more your spirit lives on. Jim was a very connected guy. He was a good guy." I finish my speech, clear my throat and wait.

"So, how are you doing now? Have you met anyone else?" Cathleen looks at me with hopeful eyes. I feel my body start to float, but I expose more anyway.

"I was seeing this other fellow, Scott, for two years. He's a mountain guide like Jim was. He asked me to marry him last summer." I pause here because their faces light up. "But then at Christmas he got cold feet and we went our separate ways." Their faces fall again.

A minute passes as all of these feelings bounce around between us and find a place. I bend over my stewed lamb and couscous. It's uncomfortable at first to peel back onion layers. But as you get used to being connected to someone more deeply, a tenderness develops in the relationship. Cathleen, Jennifer and I venture to the next level.

The next morning, I walk to the weekly *marché* where stalls fill the cobbled square. The smells hint at where I am before I've arrived: the meaty smokiness of the sausage stall where oblong casings hang from above like a fringe framing the smiling white-aproned vendor, who balances a fresh sample between his thumb and a sharp knife. The earthy, humid, sweet lingering of the fruit and vegetable stand where the plump, ruddy-faced farmer's wife convinces me to buy the best field strawberries ever. The pungent, salty assault of fish at the slippery seafood section, where a man dressed in waterproof overalls sprays the floor with a hose regularly. The sweaty-sock smell of fresh cheeses. Within half an hour, little plastic bags hang from my arms like Christmas-tree ornaments.

Back at my apartment, I survey my loot and consult the cookbook I've just bought, *The Best of Mediterranean Cooking*. On the counter, I line up the main characters: egg, eggplant and onion. Cathleen and Jennifer will arrive for dinner at 7 p.m. I hum as I cook, and when the dish is ready, I play guitar and sing until my guests arrive.

On Sunday I force myself to meditate, do yoga and write before I pull on my stretchy capri climbing pants and a tank top. In my knapsack, I stuff a windbreaker, a water bottle, snacks, money and sunscreen. The local climbing group is waiting outside their clubhouse on the other side of town. Inside my head I practise my French greetings. I'm quite fluent in French, but I am nervous. I coach myself. Good for me – I found some people I can go climbing with. I'm stepping out. That's brave.

"*Bonjour. Comment ça va? Je m'appelle Sue.*" I set my pack down to shake hands. The two fellows are in their late 20s. Gérard is a clean-cut, motorcycle-riding accountant who started out training sled dogs and Michel is a gentle, brown-eyed architect who smiles shyly when he grips my hand. Christine shakes my hand vigorously, "*Bonjour, bonjour.*" Her green eyes sparkle and her spiky blonde hair does a jig. Her leg muscles bulge under her skintight climbing shorts. As we drive to the climbing crag, they burst into laughter every few minutes. Pretty easy audience. I relax into my seat and do my best to follow the quick dialogue. When they speak to me directly, they speak more slowly.

We arrive at the treed river that borders the smooth, steep gorge known as Chateauvert. Climbers dot the rock face like coat hooks. My palms sweat; I run my tongue along my lips. At the base of the climb, we sit on boulders in the dust to yank on our snug climbing shoes. Climbers call in French to the right and to the left of us. I stand up to buckle my harness, my "natural laxative." My bowels rumble from the impending fear. The rest of the group laughs at some joke.

I breathe deeply when Gérard hands me the sharp end of the rope and asks if I want to lead. I ask to borrow a helmet. More laughter. Apparently helmets are not à la mode. I hand the sharp end back and tie the other end to my harness. I'll belay. Gérard squeezes my *mousqueton* (carabiner) to make sure it is locked and I file the new word. As he labours up the face and reaches the hardest move, the crux (named after *le crucifix*), I call encouragement.

"*Je suis vaché*," he cries, which I learn means exhausted. I use the term frequently that day. The rope goes taut, and it is my turn. I rub my hands together to dry the sweat, double-check my tie-in and place my hands on the warm rock. Breathe. The trillions of grains of sand and water that have formed the rock push strength into my limbs. "*Je grimpe!*" I call out as I leave the ground.

At the crux, my arms burn and fear takes over. What if I fall?

"*Vas-y*," Gérard cheers with a grin. His spirit feels so light that I finish the climb. Up and down we go all morning. I even lead a pitch sans helmet, and sweat puddles in my cleavage. At lunch we wade into the river and float in an eddy, spouting water *comme des baleines*. After a siesta under the willow trees, we walk to the nearby château for ice cream. *Vachée* from a morning of climbing, I take a long break in the shade and paint. At 9 p.m. we pack up our climbing gear and head home.

Good for me.

Tomorrow we begin to paint in class.

"Van Gogh copied the masters' paintings for 12 years before he adopted his own style. Today, you will copy a master." The art teacher motions to a cupboard full of poster art prints. I choose to copy Paul Cézanne's rendition of Mont Sainte-Victoire, done right out the back door. My perfectly detailed, perfectly mountain-like pencil drawing peeks at me from my sketchbook. It takes another hour to transfer the sketch to my larger canvas. Oil colours ring my palette, waiting. I jerk the flat palette knife from one primary colour to the next, mixing. All of nature is made up of red, blue and yellow in different combinations. Sunset, sunrise, autumn leaves, Mediterranean Sea. Everything. Several times my brush ventures to the canvas, but it never makes contact. I huff, wheeze, cock my head from side to side, back up to get a different perspective.

Like a jittery hen scratching in the dirt, I swipe at the canvas. Too dark. Try again. Still too dark. In one hand I hold a rag that threatens to smudge my strokes, in the other my brush floats in the air, pecking every so often. Most people have painted at least half of their canvas. I breathe faster and slap my brush down on the palette, push my hands across my apron and flop back against the chair.

Cézanne's painting stands regally beside my pitiful attempt. His Mont Sainte-Victoire is faithful to nature in its colour relationships and full of his own expression – balanced, peaceful and harmonious. Mine looks like crap – broken, divided, incomplete. Is that who I am? Broken? Fearful? Full of pain? I grit my teeth and think of ways to hide my mountain, to destroy it. I want to cover it up or throw paint at it. What am I angry at? The mountain? For killing Jim?

This mountain where Jim died, how can it be harmonious? How can I weave together muted greys to join heaven and earth? How can I express peace and calm when what I feel is anger and discord? How can I give colour and life to this mountain when I see it as death?

I push aside the oil colours and place my sketchbook on my lap. Today, I will give my anger permission to surface. Without looking at Cézanne's work, I pick up my brush and slash water-colour paint on a clean page of my sketchbook. I gaze around to see if anyone notices the tears welling in my eyes. No. Keep going.

"Oh, what do we have here?" my art instructor whispers over my shoulder.

I shift so that I can see him and laugh nervously. "I couldn't paint the mountain that way. I have to do it this way first." I feel like a kid who has done something wrong, who has failed.

"That's great. You do what you need to do." He looks at me with a slight query but no judgment. On my paper, blood-red colour flows down the mountain like lava, outlined in black anger. I have painted the words "discord, death, red, fall, broken heart, pain" in the stormy blue sky. One more time, I think to myself. This time in black. In a few minutes, my second watercolour is complete. Black with words scattered about: anger, why, empty, hopeless, fear, alone, sadness, tears. I flip back and forth from one painting to the other and smile. I did it.

After we have all struggled to put paint on paper, the art instructor leads a seminar on colour.

"What colour is this leaf?" He sits before us holding a simple, oblong green leaf against his white palette. Silence, as it seems like a trick question.

"Green, right? It's green," he answers himself and squeezes some green oil paint onto the palette. Holding the leaf beside the colour, he asks, "So, is it green?" The leaf looks nothing like the colour.

"Okay, so it's not green. What is it? It's grey. That's right. The world is made up of shades of grey. And how do we get the grey of this leaf? We add its complement." He leans over his palette, carefully mixes red in with the green until he has matched the colour of the leaf. Several ah-hahs sound from the audience.

We paint all afternoon, but my unfinished painting of Mont Sainte-Victoire is so imperfect, I purse my lips at it. On the way home I try to be patient and look at my surroundings with a keener eye, to see the truth. But my thoughts return to the chocolate éclair and the ice-cream bar waiting at the corner store. I am scared of discovering all of the colours in nature because I am scared of discovering all of the pain in my heart.

Painting is going to open something for me, I'm sure of it. Keep going. Be patient and gentle with my brave heart. When confronted with uncertainty, do not get afraid; learn. You have to let go. You must commit to painting the truth.

How do baby birds know when to learn to fly? They wait in the nest until it is time and they take off. Why don't I know when to fly? Maybe I do and I'm just not listening for the cues.

The next day is "fieldtrip Friday" and my skirt sticks to the back of my thighs as we bus to the hilltop medieval village of Gordes, popular with famous people and the world of Peter Mayle, who wrote *A Year in Provence*. Narrow streets spiral past white and grey stone houses to the top of the heap where a 12th-century fortified castle encloses the city hall. We prattle on about the view of the Luberon Hills, compare purchases from the village market and sample the local jams, cheeses and olive oil. I buy a wide-brimmed straw sunhat and some olive-oil soap. Some of our sweat dries in the air-conditioned bus from Gordes to a Cistercian monastery, l'Abbaye de Sénanque.

Our chatter dies down as we wander between rows and rows of blooming lavender to the massive limestone archways of the monastery. We stop to suck in the sweet smell. Inside, I pull my shawl over my shoulders and tilt my head back to follow the square rooms up to arches and finally into round domes. Monks dressed in earth-brown robes glide by. It's quieter and slower than a library.

En route back to Aix, most people sit in silence, gazing out the windows at the golden hayfields, limestone houses under burnt-red clay roofs, lavender fields and dark-green cypress trees illuminated by the sun. No wonder so many people come to Provence to paint.

Back at the art studio we pack up our rickety, foldable easels and clamber into a van to drive along the same route Cézanne clipped along in his carriage one hundred years ago. It is a 10-minute drive to our destination, the town of Le Tholonet, where we unload beside a small creek surrounded by giant plantain trees. Across the road, hayfields run into crags of rock in the foothills of Mont Sainte-Victoire. This is painting *en plein air*.

My eye catches a footbridge leading over the creek into the forest. Flannery O'Connor writes in her essay "The Nature and Aim of Fiction" that painters should see the subjects in their paintings as characters in a story. As I tighten the screws on my easel, my eyes dart around, seeking the essential in the scene. Do I leave the ferns in? How do I know what to leave out? I pinch my eyebrows together to observe honestly with all six senses, to find the movement in the scene. Water moves, that seems a given. In my journal I list the possible characters and their personalities:

Bridge: stately, solid, protective, scarred, bossy, anal

Creek: energetic, happy, young, athletic, noisy

Ferns: wild, wanting, talkative, thin, tough

Plantains: tired, motherly, achy

Ivy: needy, unsatisfied

Sky: calm, peaceful

Sitting on the grass, I muse over the storyline. What happens between these characters to create heat and movement? The bridge momentarily bars the water on one side, causing an eddy, but the water escapes with a raucous laugh. The plantains scold the bridge while the ferns race the story from one to another. Where is the water going and why does the bridge want to stop it?

Great, so I've got my characters and a scintillating storyline. Now for the master creation. Every few seconds, I check to see that my painting looks like the real thing so that people can tell me what a good bridge I've done. After one hour of careful, deliberate, faint paint strokes on the canvas, I am pleased with my well-behaved, content characters. It looks like a bridge over water. But I don't sense movement, or heat, or a mysterious sixth sense, or much personality. There is nothing confrontational or committing about my painting. I am absent. Frustrated, I assault a clean canvas with paint, raking my arm back and forth as if to heavy-metal music. Sometimes it's easier to find the essential, the hotspot, the personality, if you paint quickly, because the ego does not have time to override creativity. My second painting is an unrecognizable mess of colour. Good grief.

My story percolates in my brain while I prepare my paints and root to my spot.

When the instructor gives the cleanup warning, I cannot believe three hours have gone by. I was in the zone. Rock climbers describe "the zone" as intense concentration on a task that cleans the mental slate of extraneous thought and demands pure reason. Somehow I forget myself when I paint, and there is a certain beauty and timelessness in forgetting yourself. Flannery O'Connor writes that the only way one can discover the spirit, the essence, of something is to "intrude upon the timeless, and that is only done by the violence of a single-minded respect for the truth." I hold my painting at arm's length to see if it is truthful. I can't tell, but something feels different.

Seeing the truth takes reason, courage, time, practice and an open heart. Maybe being open to seeing the truth is just as important as actually seeing it. Someday I want to experience the reality of the world with all six of my senses and paint it in a way that is true to my heart and soul. Dante describes life as the relationship between "substance" and the "accidental." Perhaps if I study nature enough to see its grace, I will see how life, death, love and compassion join everything in the universe, and I will be aware of the essential in life – the substance – and what is not essential – the accidental – and present their relationship truthfully.

Seeing the real world through spirit and mystery requires a deeper vision and understanding. There are feelings I cannot face right now.

My time in the zone organizes my thoughts, settles my ego and gives me perspective. I don't want a part-time relationship. I don't want to drive back and forth from Vancouver and Whistler. I want one home in Vancouver with an art studio. There are three weeks left for me in France.

For hours every day I paint in order to complete the required 30 canvases. In 40°C heat I walk for one hour to the exact lookout where Cézanne painted to capture Mont Sainte-Victoire. At the end of the course, we host an exhibition of all of our work. Two of my rock-climbing buddies come, and I lead them through the studio and point out my paintings, saying they aren't very good. They linger on one of my paintings but not as long as on others'. I want mine to be the best, to get accolades, to be the most popular, but I feel a certain pride that they are mine. I have still not quite grasped the lesson that it is not all about me.

Two days before my flight leaves for home, I meet with the instructor for a one-on-one evaluation. As I wait outside the studio for my turn, I overhear the instructor complimenting one of the other students. "Just keep doing what you're doing. You're on the right track." I rock back and forth and consider making a run for it. I ache to hear that I am on the right track.

"Hi," I smile and sit down next to him. He looks up briefly and returns to his Rodin thinking posture in front of my paintings all lined up in a row.

"Hey, Sue. How's it going?"

"Good," I lie and match his pose.

"So, there they are." He waves his hand at six weeks of my work.

"Yup." I raise my eyebrows and nod my head. I sneak a peek at some of the more vibrant works belonging to other students around the room. My paintings look pale, one-dimensional and ghostlike, and I look down and clear my throat. If I reached out to grab the substance of my art, my hand would pass right through like mist.

"You know the way you paint, such small detailed brush strokes, reminds me of Renoir." He mimics painting holding his hand up very close to his face. "Renoir was arthritic, you know. Near the end of his career, he painted from a wheelchair."

Sweat builds behind my knees. "Oh, right, well, I am very detailed," I confess. "I look at Elly's painting and she seems to say so much with so little, like Cézanne. I wish I could paint like her." I press my lips together in hopelessness.

"But that is Elly. You have to paint like Sue."

"I don't know how to do that," I mumble.

"That's why you must keep painting. It will come." He smiles and begins a technical discussion about one of my portraits. I nod and agree every now and then, but my mind skips to images of my next painting. When my report comes, I receive an A+. I know I'm not the best painter in the course, not even close, but I made progress and tried hard.

FORTY-ONE
HOME

After the flight home, I arrive at my parents' doorstep. Dad offers to drive me the 30 minutes out to my aunt's acreage to pick up Habby. When my aunt opens the door, I crouch in ready position for the usual greeting. Habby races at me, licks my entire face with the vigour of a carwash, hopping up to get just that milli-metre closer, interspersing licks with gentle nibbles of my nose. I laugh and try to keep my mouth closed against his gigantic tongue. Soon we roll on the floor.

It's almost dinnertime by the time we get back to my parents' house, and I've got two more hours of driving to get home to Whistler.

"You look tired. Why don't you stay here overnight?" Dad looks worried. Why do I rush home to Whistler? Because I want to be there if Jim comes home. Well, there's no rush.

"Okay, yeah, that's a good idea." I unpack just enough for the night. Dad looks relieved. I sleep solidly for nine hours with Habby curled up on the bed against my legs. It's comforting to have a warm body in bed with me.

In the morning, Dad puts his arm around me and asks, "So, are you moving back to Vancouver?"

"I'm not sure how I would do that. I'm not ready to sell the house."

"You could rent out the house in Whistler so that you could rent or buy something in town." My throat tightens at the thought of a stranger living in my home. That would really be giving up on Jim. But part of me gets excited about a space of my own in

Vancouver. I envision a spacious, bright place, close to the beach, where I can paint, write, meditate and do yoga. I say nothing.

"I think it's time to take a break from your house, just to see how it feels. I think it's an important step." Dad looks at me earnestly. The lump in my throat aches. I nod. Scary. I could use logistics to dampen the idea, such as the money and time it would take to move. But I know moving is my next big challenge because the idea keeps surging up from a deep place within me, my sacred root, my inner Jim. Tears fill my eyes, and Dad squeezes my shoulder. I drive home to Whistler.

At five o'clock the next morning a sliver of a moon hangs in the blue sky over Whistler Mountain. I've lain awake in bed for hours with jet lag and the anxiety of being home. The walls, furniture and linen reverberate with memories of Jim. I fear my heart might stop beating from the intense pain.

Without my daily painting and cooking regimes, I search for purposeful activity. When faced with adversity, the heroines in *Little Women* fell upon their mantra "hope, and keep busy." I get my hope from Habby and from my inner voice, my inner Jim. In my journal, I list things I enjoy doing with the goal of reaching 20 items. My pen keeps going to 29: playing guitar, walking with Habby, reading, writing, drawing and painting, yoga, cooking, laughing, dancing, biking, rollerblading, visiting friends, exploring the wilderness, hugging Habby, loving, listening to music, sitting in the sun, learning, climbing, ski touring, making love, being out of breath in a beautiful place, eating chocolate, drinking red wine, travelling, watching a video. These activities make up my safety map.

My routine becomes my tradition: wake up, meditate, write in journal, do yoga, walk Habby, breakfast, work at organizing my sixth Kilimanjaro trip.

My friends call to touch base, and it strikes me how much I learn from them. From Terri I learn compassion and understanding. From Susan I learn resilience and hard work. From

Marla I learn that honesty and consistency allow clear communication and strong relationships. From Andrea I learn that self-confidence allows you to reach your potential. From Rose I learn not to take life and myself too seriously. From Jenny I learn the power of intellect to become self-aware. From Heather I learn how self-love allows you to love, understand and encourage others. From Karen I learn that to have a friend you must reach out and be a friend.

Learning is one of my survival tactics, as is having purposeful activity, not just busyness.

FORTY-TWO
JOE

Relax and romance will flourish.
—MY CHINESE FORTUNE COOKIE

The teaching term begins after the Kilimanjaro trip, and I settle into a routine and try to ignore my loneliness. A friend sets me up on a blind date. I sit in my car for 15 minutes before I gather the courage to go into the restaurant. The man never met Jim and is not from the mountaineering community. My body waits like a loaded gun for the moment when I tell him about Jim, my true love. Each word describing my dead husband builds a wall between my heart and the unknown man sitting opposite me. After our evening together, he does not call or e-mail, and I do not expect him to.

I cry at home, alone. I regard myself from a distance and wonder Who is this crippled mess of fear and pity? Enough of mountain guides. I am going to find myself a businessman. I laugh at the absurdity of my quest. But I am tired of being stuck and am ready to commit to change. I date a few more men and decide that if I have not met the right person within a year, I will have a baby on my own. I am 38 years old.

Six months later, I join a group of friends and strangers for a backcountry ski week at a cabin near Nelson, in the interior of British Columbia. We meet at a restaurant before flying in by helicopter. My friend introduces me to Joe, who grasps my hand firmly and nods his head once. He seems a bit stern and short. Joe confides to me later that he thought I might be gay.

Twelve of us settle into the cabin and take turns cooking meals. I set the alarm for six o'clock to make breakfast the next morning for the group, but there is no need. At 5:30 the tap runs and dishes clink. Who the heck would be up at this hour? I stomp downstairs, growling, and there is Joe, sitting at the table. "Would you like some coffee?" He raises his mug and smiles.

"No, thanks, I don't drink coffee." Thoughtful guy. Nice. I smile back. But he gets up too early.

For the next few days, we ski fluffy powder under blue skies. Joe drags his out-of-shape body up the slopes and drives his tele-mark skis down, undeterred by several face plants. Strong. He's got chutzpah. I like that.

At après-ski, Joe produces copious amounts of alcohol and shares it with the group, laughing easily. Generous. And funny.

On the third day, we ski a deliciously puffy steep slope. I part-ner up with my girlfriend for safety, and we giggle with each turn as our skis kick powder up into our faces. Joe arrives just behind us at the bottom. He beams and plows through the deep snow toward us.

"Wasn't that great?"

"Wow."

"We're going to go up again. Want to come with us?" Joe looks eager but then sees his sister on a high line heading back to the hut. They wave to one another and Joe turns to us.

"I'd love to but it looks like my sis and her hubby are going back. They've been good to me, sticking with me. I'll head back with them." And he's gone. Loyal. I watch him go for a minute and turn to see where he is a few times as we ascend the slope.

That evening, we have a party and dance until late. As I drink more, I gravitate to Joe's spot on the dance floor and we bump against each other in rhythm to the music. We step outside in sock feet onto the snowy deck to cool off.

"Here, you can step on my feet if you want." Joe offers. I giggle as I balance on his toes, hands braced on his chest. He catches

me around the waist. We look at each other for a second and
then laugh and start to tell jokes. After everyone has gone to bed,
Joe and I sit on the couch and talk.

"So, where did you grow up?" I tuck one leg under me and
turn to face him.

"Minneapolis. Well, just outside of Minneapolis, in a place
called Anoka, on the Mississippi River."

"What's it like there?"

"They say it's the closest thing to Canada in the States.
Moderate politics, friendly people. The winters can be harsh.
Some companies take their employees up in a chartered airplane
just to get above the clouds to see the sun. There's a whole system
of covered walkways for people to get from store to store when
it's too cold to be outside. I grew up on the river, fishing, swimming and exploring."

"What do you do?"

"I started out in law and practised for five years but then went
into small business start-ups. What about you? Where are you
from and what do you do?"

I wonder for a second what that means, small business start-
ups. "I grew up in Vancouver, taught French and German for six
years, got my backpacking guide certification and do some guiding, and I teach outdoor education now to high-school students."

Joe perks up when I mention guiding. "What sort of guiding
do you do?"

"I've done some ski-tour guiding and heli-ski guiding, and
now I do an annual trip to Mount Kilimanjaro in Africa."

"Wow. Ski guiding. Africa. You're hard core."

I chuckle and deny it but know he is impressed, so I don't tell
him that my ski guiding was only as an assistant and that I was
just a tail guide for heli-skiing.

"What does that mean, 'small business start-ups'?" I divert the
attention back to him. He answers in a lingo I am not familiar
with, but I nod my head to keep him talking. He made a lot of

money in the dot-com boom, millions, and then lost most of it
when the market crashed.

"Are you married?" He doesn't wear a ring but I ask anyway.

"Divorced. Five years ago now. We married young, when I
was 24."

He is two years older than me, lives in San Diego and has
three kids. His ex-wife remarried and moved to Maryland with
the kids. Joe stayed in San Diego. When I ask him if he misses
his kids, his eyes tear up.

We play one another songs on the guitar. Joe picks the clas-
sical "Bourrée" by Bach. I choose a folk song by Ferron. We discover that we both love the book *A Winter's Tale*. And the movie
A Princess Bride is one of our favourites. That night, I lie awake
picturing his handsome, strong-boned face, his bright, steel-blue
eyes and his smile.

Over the next few days, we sneak off to the sauna together,
hang back in the ski line to kiss and persuade our roommates to
give us some privacy. At the end of a week of ski touring together, Joe drives west with me to Vancouver, to my parents' house,
instead of heading south to San Diego. My parents raise their
eyebrows slightly when the bed in Joe's room is not slept in the
next morning.

Every other weekend, Joe flies up from San Diego and we
snowshoe, ski, hike, rock climb and camp in Whistler. We go out
for long dinners, drink lots of wine and spend hours in bed. Each
time I pick him up from the airport, my heart does a little flip.

Exactly 60 days after we first met, we canoe on Alta Lake
behind my house. Joe has packed a picnic of soft cheeses and
wine. I steer in the stern, Habby sits in the middle and Joe powers in the bow. At one end, the lake meanders into a reedy marsh
before forming the River of Golden Dreams. Grasses reach way
above our heads, and the canoe turtles along through lily pads.
Joe relaxes on the floor of the canoe, his legs draped over the seat
and his paddle barely dipping into the water. "It's a good thing

you've got that mondo rescue knife on your life jacket. The River of Golden Dreams could be pretty dangerous." He smirks and raises one eyebrow. He's so cute.

"I imagine for a strong Minnesota River Man such as yourself, this river will be nothing."

We nudge to a standstill against the grassy banks. The slight jolt jars Joe upright, and he stops laughing. He looks around at the snaking quiet water. We are alone. He swivels onto his knees, slides a hand into his pocket, leans over Habby and reaches out a little open box with something very sparkly inside. Habby licks Joe's face just before he says, "Will you marry me, Sue?"

I take a deep breath, look Joe in the eye and say, "Yes."

The next day at school, I tell my class of students about Joe's proposal. The girls echo a soft, "Oh."

There is a silence and then one of the boys says, "That would have been a really uncomfortable paddle back if you'd said no."

PART 5
HEREAFTER

It may be that some little root of the sacred tree still lives.
Nourish it then
That it may leaf
And bloom
And fill with singing birds!
—BLACK ELK, EARTH PRAYER

The American/Canadian 1993 K2 Team led by Stacy Allison. Jim is on the far left.

The Right Honorable Ramon John Hnatyshyn, Governor General of Canada from 1990–1995, receiving a gift from Jim after the Meritorious Service Medal ceremony in Quebec City.

Porters carrying loads to high camp on Mount Kilimanjaro, 1995.

Sue feeling sick at sunrise on the summit of Mount Kilimanjaro, Tanzania, 1995.

Mount Kilimanjaro, the highest peak in Africa, 5895 metres, seen from the plains of Tanzania, 1985.

*Sue hiking the lush forests of the Indian Ocean island of
Mauritius, 1995.*

Sue and Jim ski mountaineering in the Himachal Pradesh, India, 1995.

Sue and Jim after a big dump of snow in the Indian Himalaya, 1995.

Sue visiting a stupa, *or* chorten, *a Buddhist religious monument, in the Langtang Valley of Nepal, 1995.*

Sue demonstrating the Katadyn water filter for the local kids en route to rafting the Karnali River, Nepal, 1995.

Sue and Jim taking a break from the rapids on the Karnali River, Nepal, 1995.

Rafting the Karnali River, 1995.

Jim and Sue on the summit of Mount Edziza, BC, 1995.

Jim piggybacking Sue to keep her blistered feet dry, Mount Edziza Provincial Park, BC, 1995.

Sue climbing in the Tantalus Range, BC, 1996.

Sue mountaineering in the Tantalus Range, 1996.

Sue exploring Denali National Park, Alaska, 1996.

Sue gazing at Mount Denali, Alaska, 6196 metres, the highest peak in North America, 1996.

Sue and Jim's wedding, the whole Haberl family, at Cecil Green House in Vancouver, BC, June 30, 1997.

Sue and Jim exchange wedding vows, 1997.

Sue and Jim's home in Whistler, 1997.

Sue trekking in Morocco, 1998.

Digging in deep on Klutlan Glacier, Alaska, 1998.

Sue after the descent from Mount Bona, Alaska, 1998.

Keith contemplating the melted-out camp of their ill-fated April expedition. Mount Ultima Thule, Alaska, June 1999.

Packing up the Beaver to fly back to the lodge after saying good-bye to Jim. Ultima Thule, Alaska, June 1999.

The first time Sue and Jim met, in Gwaii Haanas National Park in Haida Gwaii (formerly known as the Queen Charlotte Islands), 1982. Jim, far right; Sue, middle back.

Sue and Susan paddle in Haida Gwaii, July 1999.

Sea lions in Haida Gwaii.

Haida Gwaii.

Sue with Dad Haberl and Habby on the first anniversary of Jim's death, spreading his ashes at Blueberry Point in Whistler, April 29, 2000.

Sue with Jim's younger brother Kevin at Mawenzi (4300 metres) on Mount Kilimanjaro, August 2000.

Sue and Habby, climbing at Red Rocks, Nevada, spring 2001.

Skiing the Haute Route in France/Switzerland, April 2001.

On the Haute Route in France/Switzerland, spring 2001.

Scott explores the wilds of Fiji, 2002.

Sue leads the Ascent for Alzheimer's team up the Gokyo-Ri valley, Nepal, 2001.

Almost at the summit of Gokyo-Ri, the team takes a quick break and then pushes on to their goal.

Villa Delia in Tuscany: Umberto's cooking school, 2003.

Sue sampling wine at Villa Delia, 2003.

Art school at the hillside village of Anversa, Italy, 2003.

Art school in southern France: the lavender fields of l'Abbaye Notre-Dame de Sénanque, 2003.

"Mama Banana." 100 × 75 cm. Acrylic painting by Sue Oakey.

Ski touring at Powder Creek, BC, and meeting Joe for the first time, 2004.

Preparing for a day of ski touring at Powder Creek. Joe is on the far left.

Sue and Joe's wedding reception at The Edgewater in Whistler.

Sue and Joe snowshoe to Rainbow Lake at Whistler with their siblings on their wedding day, January 15, 2005.

Sue and Joe raise the first wall panel of Jim's memorial hut in the stunning Tantalus Range near Squamish, BC, 2006.

Jim's memorial hut in winter.

The grand opening of Jim's memorial hut in the Serratus–Dione col of the Tantalus Range, June 2006. Elevation 2073 metres.

Samuel Remember Baker is born on August 24, 2006.

FORTY-THREE
THE PERFECT HEART

No memory of the past touched him for
his mind was full of a present joy.
— JAMES JOYCE, *DUBLINERS*

My parents host a "Meet Joe" party. I scurry through the kitch-en and overhear a good friend of mine who has Joe pinned in the corner say, "So, do you do your own laundry?" Joe laughs and answers yes. My friend nods her approval. Joe goes from conversation to conversation, meeting people, getting to know my friends and family. Dad examines the unorthodox label of a wine bottle and hesitates to pour a glass. Joe interrupts the con-versation he is having just long enough to say to Dad, "That one is fine." Dad nods at me and is impressed.

At the end of the evening, one friend leans in and says, "I'm glad Joe shows his affection for you. Jim was so affectionate with you, and I know how much you loved that." When everyone has left, Joe goes downstairs to get ready for bed. My parents and I sit around the table.

"Joe sure is bright," Dad says.

"And he's witty, too. He's savvier than Jim was, don't you think?' Glenda says.

"Yes," I agree reluctantly. I'm happy that they like Joe and that they approve, but any comparison to Jim triggers my guilt. In my heart I pledged to love Jim forever, not just until death do us part, and now I am going to marry someone else.

Within four months, Joe quits his job in San Diego and moves to Whistler. Within one year, we exchange vows at a quiet ceremony in our Whistler home in front of our families. We host a larger reception at a local restaurant with 50 friends and family members. Jim's parents, brothers and best friends are there. There are speeches and crying. One of Jim's brothers says he was skeptical when Joe first arrived on the scene, but having spent time with him, knows he is a good guy. Jim's best friend says Jim would be happy seeing me with Joe. Jim's name comes up several times. I wonder if it bothers Joe, but he keeps a poker face. After all, they are honouring Joe, too.

People hug me with such unbridled happiness that I realize my wedding to Joe allows them to say one last goodbye to Jim. Jim and Sue are no longer. It is now Joe and Sue. And I sense relief in their tears. They have watched over me for almost six years, on Jim's behalf, and now they can pass the torch. I'm okay now.

I feel strong when I go to the front of the room to address my friends and family. But I begin to cry as soon as I open my mouth:

> People are defined not so much by the job they do but by how they dust themselves off and pick themselves up after a big fall. I feel I took a big fall. And as I've been picking myself up, loving hands, and one big paw, have reached out to me all along the way. I am defined by how my heart connects to all of you, my loved ones. Thank you. And now I have Joe. I would like to read a fable I've read to my students called "The Perfect Heart." The author is unknown:
>
> In a faraway land, there lived a people who carried their hearts in their hands. One young man began to achieve some fame. "I have the most

perfect heart," he proclaimed. Truly it was a sight to see – magnificently shaped, hard, smooth and flawless. His heart became the standard of perfection and people travelled from far away to view this wonder. And they would steal a glance at their own hearts, each now clearly aware of its flaws, embarrassed to let anyone else see them.

One day, an old man stepped up to the young man and said in a voice for everyone to hear, "I have a more perfect heart than yours."

A murmur ran through the throng, then a hushed silence. Every head craned forward. Every eye watched intently as the old man brought forth his heart. The young man looked at the old man, bent and wrinkled with the passage of many years. Then he looked at the heart tenderly cradled in gnarled fingers and burst out with laughter. "Senile old fool. This is your perfect heart?" he sneered. For sitting on the palm of the old man's hands was a heart as bruised, tattered, misshapen, scarred and ugly as anyone could ever recall.

"My heart is more perfect than yours," the old man repeated, looking the young man square in the eyes. The laughter in the crowd died out as they pressed close to listen. Something in the serene way the old man spoke must have caught the young man's attention for his expression changed. Puzzlement replaced the sneer.

"My heart is more perfect than yours," the old man said once again, "because it is alive, and life is not pretty. It has been used as hearts are meant to be. This scar was left by a parent's anger. This bruise by the death of my wife. These scars by the pain of some dear friends. These pieces that do not quite fit were given to me by people I have met along the way, and they carry a piece of my heart with them. These tatters are from doing what my heart said was right and rubbing against a world that said it was foolish. These holes are from people I loved who did not love in return. But I still gave them a piece of my heart. This heart is like this because I have taken the risk to care. That is why my heart is more perfect than yours."

The young man looked sadly at his own heart. He began to walk away, head bent toward the ground.

"Wait! I am not finished," said the old man. The young man stopped and turned back. The old man stepped toward him. "Do not go without this," he said and pressed a piece of his heart into the young man's palm. The young man looked into the old man's eyes. As all the people watched, the young man tore a piece from his own heart and handed it to the old man. He smiled, and without another word, turned and went.

After reading the fable, I pause and look at Joe. "Thank you, Joe, for taking a chance on my heart."

Joe and I begin our perfectly imperfect life together.

Friends share their views. "I felt bad for Joe at your wedding reception because there was so much talk of Jim."

"How is it for Joe living in the house that you and Jim built?"

"Does he feel like you compare him to Jim?"

"What about your working on Jim's memorial hut? How does he feel about that?"

It is not easy for Joe, although he maintains a brave face. I do compare him to Jim because that is my excuse for not opening my heart to him when I feel scared. My escape route. I am still in survival mode. Once you've been in survival mode for years, rationing energy, love and food and waiting for rescue, it is difficult to transition to regular life. A learned fear is harder to overcome than an innate fear. My fear of being abandoned lies right under my skin and explodes in anger. "If I get angry, just tell yourself that I'm probably scared," I coach Joe. And I coach myself to be vulnerable, to tell Joe that I love him, to be affectionate with him, to kiss him first, to let him be who he is and to show him all of me. To trust him.

I cringe when my friends and family mistakenly call Joe "Jim." I ask Joe if it bothers him that a painting of Jim hangs in our living room. I ask him if he feels uncomfortable in our house. But these are unfair questions. Joe is patient, and when I show signs of embracing the present, he looks excited. I do my best. I sell my furniture so that Joe can bring his up from San Diego. He paints the inside of the house. I venture that maybe if we save some money, we can sell the house and buy another one. His face lights up, and I try to ignore it. He stands by me when we go to the annual memorial dinner for Jim. He holds my hand when I cry.

Water finds its own level, and my soul has found another sad soul in Joe. Joe is patient with my grief and mourning, and I am patient with Joe's complex dealings with his ex-wife and his pain over not seeing his children.

I become pregnant and full of joy.

FORTY-FOUR
CHANGE

You cannot plant an acorn in the morning and expect
that afternoon to sit in the shade of an oak.
—ANTOINE DE SAINT-EXUPÉRY

I am eight months pregnant when, in June 2006, Joe and I fly
into the Tantalus Mountains for the official opening of Jim's memorial hut. After five years of meetings, planning and building,
we have finally finished.

As the helicopter circles to land, I look down at this beautiful shelter with the rust-coloured trim and bright silver
lettering shining in the sun – THE JIM HABERL HUT – and
something expands inside of me. When I walk through the
door, I gaze at the crisp blond finishing wood, the steel
countertops, the tongue-and-groove ceiling, and all I can
say is "Wow." Tears come to my eyes. What a beautiful honouring of Jim.

Joe and I work for five hours to assemble a wall display. With
tears in their eyes, friends watch Joe as he patiently holds pieces
in place for me. When the last piece is nailed into place, I stand
back. It is full of love.

There is a flurry of activity. The guys turn off the generator
and haul it out of sight. Tools are stashed under beds and the
floor is swept. I change into clean clothes and put on earrings.
We all gather on the snow and shield our eyes from the sun as we
peer down the glacier for signs of the whirring machine.

Six helicopter loads of committee members and Jim's

family – a total of 22 people – land in the Tantalus Range to celebrate the official opening of the hut.

In a pair of Jim's old hiking boots, Mom Haberl treads carefully away from the cutting helicopter blades. There is something
about the slow and purposeful manner in which she moves that
fills my eyes with love. As we wrap our arms around one another
I tell her how glad I am that she is there. And I think to myself
that she should never have lost a son. Dad Haberl's cheeks puff
up and he blows the air out, shakes his head slightly in wonder
and comments on what a beautiful flight they had.

After three more loads, everyone has arrived, and there are
hugs and handshakes and people mill about on the rocks chat-
ting. Ten or 15 minutes pass and there is a certain holding, a tension. Mom Haberl stalls at the bottom of the stairs to the hut.
Dad Haberl picks up small pieces of building waste in the rocks.
I suggest we go inside. Mom Haberl hooks her hand on to my elbow, and the creases around her eyes are mixed with excitement
and apprehension.

They hesitate on the threshold as their eyes search the vestibule and their necks strain to see farther. Then their feet follow.
There aren't many words spoken, but the room feels full and thick.
I follow their gaze as their eyes roam the maple-panelled walls,
the ceiling, the birch kitchen cupboards, the sleek steel kitch-
en countertops, the solid-wood dining tables and chairs and the
multi-shaped windows offering a 270° view of mountains: Black
Tusk, Wedge, Diamond Head, Serratus, Dione, Tantalus. Mom
Haberl points out of one of the windows at the first mountain
Jim climbed, when he was about 14 years old at Camp Potlatch.
Dad Haberl runs his hand down the wall and asks if there will be
finishing batons on the panelling. Yes.

Their eyes come to rest on the display, and their mouths open
as they move closer.

People wander, peer, run their hands over the new surfaces,
chat and settle down to eat their bag lunches. Mom Haberl passes

around poppyseed cake, the nieces and nephews sit around the table playing cards and others meander outside. When it seems like the eating has died down and René, the head builder, has started working again installing weather stripping on the front door, I ask everyone to gather inside.

My first words are high and strained, and I pause to see if my throat will open, but it won't. I look at Mom Haberl and her head is down and her eyes are full.

> Thank you for coming. It is so nice to have everyone here. When we first started this project five years ago, I latched on to it as a way of keeping Jim alive, a way of even bringing him back to life. But as the years have passed, I realize that building this hut has helped me to let Jim be dead, and to let his spirit be free. When a loved one dies, it seems we are left with memories, some very strong, yet memories can be deceptive after a time. And then it seems we are left with more of a feeling than anything else, a feeling of the heart. And Jim left a lot of people with a strong feeling in their heart. And I realize now that even this feeling cannot be held or contained. It is free to roam just as Jim's spirit is free to roam, in and out of our hearts, carried on the wind. And as I look around this hut, I cannot imagine a more beautiful place to set Jim's spirit free.

> And Jim would be happy to see us all here. He'd be proud of his nieces and nephews, who are winning awards in martial arts, dance and French. He'd be smiling at his parents, who recently celebrated their 50th wedding anniversary. He'd be smiling at his brothers Pat and Kevin, who have carved time out of their schedule to

come here and climb together. And he'd be smiling at my belly swelling with new life and at the
wonderful man who I love now, and he would be
saying, "Right on," because life goes on and we
are of the living. And we will miss Jim and it will
hurt, but he must be allowed to be dead. Here's to
Jim and here's to life.

Tension increases as people are rubbed raw and nobody
wants to move or speak because the pain feels so near the surface.
I invite people to begin their afternoon adventures. The Haberl
brothers take the nieces and nephews to explore the rocky Dione
ridge. Mom and Dad Haberl explore the rocky rib to the nearby
Red Tit shelter.

Kevin joins me on the snow. He says he can relate to what I
said about letting Jim be dead and letting his spirit be free. In his
uninhibited way, he looks at me with his head cocked slightly
and says, "I just don't understand why it doesn't feel any better." I
tell him that I have tried unsuccessfully to package my grief and
my pain up neatly in a box and move on. I guess being better is
often equated with feeling no pain.

It doesn't seem to work that way. As long as we love Jim it will
hurt, and it is hard to accept that it will always hurt. The trick
may be not to fight the pain, to let it be, because if you cut yourself off from the pain, you cut yourself off from the love. And you
have to be alive to feel pain. And being alive is good.

So the pain does not get "better," but perhaps it changes.
Perhaps it becomes the pain of loving and living fully as opposed
to the pain of chasing the past and trying to drag it into the present and desiring something that can never be.

The hardest thing I've done in my life is to grieve Jim's death.
The second-hardest thing has been to allow my battered heart to
love again. It is harder for me to love well now, as I have first-hand

experience of what there is to lose. But my other option is not to love at all, and that would not be living.

I do not have a fairytale ending for you. What I have is an ending full of life: joy and pain. If there is one thing I have learned through grieving, it's that death and pain are common experiences. They will never be popular, but they are real and honest and such a basic part of life. I still ache for the fairytale sometimes, to escape into the illusion, where there is only love and my heart is forever protected from pain. So, I work hard to be present for all that life has to offer. I work hard at being brave and keeping an open heart, even when I feel threatened, even when I do not get what I want. I work hard at loving myself and others well, even though sometimes it terrifies me. I work hard at not denying any part of who I am, no matter how imperfect and ugly. Some days are better than others, but I am moving in the right direction: in the direction of love, with Joe. And I hope that death does not have to drag me away kicking and clawing, frightened and closed. I hope I can succumb peacefully, with an open heart, a body deeply wrinkled and well used from life experiences, having lived fully and honestly, in spite of my fears.

Even when my heart shakes and my mind is full of fear, there's something deep inside of me, a sacred root that is attached to something universal, something so incredible and yet at the same time so ordinary about the human spirit, that is whispering: "That's right, you go get 'em, girl. Get out there and love."

And I can hear Jim. He is a part of that universal voice.

ACKNOWLEDGEMENTS

This book has been years in the making, and I am grateful to many people who have given me courage along the way. The Vicious Circle, a group of talented, compassionate writers, read my first draft at a time when I was still raw with grief, and then saw it through to the twelfth draft, over seven years. Stella Harvey, Rebecca Wood-Barret, Sara Leach, Libby McKeever, Mary Macdonald, Nancy Routley and Katherine Fawcett, thank you for your brave critiquing and friendship.

Thank you to Paulette Bourgeois, Candas Jane Dorsey, Wayne Grady and Fred Stenson for their careful and thoughtful critique. As a first-time author, I asked questions of many people in the field. I thank Angie Abdou, Merilyn Simonds, Jack Christie, Shelley Adams, Stacy Allison, Jennifer Lowe-Anker and Chic Scott for their advice.

For adding depth to my story with their writing and photography, thank you to Bruce Allen, Steve Britten, Damian Cromwell, Jayson Faulkner, Kevin Haberl, Bob Herger and Rob Orvig.

A warm thank you to Honorable Madam Justice Wailan Low, who generously granted permission for the use of Earle Birney's poem "When we must part."

I received my share of rejection letters but one publisher took the time to write to me suggesting I submit to Rocky Mountain Books. Thank you to Joan Coldwell of Hedgerow Press.

Thank you to Don Gorman and the staff at Rocky Mountain Books for supporting a first-time author. Thank you to my editor,

Meaghan Craven.

When Jim was killed, I realized what sustains me from the inside out: love and how my heart is connected to everyone in my life. These connections keep me breathing. To my family, Jim's family, my dear friends and my dog, Habby, thank you for your love and support.

Finally, I thank Joe and Sam, the loves of my life.